RUNES
—AND—
ASTROLOGY

Symbol and Starcraft
in the
Northern Tradition

NIGEL PENNICK

Destiny Books
Rochester, Vermont

Destiny Books
One Park Street
Rochester, Vermont 05767
www.DestinyBooks.com

Text stock is SFI certified

Destiny Books is a division of Inner Traditions International

Originally published in the United Kingdom in 1990 by Aquarian Press under the
title *Runic Astrology: Starcraft and Timekeeping in the Northern Tradition*
Second edition published in the United Kingdom in 1995 by Capall Bann
Publishing

Cataloging-in-Publication Data for this title is available from the Library of Congress

ISBN 978-1-64411-600-5 (print)
ISBN 978-1-64411-601-2 (ebook)

Printed and bound in the United States by Lake Book Manufacturing, LLC
The text stock is SFI certified. The Sustainable Forestry Initiative® program
promotes sustainable forest management.

10 9 8 7 6 5 4 3 2 1

Text design by Virginia Scott Bowman and layout by Debbie Glogover
This book was typeset in Garamond Premier Pro and Gill Sans with Cheddar
Gothic used the display typeface

To send correspondence to the author of this book, mail a first-class letter to the
author c/o Inner Traditions • Bear & Company, One Park Street, Rochester, VT
05767, and we will forward the communication.

✳

To the memory of the great Manx runemaster,
Gaut Björnsson; the Swedish runemaster, Öpir;
and those unknown men and women who
carried the knowledge of the runes through the
dark times, this book is respectfully dedicated.

CONTENTS

ACKNOWLEDGMENTS

I would like to thank some people who have been helpful in various ways regarding certain aspects of this book: either they have been with me at the right place at the right time, have taken me there, or have given me information that has proved insightful. They are: Freya Aswynn, Diane Seadancer Battung, Michael Behrend, Nini Bjønness, John Blackthorn, Larry Blanton, Donald L. Cyr, Charla and Paul Devereux, Richard Dufton, Hermann Haindl, Annarut Hunzinger, K. Frank Jensen, Prudence Jones, Rosemarie Kirschmann, Caterina Maedel-Deringer, Barry Millard, Colin Murray, Rupert Pennick, Robert J. M. Rickard, Deb and Jeff Saward, Bernhard Schaer, John Score, Bo Stjernström, Anthea Turner, Waltraud Wagner, Helen Woodley, and Sam Canarozzi Yada. A special thank you to Michael Moynihan for his meticulous work for the 2023 edition.

A Note on Terminology and Dating

This book refers to many terms and deity names from different cultural traditions and languages. In the case of the Norse deities, I have generally used anglicized forms of their names for better readability. At the first instance, I provide the original Old Norse form in parentheses after the anglicized form; for example, Odin (Óðinn), Njord (Njörðr), and so forth. For simpler names, such as Sól and Máni, I have opted to use just the Norse forms. With regard to the Germanic runes, I have devised a set of names that are based on the attested Anglo-Saxon rune names, rather than using reconstructed names from a prehistoric period. I explain this further in chapter 2.

The year dates in use are taken from the Christian or Common Era calendar. Often, the letters written AD (*Anno Domini,* "in the year of our Lord") or AC (After Christ) are written to denote the system in use. In this book, I use the non-Christian terminology for this year-reckoning, CE, meaning Common Era. The beginning year of the Common Era correlates with the 753rd year after the Foundation of Rome (AUC, *Ab urbe condita*), the fourth year of the 194th Olympiad and 3761 AM (*Anno Mundi*) in the Jewish reckoning.

There are other less well-known systems, too. Insomuch as they are no more than a matter of convenience, these systems of year-reckoning are arbitrary. Significant dates in one system—such as the year 5500 in the Jewish system, or the year 2000 in the Common Era—are meaningless in another. This problem is compounded by an uncertainty over the actual date and year of birth of Jesus of Nazareth—between 7 and 4 BCE have been suggested. Another problem with this reckoning is that the Common Era system was not used before the sixth century CE, when it was introduced into Italy. In the seventh century it reached France, but it was not in general use in England until the year 816, when the ecclesiastical Council of Chelsea brought it into general use.

The runic time cycles have no known historical beginning reference point, but the fourth century BCE is a reasonable approximation. However, some adherents of Ásatrú (northern Germanic or Scandinavian Paganism) use what they call the *Runic Era,* which adds 250 years onto the Common Era reckoning. This makes the year 1990 CE into 2240 RE. My personal opinion of this is that it is arbitrary and unnecessary, so I do not use it.

INTRODUCTION

This is a book about an ancient tradition, runecraft, and an archetypal perception, the cycles of time. Runecraft is a tradition that comes from the oldest roots of European culture. The reinstatement of the runes in the mainstream of esoteric thought has been one of the success stories of the last quarter of the twentieth century. Before that, in English-speaking countries especially, study of the runes was restricted to academic circles, which largely ignored the esoteric and magical content of runes. If they were studied at all, runes were studied in an epigraphic sense, as a historical record, largely of names carved on memorial stones and personal possessions. Their relationship to magic, divination, and spirituality was seen as outside the remit of academic study. But then came a transformation. Suddenly, the runes asserted themselves from their deeper, magical, level. The ground base of academic studies on the runes acted as a new entry-point for those who had a deeper connection with this time-honored magical alphabet. The change came when people began to work the techniques experientially rather than to study them externally—to encounter them in direct, revelatory, shamanic ways.

Northern Tradition techniques are a means of describing and using this experience. They have never been—and can never be—a substitute for it. Their strength derives not from some long-established authority, but from present experience. Because of this essential interaction, the personal nature of runecraft makes it an ever-evolving, dynamic process. Within the basic framework of meaning, there is the freedom of personal experience. This is the epitome of the creative force, a non-orthodox exploration of a system that accesses the deepest structure and meaning of existence. The spirit of runecraft is away from the rigid, fixed, and authority-decided view of the world, and toward the as-yet-unformed potential of human creativity. Any observation that can aid this vital flow of creativity and prevent it falling into the trap of claiming to possess absolute exclusive truth is of great value. There is no religion higher than the truth, and truth can never be the exclusive preserve of blinkered, dogmatic people. Runecraft is like this, being open to new developments and evolving continuously while keeping true to its eternal principles. Anything that cannot grow and change with changing conditions, while retaining its original essence, is nothing more than an empty, lifeless husk that has lost its vital force. Such systems are composed of artificially imposed beliefs and rites that exist largely to suppress the possibility of any continuing creative revelations of the spirit.

Unfortunately, most long-established systems of belief contain within them the inherent claim that they possess within their myths and rituals everything that there is to know. Over the years, devotees of various beliefs have claimed that all others are false. Furthermore, this error has led to the deliberate suppression of all people's knowledge as unnecessary, even "evil." This is epitomized by the Christian Byzantine Emperor Justinian, who in the year 529 closed down all the surviving schools of Pagan philosophy at Athens. As part of the closure, he had their libraries—which contained texts on astronomy, astrology, biology, chemistry, geography, geology, medicine, and physics—consigned to the bonfire. But even when such intolerant bigotry triumphs in one place, it can never succeed completely. The world is too large, and the human spirit irrepressible. After Justinian's burning of the books, Greek philosophy, astronomy, and science survived outside the realms of orthodox Christendom: in Hindu India; in Pagan Persia; and in Ireland, where the Celtic Church, continuing the cultured and learned ways of the

Druidic branch of the Northern Tradition, was wise enough to recognize the value of knowledge in its own right, regardless of its origin, and not necessarily in line with orthodoxy.

In mainland Europe, however, a thousand years passed before these truths, recognized in the Bardic tradition of ancient Wales and Ireland, and by Germanic and Norse seers, were permitted to be exercised openly without fear of the rack, the block, the gallows, and the stake. For those thousand years, the statements of the written word, often symbolic, were enforced as immutable reality; when direct experience showed that those words were untrue, then that experience was condemned as false. By this inversion of logic, the teaching of observed facts like the spherical nature of our planet, and the orbit of the Earth around the Sun, was called evil, as it contradicted scripture. To hold such ideas—even to make observations of the heavens—became a criminal offense, punishable by death. Clearly, this sort of inversion could not last forever, and the constraints of reality reasserted themselves in the end.

Similarly, runecraft, originating in continental central Europe, and developed in Germany, England, and Scandinavia, was largely suppressed. Because of their intimate connection with the Elder Faith, the indigenous religions of northern Europe, churchmen frowned upon the runes. But it was not possible to destroy the knowledge of the runes. Nothing has been lost, having been maintained both in folk tradition and by academic study—initially by scholarly monks and later in the universities. So, the runes have remained in unbroken, continuous use since antiquity, as a means of writing and as calendar notation, finally reasserting their esoteric side in the twentieth century. Although the runes are an esoteric system in their own right, attempts have been made in the past to "fit" the runes into other esoteric systems, for example the Kabbalists' Tree of Life. While reasonable "fits" have been made in some areas, there are serious discrepancies elsewhere. The "fits" are those parallels and correspondences that can be found in any system that deals with the underlying reality of the universe. They will have things in common with other systems that concern themselves with the same subject area. But, ultimately, the runes are a system in their own right, having a certain precise underlying pattern that is unique.

"By the Law of Periodical Repetition, everything which has happened once must happen again and again—and not capriciously, but at regular periods," wrote Mark Twain. "The same Nature which delights in the periodical repetition in the skies is the Nature which orders the affairs of the earth" (Twain 1972, 401). This truth has been recognized throughout time by intelligent people who have been "tuned in" to nature. This book deals with an important but little-studied aspect of this reality: the cyclical qualities of the runes from a standpoint of runelore and runecraft, and how they relate to specific periods within the cycles of time. Every process in the universe is basically cyclic, from the majestic rotation of galaxies over tens of millions of years, to the smallest vibration of subatomic particles. In our direct experience, we may include the cycles of the seasons, and human cycles of birth, life, and death. Systems where special qualities of time are recognized and used are often called *Chronomancy*. Here, the auspicious qualities of time, especially specific hours and days, are noted and used appropriately for the performance of certain activities. Astrology deals with qualities of time as measured by the relative position of the Earth and other celestial bodies: Sun, Moon, planets, and stars. Classically, the influences of the planets are seen as exerting an influence on the Earth and its inhabitants at vast distances, affecting every action and the very destiny of individuals. Runic astrology deals with the qualities of time and time cycles, as defined by the meanings and attributes of runes, individually and combined. An almost infinite number of factors may influence any event, yet some can be seen as more significant than others. It is this power of discrimination that distinguishes wisdom from folly.

Although certain influences are indicated by the time cycles, this does not mean that future events are fixed, and therefore inevitable. There is no place in runic astrology for helpless fatalism. Rather, the runes and the stages of cycles in progress indicate events that are in process, but that may, according to the laws of chance and by conscious intervention, be disturbed, interrupted, disrupted, or diverted in other directions before they come to fruition. The ways that things happen, the laws that govern process, are the unchanging core of universal existence. They are taught and explained in myth and folktale, and the best literary fiction and drama. They cannot change, and an understanding of them is essential if one is not to be an eternal victim of circumstances.

But in many ways, the present is qualitatively different from the past. Most notably, it is distinguished from traditional societies in the use of unnatural power sources. This is manifested in powered machines, the most transformative of which are self-propelled vehicles, including aircraft. Modern human habitation and lifestyles are conditioned largely by and for powered vehicles. But, in addition to this visible transformation, there are more subtle differences. Apart from the natural radiation from the Sun and cosmos, and the background radiation and magnetic fields of the Earth, we live in the midst of human-made electric fields from power lines, radio and television transmissions, and the emanations of radar and microwave installations. The effect that these artificial electric fields have upon the human body is only known partially, but there is an increasing recognition that all is not well with the unbridled use of this technology, especially in the way that it has separated many people from the natural cycles of time.

As we are living now, and not in some romanticized historic period a thousand years ago, our runecraft, if it is to have any relevance, must reflect the present times. We are present today, and the present is the result of the past. So it is not possible to behave as though we were living in ancient times. But then, neither is a blind acceptance of the modern zeitgeist necessary. What is needed is a creative acceptance of those conditions that are beneficial or useful to us, and a recognition that the malefic elements of modern life must be abandoned. By using the runes in a way relevant to today, we can handle the present in a creative way. A new knowledge of the runic time cycles can help us to do this.

1

THE BASIC CONCEPTS

There are, indeed, things that cannot be put into words.
They make themselves manifest. They are what is mystical.

WITTGENSTEIN,
TRACTATUS LOGICO-PHILOSOPHICUS,
PROPOSITION 6.522

THE UNDIVIDED UNIVERSE:
THE NORTHERN TRADITION

Nothing in existence exists separately—everything that is present in the universe is continuous with its surroundings and is the product of its own unique historical circumstances. This is true of everything in the world, without exception. Wherever we choose to look, there is nothing that exists now, or that has existed in the past, that is not the result of a multiplicity of events and processes, traceable back ultimately to the formation of the world eons ago. Because of this, it is only by studying history in the widest sense that we can begin to get some insights into the true meaning of anything. Naturally, this is true of the spiritual system that lies at the root of the subject matter of this book, the time cycles of the Northern Tradition, of which the runes are the deepest mystical manifestation.

The term *Northern Tradition* describes the basic aspects of natural spirituality indigenous to the lands of northern Europe. The Northern Tradition is a sacred worldview native to that part of Europe generally north of the Alps. Although the Northern Tradition is syncretic in many ways, it is nevertheless distinct and almost completely separate from the spiritual system known in occultism as the *Western Tradition*. The Western Tradition has the precise meaning of a collection of magical practices influenced in the main by the mythology and beliefs of the Middle East. The Western Tradition is usually compared and contrasted with Eastern traditions—the beliefs indigenous to India, Tibet, China, and Japan. But because of their cultural origin, the exoteric manifestation of Middle Eastern traditions tends to be imbalanced toward the male side of the feminine-masculine polarity, and the Western Tradition tends to be patriarchal in character.

In geographical terms, the Northern Tradition covers a large part of Europe. In the east, it includes indigenous beliefs and customs from Austria and Bohemia (Czechia and Slovakia). It covers much of Switzerland, Germany, and northern France, and also includes Brittany, Ireland, Britain, the Faroe Islands, Iceland, Scandinavia, and the Baltic countries (northern Poland, Latvia, and Lithuania). As with any spiritual tradition based on a continent, and not on an isolated island, the Northern Tradition has evolved with influences from various quarters. But today it contains mainly Germanic, Baltic, Norse, and Celtic strands, along with some elements from Etruscan and Greco-Roman Paganism. The elements from other systems of thought, however, are those that enhanced and elucidated certain aspects of the tradition rather than altering it materially, so the Northern Tradition still retains the essential spiritual observance of this part of Europe. Originating in prehistoric times, it has persisted and developed until the present day in the form of folk custom, the veneration of saints, farming- and calendar-lore, women's mysteries, and household magic. It has continued to evolve with the times until the present day, when it has reappeared as a living and vigorous independent spiritual tradition in its own right, with the reemergence of the runes as its most obvious manifestation. Details of the major magical elements of the spiritual path can be found in my book *Pagan Magic in the Northern Tradition* (Destiny, 2015).

At the roots of this first publication anywhere of the runic time cycles is the traditional spirituality of Britain. As it exists today, traditional British culture is an amalgam of various related elements. It is composed largely of developments of two basic ancient strands, the Celtic and the Germanic. The Celtic strand has its origin in the vigorous so-called barbarian (i.e., non-Greek or Romanized) prehistoric culture of Central Europe, which was brought to Britain and Ireland by way of Gaul (France). This came to Britain around the fifth century BCE and assimilated earlier, pre-Celtic, cultures. The Roman conquest of 44 CE and the subsequent 400-year-long occupation brought southern European organization and deities, Roman architecture and roads, the Julian Calendar, and the Roman alphabet, in which this book is set. However, this Roman influence was merely an additional afterthought laid on top of the more vigorous "barbarian" culture, which survived the basically urban-based occupation. Today, there are many continuing folk customs of Celtic origin, while most of the Roman ones have continued within the Church. Even when the Roman Empire's official—indeed only—religion became Christianity, Paganism continued in Britain, far from Constantinople. It was only after the Romans left that missionaries sent by the Christian Church in Rome felt it necessary to come to "convert" Britain. The dates of the first Christian foundations in Wales, for example, show this graphically, being mainly in the 500s and 600s, long after the Romans departed. These strong Pagan elements, mixed with the local variant of the Christian religion, are best expressed in the extensive Arthurian literature that originated in this era.

The Germanic strand of British traditional culture is more complex than the Celtic. It comes directly from "English" settlers who, from the third century CE onward, migrated from the countries now called Holland, Germany, Denmark, and Sweden. It was with this wave of settlement that the runes came from mainland Europe. Added to this is the influence of Danish and Norwegian settlement from the eighth to the eleventh centuries. All of these settlements were of Pagan people; that is, people whose religion and beliefs were basically in harmony with the cycles of nature. It is directly from these Pagan customs, both southern and northern European, that we get our cherished principles of democracy, female-male equality, trial by jury, rights to ownership, and freedom of thought and expression. Subsequently, the Christian Church became dominant, and assimilated many traditional Pagan customs into the round of yearly observance. As they were integral with the labors of the agricultural year, they could not be abolished, so the names were changed, and churchly interpretations were invented to explain the meanings of the festivals. The Pagan deities of the year then became the Church's saints or devils. Many of the male Pagan deities, or personified year markers, became saints in the Christianized calendar. As befitting the patriarchal traditions of the Church, almost all of the female deities were deemed to be harmful and dangerous by the new religion, and were said to be female demons sent to lure men away from God. But as these divine qualities are eternally present, none were lost, and their basic traditions have continued until modern times as the local customs, which nineteenth-century academics labelled "folklore." These Pagan sacred traditions and beliefs also continued in saga, folktales, and local lore, and form the basis today of our knowledge of past practices. It is the spiritual core of these indigenous customs that has reclaimed its position as the Northern Tradition, and is recognized once again as a valid spiritual system in its own right.

As a nature-based spiritual path, the Northern Tradition is expressed in the interaction between the inward experiences of people and their exterior experiences of the climate and landscape. The inner experiences are archetypal—being universal for all men and women—but the outer experiences are specific to the landscape, climate, and yearly cycle of this part of planet Earth. As with traditional Paganism everywhere, the many elements of the Northern Tradition are linked by the theme of harmony with the natural environment. In northern Europe, the cycles of the seasons are very apparent. There is a marked contrast between the light, pleasant, productive summers, and cold, dark, harsh, winters. In response to the cyclic seasonal variations, a system of natural lore arose with which people were able to come to terms, more or less, with the ups and downs of life. Personified as spirits and gods, the forces of nature became approachable. A dynamic interplay became possible between the conscious will of humanity and the natural cycles. Surviving testimony to our ancestors' interaction with both the seen and unseen environment can be found in the four-millennia-old stone circles of Britain, Ireland, and Brittany, their layouts arranged to mark and harmonize with celestial and terrestrial influences.

The Northern Tradition today is a direct continuation of this usage, tried and tested over thousands of years. They are as valid today as ever they were. Although it is implicit in the thought patterns underlying modern technical-industrial civilization that these cycles have been overcome once and for all, and the old ways are gone forever, Nature has ways of reasserting herself in so-called ecotastrophe. Humans are one type among many in Mother Earth's living continuum, just like other animals. When humans go in ways that are out of harmony with nature, then alienation and disaster occur as a matter of course. This is not because some external judge decides that humans have "gone too far" and decides to "punish" us—rather, it is the inexorable result of processes set in train by thoughtless people. Although ignored by modern industrial civilization, this has been recognized by wise people of all natural religions. "For things that violate nature can hardly come to be: and anyhow they pass quickly to destruction, even if they do come into existence," as the great first-century CE Pagan teacher Apollonius of Tyana wisely said (Philostratus [trans. Conybeare], I, xxi). The natural cycles still exert influence upon our lives, and, for those who recognize that eternal fact, the Northern Tradition remains a vital body of appropriate natural lore, which anyone today can use to their benefit.

The Northern Tradition sees the physical universe as eternal and

Fig. 1.1. The Timewheel of the Runes,
encompassing all things.

cyclic, having continuous phases of coming into being (creation) and dissolution (destruction). Because the universe is eternal, there was never a single moment in time of creation. As there was no beginning, there can be no ultimate end. The human being's place in this scheme is that there is no clear boundary between the self and the non-self. As individuals, we are continuous with the universe—physically, spiritually, and consciously. Because of our non-separation, we can view being in many ways, and have a part of that divine living quality that permeates all things. The universe is a single living entity, which, though largely incomprehensible, is comparable to a living being. All things within it, living entities that we may recognize, from plants and animals to sprites and gods, are aspects of the single living One. This knowledge automatically demands respect for all things natural. Basically, then, the Northern Tradition is a holistic system, integrated with reality.

In contrast to the Northern Tradition, the "modern ethos"—that is, the concepts that are the result of many centuries of thought and practice in the Western (European-American) scientific-industrial tradition—is basically fragmental in its worldview. Its fundamental underlying view holds that all things are composed of smaller, discrete parts, which can be broken down into smaller and smaller particles, atoms, and subatomic particles. Then these are considered to be independent entities in their own right, often in absolute opposition to one another. Of course, it is necessary to separate things in order to view them and to live from day to day. Dealing with the totality of reality at one time is impossible. Division is useful when dealing with things on a practical or functional level, but when applied inappropriately as a general concept, it leads ultimately to a breakdown of everything. This fragmental separate-atomic view of things lies at the root of all modern science. It is considered implicitly the "true" basis of reality to the exclusion of all other viewpoints. Science has operated in the main by isolating parts of the whole and studying them separately, then trying to understand the whole as if it were assembled from these separate parts.

But because in certain areas of study this technique has succeeded and produced the technical civilization that exists at the moment, this fragmental, life-denying viewpoint has been put forward as the "real" way that things are in "ultimate reality." Instead of understanding the universe as an interconnected whole, as an unbroken continuum, science views our environment as a collection of separate parts. For example, in this viewpoint, beginning and end, birth and death, hot and cold, dark and light, female and male are seen as absolute opposites rather than polarities of the same continuous whole. Scientific expressions like the "building blocks of life," and atomic theory, where a small aspect of the real continuum is studied artificially in isolation from the context in which it really exists, can easily give a false impression that existence is "nothing but" an assemblage of parts. It is extremely difficult for someone brought up amid Western scientific thought to think of an organic structure as being "whole"—that is, *not* composed of separate parts—and even our language gives us problems in describing "whole" structures without resorting to the "naming of parts." This idea is reinforced by modern manufacture, where every artifact of any complexity is assembled from component parts, which may have been made individually in factories greatly distant from one another. As children, in our formative years, we played with building blocks and construction kits that also molded our worldview into thinking that things are made up from independent, separate, parts. This is also seen in the idea current in some religions that "God made the World," a poetic description that tends to be visualized in the simplistic way of assembly from a kit of parts. On a larger scale, this idea that whole things are in reality composed of separate parts makes it seem natural to disrupt and dismember nature. The continuous surface of our planet has been divided up into a collection of separate parts, either individually owned, the property of companies and corporations, or as fragmental nation-states, often divided in such a way as to take no notice of natural discontinuities and divisions. This "property" is divided up so as to be accessible to exploitation, such as the fragmental removal of minerals.

In the Western worldview, the products of human intelligence—science, art, education, medicine, architecture, language, philosophy, and so on—have been broken down likewise into small areas of specialization. This has led necessarily to a general acceptance that they *are* separate from one another in essence, which is clearly a misperception. When new insights have arisen, new fragmentary areas, called "interdisciplinary," have been created, with the effect of making further fragmentation. Unfortunately, because of these cultural reasons, many people see the boundaries of things as being absolute. But, on the contrary, except as definitions for human use, they are illusory. The problem of the prevailing worldview, however, is that it causes everything to be broken up into fragments, so as to seem to correspond with the fragmented thought system. Because all of the scientific "evidence" for the nature of things has been gained by fragmental means, the information gained tends to reinforce the fragmental hypothesis. By these means, fragmentation seems to have obtained a separate existence of its own, independent of human life and consciousness. However, this is not a correct analysis, for everything gained by human means has the human element in it. In modern science, there is a deliberate attempt to deny this fact. Science strives to get away from human and humane ways of perception (as if that were desirable, even if possible). But by attempting to deny the human element, one also denies implicitly the human usefulness of such knowledge. In addition, because the human element was paramount in ancient times, and ancient thought is based exclusively upon it, the holistic wisdom of the ancients is excluded from the modern viewpoint. This is a tragic mistake, for had the ancient ways been retained, and further refined, then many of the world's present ills would have been avoided. We can find these holistic, nonfragmental truths in the writings of many ancient sages of all lands. In Europe, the best recorded ancient philosophical ideas come from Greek Paganism. For example, Anaxagoras stated (Frag. 6): "all things will be in everything; nor is it possible for them to be apart, but all things have a portion of everything" (Burnet 1892, 283); Aristotle wrote in his *Metaphysics* (XII, 10): "All things are ordered together . . . and the world is not such that one thing has nothing to do with another, but they are connected" (Kaplan 1958, 153); and Empedocles (Frag. 8) saw that everything was intimately connected in the universal continuum as an endless recycling process:

> There is no birth of all things mortal, nor end in ruinous death;
> But mingling only and interchange of mixed
> There is, and birth is but its name with men. (Leonard 1907, 452)

This older worldview exists in myths all over the world. Tales of a former Golden Age reflect a prefragmentary time of wholeness. These legends are images of the true and natural state of human existence that was in being before the perceived split between the human and the natural. When this split came, it was commemorated in myths such as the Jewish "fall of man," and the Greeks' "destruction of Atlantis." In this schism between humans and nature, we have been separated from the animals, which still experience reality in this unbroken manner. We have lost this spontaneity in life. After this, human beings are felt to be in a state of loss, having been rejected by nature or the gods, and being compelled to eke out a precarious separated existence in the wilderness. But even in this fragmented state, we humans are offered comfort by these myths, and a means to transcend the split. This comfort takes different forms in different cultures. Some place their faith in a savior god, who is visualized as coming to Earth as an avatar to spread enlightenment and pave the way for a return to the Golden Age. Among notable spiritual teachers described in this way are the Buddha, Zoroaster, Mithras, Jesus, and Krishna. But there is a danger in this belief in external saviors. It is the seeming readiness of people to abdicate their own personal responsibility for their lives, and to praise or blame others instead of themselves when things go right or wrong. In ancient religions, the non-self-reliant doctrines of the scapegoat and vicarious atonement come from such an abdication of personal responsibility, as have political dictatorships in more recent times.

Other cultures have developed a more direct and self-reliant method—shamanism. The Siberian Tungus word *šaman* is the origin of our word *shaman*. It defines a person who uses specialized ecstatic techniques to mediate between the human world and the realm of that part of the universal whole described variously as spirits, demons, or gods. Before the creation of established priesthoods, the shaman's position in society was one of priest, healer, magician, astrologer, seer, and diviner—a vitally important character in tribal society. Because they touch a common core of human experience, the salient features of Siberian shamanism are paralleled in all human societies. Shamanism involves ritual separation from the everyday world, and the acquisition of the ability to see through and beyond the normal human boundaries of time and space. This separation can be attained by an initiatory pilgrimage to an isolated sacred place, a numinous place of power where the boundaries between the realms of the mundane and the transcendental are weak.

Usually, institutionalized tribal shamanry has been hereditary, but, even where it has not, it has certainly involved a handing on of the craft from master to apprentice. At his or her initiation, conducted at the appropriate place and time, the new shaman was said to be adopted by a divinity or spirit, usually in animal form, through whose agency the magic, divination, and healing would be accomplished. However we interpret the nature of this spirit, it is clear that the shaman has access to knowledge and powers concealed within the inner parts of nature, direct access to the living One that is the universe. When initiated, the master gave the new shaman the clothing and paraphernalia of his craft—a drum, staff, and other magical objects. Then, the master shaman revealed to the initiate the locations and character of the different classes of spirits, along with methods of befriending, propitiating, or outwitting them.

In different cultures, the shaman's initiation has taken different forms. Some have involved dangerous practices of self-torture. Others, such as the Ostyaks of northern central Asia, have had hereditary shamanism, in which the education of the sons by the father shaman was a lifelong instruction in the craft. Spontaneous shamanry has always been highly important, too, and it remains so today in our modern culture where shamanism has been marginalized or dismissed as worthless primitivism. But shamanism is inherent in the human constitution, and is present in every generation. Only its outward manifestations are different. In the modern era, we are nearest to the Altai of central Asia, who assumed the mantle of the shaman spontaneously, without ceremony. Any person who suffered serious injury or near-death illness, who experienced certain revelatory things while injured, and who subsequently recovered, had received the power of the ancestors and was a shaman. This is the way that shamans come to be in modern times.

Once chosen, by whatever means, the shaman undertakes seer's journeys in order to make direct contact with the transcendental powers that underlie existence. Through these journeys on both the physical and astral planes, the shaman is brought into contact with the deep ecology of this and other worlds, becoming one with the One. Inner and outer experiences merge to transcend both. By these means, the shaman reintegrates his or her experience with that of the animals, whose unseparated experience of the world is ever-present. When in any self-induced extreme state, bodily or psychic, a shaman can converse with the inhabitants of the nonmaterial world. From this dangerous terrain, the shaman can obtain knowledge valuable to himself or herself and the human race at large. Through their specialized techniques, shamans reintegrate themselves into the natural world in a manner not possible through intellectual thought. By shamanic techniques, many things useful in the everyday "this-world" have been brought back from the "otherworld."

One of the most important systems bridging the gap beween these worlds is that of the runes. The runes offer a means of transcending this split, for they are shamanic in origin and use. According to Northern

Tradition scripture, they were gained by Odin (Óðinn), who underwent a form of shamanic self-sacrifice. Odin was hung for nine days and nine nights upon a tree, after which he fell, screaming, from it with a full understanding of the wisdom of the runes.

When they are described as an "alphabet," the runes may at first be seen as being part of the fragmental worldview, dividing up the various areas of human and nonhuman experience into discrete elements. But their alphabetic sequence is one of progression. Although the runes are connected with seemingly separate entities, they do not stand for single concepts, as in scientific or mathematical languages. Rather, they access deep levels of universal structure and their corresponding levels in the human psyche. They are symbols of different aspects of reality.

THE PRIMAL STRUCTURE OF ALL THINGS: ORLOG, WYRD, AND THE NORNS

Although we have free will in our lives, we are all subject to *Orlog,* that is, the combination of events, structures, and things—everything that has ever been—which goes to make up that which is now, the present. Whatever has been, even down to the smallest, seemingly insignificant event, like the fall of a leaf millions of years ago, is encoded within that which makes up "now." For, if any event had been otherwise than how it was, then the present would not have been exactly as it is now, however slight the difference might be. Orlog (sometimes spelled in its Old Norse form, *ørlög*) may be translated roughly as "destiny." The original word *ørlög* incorporates the word *ør,* which is cognate with the name of the second rune, Ur, meaning "primal," and the word *lög,* which means "law" or "layer." Thus, the whole word means "primal law" or "primal layer." Human laws are the underlying structure upon which society operates, and in the natural world, the human idea of law has been used to describe the underlying principles upon which the universe operates. As primal layers, these principles or natural laws lie beneath the obvious surface of things but are their inner reality. But although Orlog is sometimes translated as "destiny," in the Northern Tradition, there is no inference of predestination, or fatalism. Every person is an individual blessed with the creative human faculty of free will. The only constraints upon this free will are the circumstances in which we find ourselves, including the cyclic influences in time, which are studied in astrology and chronomancy. This combination of events, persons, and things composes our own personal *Wyrd,* or fate. But of course, we can transcend this fate by our own personal actions.

For example, our present culture is the result of its own Orlog, every influence upon it making it what it is today. We use the Roman alphabet to communicate in print, and numerals that are derived ultimately from Indian mathematics. These each have a specific historical origin and development and are in use today because of a combination of historical and functional reasons. The mystic alphabet of the runes in this book is being described in modern English, a language that contains many words from disparate sources the world over, each of which has its own place in the present, and its future potential is known as its Wyrd or destiny.

The Old English word *wyrd* is directly related to the modern German verb *werden,* which means "to become," and although it is impossible to understand Wyrd intellectually, the multiple elements of Wyrd are often visualized as a web or woven material composed of many disparate threads. A connection can also be seen between the word *wyrd* and the Old High German words *wirt* and *wirtel,* meaning "spindle." Many cultures have the tradition that spinning thread on a spindle and weaving on a loom are connected allegorically or magically with time and destiny. Spinning is an act of creation in which the disordered, and unusable, fibers of wool or flax are transformed into an ordered, and usable, thread. There are two tools necessary for spinning—the spindle and the distaff. The spindle is rotated to spin the thread and the spun material is gathered onto the distaff. Clearly, the rotation of the spindle has a parallel in the apparent motion of the starry heavens in rotation above the Earth. In the north, where this is easily observed, the spinner has been associated esoterically with the heavens, and, by association, with the seasons. The turning spindle, like the mill, is a model of the universe. It operates with a rhythmic, reciprocating, cyclic motion from which comes an unbroken flow of thread, symbolizing the continuum of undying existence. The spindle of the heavens, around which the fixed stars appear to rotate, is marked by the Pole Star. This is known by various names, such as the Lode Star, God's Nail, and the Nowl. It is the guiding star of the navigators of old, upon which traditional East Anglian gardeners still orient their rows of seeds at planting time.

As images of the cosmos, the spindle and distaff are sacred to the goddess Frigg, and to the Norns. Frigg's Distaff is the Northern Tradition name for the three stars now known as the Belt of Orion, with their Arabic names, Anilam, Alnitak, and Mintaka. The rising point of this important constellation is due east. It is close to the two fire-stars of wintertime, the Torch Bearer (Procyon), and the brightest of them all, Loki's Brand (Sirius). Further details of the traditional astronomy of northern Europe can be found in chapter 7. The famous twelfth-century Pagan mural of Frigg in the cathedral at Schleswig shows the goddess riding astride a distaff. Spinning was also connected with the passing of time in general. This is because spinning is one of the earliest manufacturing technologies where the amount of time taken had an obvious direct connection with the amount of thread produced. The length of thread spun was a direct measure of the amount of time spent in making it. Perhaps spinning was the first directly quantifiable work ever done by humans. Whether or not this is the case, from spinning comes the symbolism of the thread of time, which exists in many cultures.

In the Northern Tradition, Wyrd, the working of Orlog, is activated through the mediation of the Norns. These three Norns, the goddesses of fate, are not under the control of the gods, but of Orlog, to whom all things, including the gods, are subject. They are the three Weird Sisters, named Urd (Urðr), Verdandi (Verðandi), and Skuld, whose names mean, respectively, *That Which Was, That Which Is Becoming,*

Fig. 1.2. The Weird Sisters, an engraving from the Elizabethan *Holinshed's Chronicle*, illustrating the story of the Scots King Macbeth. Here, unlike Shakespeare's misogynist rendering of the Norns as three repulsive witches, they are depicted as fine ladies, attired accordingly with their roles as past, present, and future.

and *That Which Will Become*. Urd is depicted as an old woman, looking backward to the past, Verdandi is a young, vigorous, active woman, fearlessly looking straight ahead of her. Skuld, the uncertain future, is heavily veiled, with her head turned away from Urd. She holds the book whose pages remain unwritten in, the unused parchment scroll or the blank tape. The work of the Norns is expressed in an old rhyme, where each speaks in turn:

> *Early begun,*
> *Further spun,*
> *One day done.*

The first two of the Norns, Urd and Verdandi, are considered to be benevolent and creative, but the third, Skuld, continuously undoes their work, ripping it apart and scattering it to the eight winds. On a functional level, the three Norns teach us to learn lessons from the past, to make good use of the present, and to be aware of future problems and threats. Symbolically, their principal function is to weave the web of Wyrd—fate or destiny—which is under the control of Orlog, the eternal law of the universe, the supreme power, without beginning or end, to which all, material and nonmaterial, mundane and divine, are subject. The thread they weave is that which has been spun by the goddess Frigg, Queen of the Heavens and ruler of time. According to tradition, the Web of Wyrd is so large and complex that it stretches from one weaver on a mountaintop in the east to another who stands far in the western ocean. This is the fabric of time, created and measured by the passage of the sun over the earth. The threads of the Norns' woof are cords that vary in color depending on the nature of the event being woven. A black thread, ranging from north to south, portends death. This black thread is the cutting off of a human life between the day's range of east and west. Cosmologically, this "loom of creation" is related directly to the apparent motion of the sun through each day and also through the year. This is one of the many symbolic meanings of the labyrinth, more specifically the ball of thread, the *clew* or clue to the puzzle. It is this thread that, in many cultures, the hero uses to find his way through its gyres. In weaving symbolism, the sun weaves the fabric of time on the loom of the earth. The warp, running north–south, is laid down by the Earth Mother, and the sun goddess completes the fabric by weaving the east–west threads. The intervention of other conscious beings, human and supernatural, creates the patterns known as the "rich tapestry of life."

The spindle-distaff model of the heavens, and the origin of Wyrd, is largely female-oriented. In some ways, it is a parallel of the mill, which is largely male-orientated. The mill is the Northern Tradition model of the cosmos. It is vital to the everlasting food supply of the human race, for the mill grinds grain into flour, the staple food of agricultural humans. Symbolically, it is a microcosmic reflection of the cosmos as traditionally conceived. Although the windmill was invented in northern Europe, the vertical watermill is far older. The working parts consisted of a channel beneath the floor of the mill, through which water was channeled. The flowing water drove paddles connected directly to an axletree, which carried the power upward through the center of the immobile lower millstone to the upper millstone, which was connected to it directly. The upper millstone rotated above the fixed lower one. The mill was thus a model of the cosmos. The Earth was the lower millstone—immobile. Through its center, the nowl, passed the cosmic axis, linking the lower, chthonic, watery underworld with the upper, starry, heavenly upperworld. In the underworld, the dragonlike power of flowing water, the serpent Nidhogg (Níðhöggr), at once powered the mill and threatened it with slow decay, as wood rots in water. In the Northern Tradition, the divine master of the mill is called Amledi or Amluth, the mythic forerunner of Shakespeare's Hamlet. According to some interpretations, Amluth is invoked on a surviving Frisian talisman, the runic-inscribed yew wand from Westeremden, dating from around the year 800. According to other sources, nine giantesses worked the mill. These were the nine mystical mothers of Heimdall, god of orderliness.

When properly managed, in harmony with natural law, the mill ground out peace and plenty. Its disruption means the breakdown of society, bringing the myth of the mill beneath the sea grinding the salt that makes the ocean briny. The bones of people are ground in the demonic mill of the giants. This is the Mill That Grinds Exceeding Slow, bringing suffering and death—grist for the mill. The fairy-tale "Jack and the Beanstalk" has this element where the giant proclaims:

> *Fee, Fie, Fo, Fum!*
> *I smell the blood of an Englishman,*
> *Be he alive, or be he dead,*
> *I'll grind his bones to make my bread!*

"Jack and the Beanstalk" is an "ascent of the cosmic axis" story, where the hero visits Jotunheim (Jötunheimr), home of the giants. The first line of the rhyme is the last remnant of *galdr* or runic calls in non-mystical English, invoking the power of the first rune, Feoh, for wealth.

POETIC SCIENCE:
NORTHERN TRADITIONAL COSMOLOGY

The ancient wise people of the north of Europe recognized many important facts about the structure of the Earth and cosmology that are now given scientific names. Their way of describing things was in terms that could be understood by anyone, yet still incorporating the salient points of reality. The runemasters of old saw the fundamental structure of all things in the primal seed, expressed as the rune Hagal, the cosmic diagram. In antiquity, this was described as the hailstone, written in the microscopic form of ice crystals, which could not be seen until the invention of microscopes many centuries later.

The northern creation myth tells of the coming into being by the dynamic interaction of opposites. During the first phase of this cycle of existence, there was a yawning abyss, the gaping void, Ginnungagap. However, this void was not formless, but contained potential polarities within its whole everything/nothingness: it also had absolute orientation, expressed as the north–south axis. The concepts of north and south are rather those of the polarities than actual physical directions, which may not be defined in the absence of matter. To its north lay the zone of the static principle of coldness and crystalline form, Niflheim. To its south, Muspellheim, the zone of the active principle of energy: fire. Between these two polar zones, in Ginnungagap, the principles of ice (static, crystalline form) and fire (unformed energy) came into contact, and from this, matter was formed. Modern physicists have talked of matter as being "frozen light," and this is what is described in the northern creation myth.

Astronomically, the ancient northern wise women and men knew that the stars generated their own light—something that is taken for granted now. Sisebut, king of the Visigoths (western Goths), argued this in a didactic poem written at Toledo in 614 CE, though the orthodox "wisdom" of the Church fathers asserted that the stars reflected the light of the sun. The description of the shield Svalin, which, in northern mythology, was said to protect the Earth from the harmful rays of the sun, can now be seen as a poetic way of describing our planet's ozone layer—currently threatened with destruction through industrial pollution. Also in northern legend is the world serpent, Jörmungand. He was cast into the ocean, where he grew to such dimensions that he could encircle the world, biting his tail. In this sense, he is the alchemical serpent, Ouroboros. But when he moves, which he does occasionally, then undersea earthquakes and tidal waves are generated. On a geophysical level, Jörmungand represents the mid-oceanic ridges, which were not discovered scientifically until after World War II. Tectonic movements of the ridges are the origin of undersea earthquakes and tidal waves. When we look at the old myths in a new light, we are often surprised at the wisdom they contain.

HAGAL— THE GRAIN OF REALITY

When things are done in accordance with the natural order, they are fresh manifestations of the eternal One. The eternal can manifest itself in a seemingly infinite number of ways. But the effects of Orlog occur within the framework of what is possible. In the Northern Tradition, this framework is described by the rune Hagal or Hægl. Esoterically, this is the Mother Rune. It is called this because, in its early form, it has the geometric form from which all of the other runes may be generated. Basically, Hagal means hail, water, solidified by cold in the air, which then falls from the sky. The mystery underlying Hagal is expressed in *The Old English Rune Poem:*

Hail is the whitest of grains,
It sweeps from the sky,
Whirled by the blowing wind,
It then turns to water.

As the hailstone, Hagal symbolizes the primal seed of manifestation and transformation. Paradoxically, it is solid as it falls in the air, but when it reaches the ground, it becomes liquid water. The hard, damaging hailstone reverts to its life-supporting liquid phase. On a symbolic level, Hagal is the underlying structural pattern of all things. Although this pattern is generally unmanifested, it is that intrinsic framework of reality without which there would be no existence. On a more intelligible level, Hagal's form underlies the basic geometric structure of the physical universe. The Hagal pattern pervades nature as the archetypal matrix known as the *hexagonal lattice,* the most basic configuration of self-ordering systems like crystalline molecules. In Northern Tradition sacred geometry, this pattern is the *Hagal Grid* (Fig. 1.3). The Hagal Grid is composed of an overlapping hexagonal lattice with the overall form of a hexagon. This is composed of 19 foci that enclose 24 equilateral triangles between the links, 19 being the number of the Metonic cycle of Sun and Moon (see Chapter 6), while 24 is the number of runes in the oldest runic row known as the *Elder Futhark* (see next chapter). At the center of the grid is a sevenfold figure, which symbolizes the seven days of the week and their corresponding astrological "planets." Around it, the other twelve foci signify the twelve months of the year. The complete Hagal Grid pattern is also the basis for every runic character, which can be made by connecting the corresponding foci of the Hagal Grid. It is not for nothing that to runemasters Hagal is known as the Mother Rune.

In the natural world, Hagal is omnipresent when natural patterns self-organize. Hagal's form can be found in crystals of ice and quartz, in surface cracks in many materials, in the cellular structure of plants and the wax honeycombs of bees. The archetypal form of Hagal is a

Fig. 1.3. The Hagal Grid.

six-branched character, which is precisely the geometry of snowflakes and larger ice crystals, recognized intuitively by the ancient runemasters more than a score of centuries before the first microscopists described them scientifically. When ice forms on a lake surface, it does so as a horizontal hexagonal lattice. This may not be apparent to most people, but the observation of natural processes was part of the training of the runemasters of old, as today. The ice on freshwater lakes is sometimes found divided into six-sided prisms, the edges being defined by lines of air bubbles trapped in the ice. Large blocks of Arctic ice are known to break up into six-sided vertical columns and look like a glassy version of the well-known columnar basalt rocks. The fernlike forms of ice crystals inside a window on a cold winter's day are composed basically of an array of elements of the Hagal hexagonal lattice. The hexagonal lattice occurs also in patterns of convection, where a fluid is heated, and "cells" of rising and falling fluid are formed. This phenomenon can be seen in cooking and the drying of thick coats of oil-based paint. It remains, "fossilized" in the structure of many igneous rocks, such as the basalt that forms the Giant's Causeway in the north of Ireland. In a macroscopic form, parts of the cracked icy surface of Europa, one of the major moons of Jupiter, have an underlying hexagonal lattice pattern.

The research conducted in the 1930s by the Japanese scientists Terada and Watanabe, mentioned in Robert Temple's book on divination, *Conversations with Eternity,* investigated the importance of the hexagonal lattice in the formative processes of life. Beginning with an investigation of the nature of cracks in pavements, they moved on to the basically similar patterns in organic structures. Terada and Watanabe found that when any solid structure, such as a paving slab, cracks, then the pattern of cracks will conform to parts of a hexagonal lattice ("quasi-hexagonal cells") along the line of stress. Physically, the crack is a place where a macroscopic discontinuity is produced in a field that apparently is uniform and homogenous, but that is subject to microscopic fluctuations. Whenever these fluctuations occur, they are subject to the basic laws of physics, and the cracks produced also conform to those laws, producing a hexagonal lattice, which is especially noticeable when the cracks fill up with some other matter. In an article titled "Crack and Life," Terada followed up the studies on pavements by investigating other phenomena including patterns in living systems. They studied the patterns on the skins of some animals, and came up with the conclusion that they represented the places where the surface of the embryo had cracked during growth, for they conformed broadly to a hexagonal lattice.

In 1984 I worked on self-ordering systems in living algal cultures with Professor John Kessler of the University of Arizona. During studies on the fluid-mechanical phenomenon known as vorticity, we conducted some experiments on self-ordering systems in thick cultures of motile marine algae. This very interesting phenomenon is where patterns are produced in a homogenous culture of living cells in water by the subtle interactions between the organisms' swimming characteristics and the shape of the container in which the culture is held. It is not heat-driven convection, but a dynamically produced phenomenon unique to self-propelled living organisms. Using the saline-tolerant alga *Dunaliella salina,* a thick culture composed of millions of cells was placed in a shallow container and allowed to stand. After a couple of hours, patterns appeared in the cultures where the swimming microorganisms were circulating. The size of the "cells," that is, the diameter of the area of circulation, was found to be dependent upon the depth of the medium. But whatever the size, the general overall tendency was to form a hexagonal lattice.

From the foregoing, it can be seen that the hexagonal lattice, expressed in the Northern Tradition as the Mother Rune Hagal, is the archetypally basic pattern of the universe. In geometry, Hagal is a fundamental pattern, produced from the inherent sixfold division of the circle. Drawn with compasses, the radius of a circle divides the circumference into exactly six parts. From this, the hexagon, the hexagram, and several other major geometric figures can be produced. Another aspect of the rich symbolism of Hagal is as indicating the six directions of space. Traditionally, these are forward and backward, left and right, up and down. Here, the Mother Rune is at the center of all things, which in traditional cosmology is the navel of the world, known in geomancy as the *omphalos* or *nowl.* As this central point, the intersection of the cosmic axis with the earthly plane, Hagal denotes the access-point to other states of consciousness and alternative dimensions. Hagal is an entrance to the cosmic axis, which is the link between the upperworld, the middle world and the lower world. Physically, such points were represented in the landscape as crossroads, often marked by a standing stone, perron, or cross. Each such nowl point is the local center of the world, and other things are arranged around it accordingly.

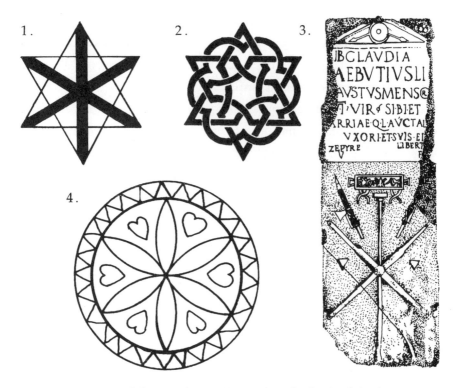

Fig. 1.4. Versions of the Hagal rune: 1. Hagal as the basis of the hexagram;
2. The *Lacey Fret*, from Lancastrian heraldry; 3. Tombstone of the Roman
surveyor, Lucius Aebutius Faustus, showing his *groma* as the Hagal pattern,
Ivraea Museum, Italy; 4. Magically protective *Hex* sign from
a traditional "Pennsylvania Dutch" house, USA.

An intriguing Hagal-nowl connection can be found in representations of the old Roman surveying instrument known as the *groma*. These are known from Roman tombstones, which often have depictions of the tools of the trade of the deceased. The memorial of Lucius Aebutius Faustus at Ivraea, Italy, has a *groma*. This tool was an ingenious technical instrument that enabled straight lines at right angles to one another to be laid out across the ground from any point at which it was set up. Derived from the ancient techniques of augury used in the Etruscan Discipline (see chapter 2), it consisted of a cross-shaped portion supported by a stick or post. In use, it defined the four cardinal directions and the perpendicular axis of up and down. When dismantled, as shown on the tombstone (Fig. 1.4) it makes the form of the Hagal rune. The six-branched form of Hagal mirrors the mystery of the microcosm and the macrocosm, in which the greater world (the universe) is reflected in the lesser world (the human being). The older form of Hagal is analogous to the serpent-bearing *caduceus* staff of the southern European god Hermes/Mercury, deity of the transformative flux in the universe. Hagal is also connected with the cosmic axis by being associated with the world serpent. In Northern Tradition cosmology, this worm, called Nidhogg (Niðhöggr), winds itself around the base of the World Tree Yggdrasil, continuously gnawing away at its roots, threatening its stability. Thus, the serpent, agent of decay, threatens the stability of existence. Often, the worm Nidhogg is equated with Jormungand (Jörmungandr), the World Serpent. Whether it is in the form of Nidhogg or Jormungand, the snake symbolizes the threat of potential sudden catastrophic change inherent in all seemingly stable systems. In the rune Hagal, this is the rapid transformation from its static crystalline form to its flowing liquid form. There is an allusion to this image of serpent/Hagal in *The Old Icelandic Rune Poem,* which says:

> *Hagal is a cold seed,*
> *And a fall of sleet,*
> *And a disease of serpents.*

In the runic row, Hagal is the ninth rune. Nine is the most sacred number of Northern Tradition spirituality, signifying completion and wholeness. Hagal, as nine, symbolizes the universe, manifested in the nine worlds of Yggdrasil. Unlike most of the other runes, which are invertible and reversible, Hagal's shape remains unchanged whichever way we look at it. This unchangeable shape symbolizes the eternal cosmic harmony, which is attainable by those who care to use the appropriate techniques.

DIVINATION AND THE RUNES

Today the runes are widely known for their use in divination, as an oracular technique. The passage from Tacitus's *Germania* (chap. 10), written at the end of the first century CE, concerning the ancient Germanic tribes' use of "lots" for divination has often been interpreted as an early reference to the runes as an oracle. But the basic concept of divination is the same whether the runes or some other system is used. Divination is to do with time. It is a means of defining the character and qualities of the present time, of discerning the processes current at the present time, and the tendencies and potential development of those processes in the future.

When divination is seen as "telling the future," that is a simplistic interpretation—as if "the future" is the next page in a book already printed, or the next track on a record. This is a fatalistic viewpoint, imagining that we have no free will, but are programmed robots in some sort of film whose purpose of existing is presumably to entertain the unseen beings for whose benefit the show has been brought into being. Then, even our acts of divination would be part of the program, and the whole of existence would be an insufferable sham. Naturally, Northern Tradition spirituality utterly rejects this view, which assumes that our existence is some sort of cosmic showbiz. The Northern Tradition recognizes free will within our personal Wyrd and general Orlog. But neither is the future a random unknowable. While it must be recognized that catastrophes are possible, and the processes of the present may be interrupted, even terminated, by some major foreseeable disaster, in general, the processes in train now are leading toward certain results, and these may be predicted. Things that will come about as the result of processes already in action are only "going to happen" *if* those who can alter or prevent them do nothing. Everything we do is important, for each action, however small, affects the course of events. Even a divination is part of this process. In divination, as well as other areas, runecraft is a vital, living tradition that is developing rapidly as new insights are found. Today we investigate and find new insights, new parallels, new ways of using the runes. But, because these new ways are within the traditional framework of the ways things go, they are as authentic as if they were dug out from a 2,500-year-old burial mound.

2

THE RUNES AND THEIR MEANING

Runes shalt thou find, and fateful signs,
That the king of singers colored,
And the mighty gods have made;
Full strong the signs, full mighty the signs,
That the ruler of the gods doth write.

HÁVAMÁL (TRANS. BELLOWS)

All over the world, people have devised devices and techniques that give some insight into the hidden processes of life. This recognition is at the base of those sacred traditions in which knowledge and wisdom are valued. There are many symbolic techniques that allow people to interact with the unseen, of which alphabets are perhaps the most developed. In the West, there are five main alphabets that have magical connections: Hebrew, Greek, Glagolitic, Ogham, and Runic. Although they were or are used in everyday life for written communication, they all began as sacred symbolic alphabets in which every character had an array of meaning far beyond the mere sound it represented. The runes, which originated in central Europe about 2,500 years ago, are the prime example of such an alphabet. Strictly speaking, the runes are not an alphabet at all. An alphabet begins with *alpha* and *beta*—A, B, and so on. The runic rows do not have this Greek-derived character sequence, but a different one. They are known as the *Fuþark* because the characters (or *staves*) are arranged in a specific order, which begins F, U, Þ, A, R, K. As the third runic stave (Þ/þ) is equivalent to the sound "th," a common alternative transliteration is *Futhark,* which will also be used in the present book.

However, the word *alphabet* is used now (incorrectly) to refer to any system of writing comprising separate individual characters with phonetic meanings. But whether we call their array an alphabet or a Futhark, the runes are far more than mere phonetic sigils designed for information interchange in so-called "barbarian" central and northern Europe. They encapsulate symbolic meanings that go far beyond the modern materialist images of practical necessity.

The connotations surrounding the word *rune* itself provide evidence for this. They are far removed from the idea of a *character* or *letter,* words used to describe an individual *stave* in more prosaic alphabets. The *rune* is a precise concept in its own right. The word itself possesses associations with the carefully guarded inner secrets of the esoteric mysteries. This is apparent in the old languages of northern Europe, where it is directly cognate with words meaning "to whisper" such as the archaic English verb *to rown* and the modern German verb *raunen.* There are also related words in the Celtic languages, including Old Irish word *rún,* "mystery, secret; secret intention" (modern Irish *rún,* "intimate friend"), and Middle Welsh *rin,* "secret, mystery," "privacy, intimacy," and "magic spell, charm" (modern Welsh *rhin,* "virtue, essence"). The leaders and councilors of Anglo-Saxon England called their discussions "runes" (*rūne*), where the runes were used for divination when problems arose. For instance, the meeting where Magna Carta was signed in 1215, which guaranteed the citizens of England certain civil rights, was held at a traditional site of royal councils, Runnymede, the "Meadow of the Runes." This site was the place of former runic consultations in Anglo-Saxon times.

At the basic level, a *rune* is literally a mystery that comprehends fundamental secrets of the inner structure of the reality. Each stave, which we call a rune, is a storehouse of knowledge and meaning, which is apparent only to those who study runecraft in all its aspects. Each individual rune expresses an amorphous yet eternal reality, which is revealed in the world of our experience as the specific things or processes characterized by it. Unlike many rigid magical disciplines, the runic system is dynamic, creative, and developing. At a fundamental level, the meanings of the runes are fixed, yet every day new things are made and new experiences, new juxtapositions, and new relationships occur. No time or place is ever like any other, and accordingly, the action of the runic archetypes is affected by the specific conditions there.

In its symbolic use, runic is an analogue of reality, where each character describes a set of events. But because of this fundamentally fluid nature of reality, one cannot ever make the definitive statement about the meanings of the runes. While it is clear that some runes do not have certain meanings, runecraft is less rigid on the inclusiveness of runic interpretations. This creative, nondogmatic approach is a characteristic aspect of the Northern Tradition. It was stated openly in the laws of ancient Wales regarding the shamanic diviners known as the *Vates* (seers). Unlike the Druids and Bards, these *Vates* were not initiates, but had been "chosen" in some way through personal hardship, injury, illness, or other catastrophic revelation. Thus empowered and recognized by others, they were charged with bringing into the traditional esoteric milieu any new things that they knew intuitively were appropriate and valuable additions.

Over the years there have been heated arguments over the origin of the Futhark, in which sometimes chauvinistic nationalism and even racism have played a greater part than scholarship. But whatever the claims, it has been established without doubt that as an alphabet the characters (or *staves*) of the runes are derived from the North Italic script. This North Italic writing was used by Etruscan merchants who carried it from Italy across Central Europe to the Baltic when trading for amber. The Etruscan culture was very influential. Throughout Europe, the geomantic system known as the *Etruscan Discipline* became the basis for traditional town foundation until the late Middle Ages. The eightfold division of the horizon, upon which the day and year wheels are based, came to full development in Etruscan esoteric tradition. Central European Celtic and Germanic workmanship of the first millennium BCE shows many motifs derived from Etruscan crafts. The famous beaked bronze jug known as a *Schnabelkanne* (dating from 400 BCE) in the Salzburg Museum is a magnificent example of such influence, and there are many similar examples. Also, the Etruscan-Runic link has been proved archaeologically. In 1812, twenty-six bronze helmets dating from the fourth century BCE were excavated at Negau in Austria-Hungary. Engraved into the helmets were inscriptions in Germanic words but written in North Italic script. From this time onward, the phonetic use of the runes was developed.

However, the runestaves as we known them were not just taken directly from North Italic script, for many of them existed already as symbols. In northern Europe, especially Scandinavia, during the late Bronze and early Iron Ages (1300–800 BCE) the pictographic rock-carvings known as *Hällristningar* were created. From the *Hällristningar* came sigils that were incorporated in the first runic "alphabet," created in about 350 BCE. Consequently, this collection of pre-runic signs, sigils, and symbols is sometimes given the alternative name of the *Rune-hoard*. Examination of both *Hällristningar* and North Italic makes it clear that the runes are derived initially from two separate sources, amalgamated in a skillful way that tapped the common, deeper, level of the two separate systems. The meanings of the runes may also be derived from the two sources, as Greek, which is related to the North Italic script, has a series of meanings, making it likely that Etruscan character correspondences also existed. But whatever the exoteric origins, the deep, common level of symbolism is the level at which the runes operate: the level of the archetypal underlying reality that is at work in all our lives, whether or not we recognize the fact.

Although it is certain that the *Hällristningar* symbols were used for divination before the creation of the Futhark, the runes as such came into being when some of the signs were taken and identified with certain transalpine alphabetic characters. This act of insight is expressed in the legend of Odin. According to Pagan scripture, human possession of the runes came about as the result of Odin's shamanic revelation by means of a precise ritual. In the song of *Hávamál*, stanzas 138 and 139 read:

> *I ween that I hung on the windy tree,*
> *Hung there for nights full nine;*
> *With the spear I was wounded, and offered I was*
> *To [Odin], myself to myself,*
> *On the tree that none may ever know*
> *What root beneath it runs.*
> *None made me happy with loaf or horn,*
> *And there below I looked;*
> *I took up the runes, shrieking I took them,*
> *And forthwith back I fell.* (trans. Bellows)

Among other attributes, Odin is the shaman-god of magic, poetry, divination, and inspiration. He is also seen as an important aspect of the One, Odin Allfather, active in the mental and physical worlds. In ancient society, the practice of shamanism cultivated the means of direct access to the worlds beyond. The techniques used included dangerous, potentially lethal, practices of self-torture—often involving the use of natural hallucinogenic or trance-inducing roots, herbs, seeds, fruits, and fungi. Odin's shamanic experience appears to have been one of self-crucifixion for the magical period of nine days and nights. The tormented resulting flash of insight, which enabled Odin to release the full potential of the runes for human use, was a rare moment in history where the two sides of the brain were linked by a unified response to a single sign.

Fig. 2.1. Odin on the World Tree. A medieval sculpture
in the vault of the crypt of Königslutter church,
Braunschweig, Germany.

Each of the runes has a name, describing an object or quality, and
that name refers to a complex of ideas and correspondences surrounding
it. The oldest version of the rune alphabet is known as the *Elder Futhark*.
It has twenty-four characters, each of which has a name that relates symbolically to some thing or quality. Using combinations of runes, every

aspect of life can thus be described or investigated. Traditionally, these twenty-four runes are divided into three groups of eight known as the *ættir*. Each group of eight is known as an *ætt,* a Norse word that also describes the eight directions, cognate with the Scots word *airt.* Each of the three *ættir* is ruled over by a Northern god and goddess. The first is sacred to Frey and Freyja, the second, Heimdall and Modgud (Móðguðr), and the third, Tyr (Týr) and Zisa.* The Elder Futhark is used for the directions and in the time cycles of the day and the year. Later, slightly different rune rows are used for the other cycles. The five additional runes of the longer Anglo-Saxon Futhork system are used in the lunar-based cycles, while those of the longest row, the 33-rune Northumbrian, are related to more arcane ones. A 19-rune row, derived from the(16-rune) Scandinavian Younger Futhark, is used for calendrical purposes to denote the 19-year Metonic Cycle of Sun and Moon.

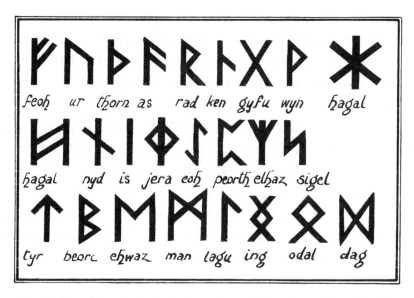

Fig. 2.2. The Elder Futhark. Both versions of Hagal are given, the six-branched form being the earlier.

---

*Zisa is a Continental Germanic goddess who was associated with the city of Augsberg. Her name suggests she may have been a female consort or counterpart to Ziu (Tyr).

Before proceeding with the runes of the Elder Futhark, a brief explanation should be given regarding their names. Based on the later evidence of rune rows such as the Anglo-Saxon Futhork and Scandinavian Younger Futhark, linguists have been able to reconstruct what the Elder Futhark rune names are likely to have been in the ancient Proto-Germanic language (from which the later Germanic languages all descend). Since these reconstructed names are not actually attested in any literary source, they are written with a preceding asterisk: *fehu, *uruz, and so on. But it is also the case that linguists do not necessarily agree on what the exact form of these names would have been, and therefore I have opted not to use them for the system I present in this book. Instead, I have assigned names based on those that appear in the Anglo-Saxon Futhork, although in a few cases the names used here do reflect older forms (e.g., *elhaz* and *ehwaz*). A chart of the runes and their names can be seen in Figure 2.2. In the explanations below, the rune name I am using in this book will appear first in bold type, followed by the reconstructed Proto-Germanic in parentheses. The Proto-Germanic forms are based on those posited by the late Klaus Düwel in the fourth edition of his standard runology handbook *Runenkunde* (2008, 7–8).

The Elder Futhark row begins with **Feoh** (*fehu*), the primary rune of the first *ætt*. Like the first letters of the Hebrew and Greek alphabets (*aleph* and *alpha*, respectively), the name of the first rune, *Feoh*, means "cattle." The real sense of "cattle" here is "movable wealth." In the traditional society of so-called barbarian Europe, the main negotiable property of a person, family, or clan was cattle. The homestead was immutable inheritable property, which could not be sold or bartered for anything. The cow is revered in Northern mythology as Audhumla (Auðumbla), the primal cow, which licked a crystalline block of salt from which arose the being known as Buri, the progenitor of humankind. Feoh is thus that primal power from which we all originate. In Book I of *The Georgics*, Virgil's account of the Birth of Man begins: "The snow-white bull with gilded horns ushers in the year" (ll. 216–18;

trans. Fairclough). The first rune, Feoh, the white bull, opens the runic cycle of the year.

On a material level, Feoh symbolizes the accretion of power and control, both directly over the herd itself and through its possession and manipulation. But, by possessing anything, we have automatically certain responsibilities that ownership brings. To own a herd of cattle wisely and responsibly entails correct stewardship. Wastefulness or greed will soon lead to disaster, either through the collapse of the enterprise or interpersonal discord. In modern times, Feoh refers to money in general, but more specifically, the ability or opportunity to gain worldly success and great wealth, and to keep it. The word *fee,* meaning a payment, comes from this source. But, as with all things, there are two polar aspects of wealth. *The Anglo-Saxon Rune Poem* expresses them both: "Wealth is a comfort to everybody, yet we all must give it away freely, if we want to gain favor in the sight of the lord." But *The Old Norwegian Rune Poem* stresses the problems of wealth stirring greed and envy, which can bring the downfall of all: "Wealth causes friction between relatives, / While the wolf lurks in the woods."

The herb corresponding to Feoh, the Stinging Nettle (*Urtica dioica*) is a good image of a beneficial/harmful thing: it can be used for healing as a beneficial herbal infusion, but it can also cause pain. Feoh's tree is one of the most magical, the Elder (*Sambucus nigra*).* The elements ruled by Feoh are fire and earth, and the deities ruling the rune are the twin brother and sister divinities Frey and Freyja, the Lord and Lady of modern Wicca, though the rune has a female polarity overall.

Ur (**uruz*) is the second rune. It represents the great European wild cattle known as the aurochs, *Bos primigenius.* This was literally the Primal Ox, once widespread in northern and central Europe, the last of which, sadly, was hunted to extinction in the 1600s. For the traditional hunting clans of ancient northern and central Europe, the aurochs

---

*Further details of the magical meanings and uses of trees may be found in my book, *Practical Magic in the Northern Tradition* (Pennick 1989), 70–84.

occupied the same place as did the buffalo for the Native American plains tribes. *The Anglo-Saxon Rune Poem* treats it thus: "The aurochs is bold with horns rising high, a fierce horn-fighter who stamps across the moors, a striking animal!"

Unlike the personal, socially controlled power of property expressed in the rune Feoh, Ur is the raw, tameless might of the Primal Ox. Ur is the boundless power behind creation. Ur signifies the primal power, an irrepressible combination of vital stamina and perseverance united as a fearsome embodiment of creative potential. Because of this, Ur can never be a personal power owned or controlled by a single individual. When it applies to human power, it is collective power, "our" power. The influence of Ur is for good fortune, personal success that is not at the expense of others and, primarily, the promotion of the common good. The sacred tree of Ur is the Silver Birch *(Betula pendula);* its corresponding plant is the lichen known commonly but erroneously as Iceland moss *(Cetraria islandica).* Ur is ruled by the god Thor and the eldest Norn, Urd. Its element is earth, with a male polarity.

Thorn (**þurisaz*) is the third rune, signifying literally the resistant qualities of the thorn tree, and a legendary type of giant known as a *Thurs.* It is a rune sacred to Thorn. On the plant, the thorn is a protective structure that operates passively or as a deterrent. In sacred terms, Thorn represents the defensive quality of the sacred Hammer of Thor, Mjöllnir. The hammer's name means "Crusher," and is a word cognate with *mill.* One of the bynames of the Greek god Zeus, equated with Thor in many ways, was "the Miller." Thorn is that divine power that is resistant to all things that threaten right orderliness. Accompanying the Thunder God's hammer sound is lightning, a sudden, unheralded change that can cause an immediate alteration in the way that things are going. Thorn is also the masculine creative energy, the wilful direction of the generative principle.

The Anglo-Saxon Rune Poem says: "The thorn is very sharp, an evil thing to grip upon, very grim for anybody who falls among them." As a rune, Thorn indicates a change of fortune, good news, or the immediate necessity for an important and far-reaching decision to be taken. In this latter meaning, it can also signify regeneration. It is associated with the Oak (*Quercus robur*), the Bramble (*Rubus fruticosa*), the Blackthorn (*Prunus spinosa*), and the Hawthorn or May Tree (*Crataegus monogyna*); its corresponding herb is the Houseleek (*Sempervivum tectorum*), a traditional protector of houses against lightning, Thor's weapon. Thorn's element is fire, and its polarity male. Thorn is the rune of the harvesters, especially the grain harvest at Lammastide. It is especially the rune of places in England named after Thor, such as Thunderfield, Surrey; Thundersley, Essex; Thorley and Thundridge, Hertshire, and generally, places with names like Thornton or Thornbury. Torshavn, the capital of the Faroe Islands, was a most sacred harbor dedicated to the god, and thus under the power of the rune Thorn.

As (*ansuz*) is the fourth rune of the Elder Futhark (in the later Anglo-Saxon Futhork it is moved to the twenty-sixth position as *Æsc* and the fourth position is filled with a variant form, *Os*, which represents an "o" sound). This powerful rune signifies the divine force at work. It has its origin in the most archaic period of the Indo-European tradition as the Sanskrit primal sound that preceded the manifestation of this cycle of the universe. On a physical level, As is represented by the Ash tree (*Fraxinus excelsior*). In the Northern Tradition, the Ash is one of the most sacred trees, being a version of the World Tree Yggdrasil, the cosmic axis. The black buds and horseshoe-shaped leaf scars of the Ash denote its dedication to the god Odin and the Anglo-Saxon goddess of spring, Eostre. As the cosmic axis, As controls the maintenance of order in the cosmos, eternal stability: "The Ash, beloved of humans, towers high. In a firm position it holds well to its place, though many enemies come forward to fight it," as *The Anglo-Saxon Rune Poem* recounts.

In addition to the Ash tree, the Linden tree (*Tilia platyphyllos*) is connected with As. Its "herb" is really a fungal fruiting body, the red and white Fly Agaric mushroom, *Agaricus muscaria,* whose hallucinogenic qualities are associated with the ecstatic techniques of shamanry. Eating this fungus can produce sensations of flying and, appropriately, the corresponding element of As is air. Its polarity is male, and its tutelary god is Odin, master of shamans. It is not recommended that readers should eat the Fly Agaric fungus, however, as fatal overdoses are quite possible.

Rad (*raido*) or Raed is the fifth rune. According to *The Anglo-Saxon Rune Poem,* "Riding is soft for a hero inside the hall, but it is more strenuous when he is astride a great horse riding the long-mile roads." Rad symbolizes both types of riding: sexual intercourse and horsemanship, but its name indicates the wheel and motion. Esoterically, it is the "vehicle" that we use to achieve something. But a wheeled vehicle is useless without a road to run on, and so a subsidiary meaning of Rad is the road itself, encompassing the way forward and the means to get there. Rad represents the transformation of energies—a transference of spirit, matter, or information from one place to another, with emphasis on personal transformation. It symbolizes conscious control of the factors that go to make up our Wyrd. This can be accomplished by the positive influence of our consciousness on the wheel of fortune. It is also the wheel of the year, with which we must come into harmony if we are to live a reasonably successful life. It is the channeling of energies in the correct manner to produce the desired results, with the emphasis on being in the right place at the right time, performing the appropriate act. Rad's ruling trees are the Oak (*Quercus robur*) and the Wayfaring Tree (*Viburnum lantana*). Its herb is Mugwort (*Artemisia vulgaris*). Rad's corresponding element is air, and the ruling divinities are Ing and Nerthus. It has a male polarity.

Ken (*kenaz*) or Cen is the sixth rune. It symbolizes a flaming brand illuminating the royal hall of olden times, and the Deal branch from which it was fashioned. *The Anglo-Saxon Rune Poem* says: "The torch is living fire, bright and shining. Most often, it burns where noble people are at rest indoors." Ken therefore signifies illumination, being the mystery of transformation, regeneration through death, and the destruction of the pine wood giving heat and light. In the darkness, Ken brings light, allowing us to see and thus is the bringer of knowledge, the inner light. It is the bringer or starter of the fire of the hearth, the power of the forge where material is transmuted by the will into something that reflects the human intellect and reflects the divine harmony. As a rune of balance through transformation, it is present at the autumnal equinox.

Its form is of a branch from a straight stave, the active principle and the polar opposite of the eleventh rune, Is, the single stroke which signifies the static principle. It is interesting to consider that in English dialect and in the Scots language, the homonym *ken* has the meaning of knowledge, and the old poetic term *kenning* means a poetic metaphoric description, such as "sea plow" for a ship.

Ken is the mystical creation by the union and transmutation of two separate entities of a third, which formerly did not exist. Ken channels protective energy, regenerative powers, and furthers positive actions. It enhances the positive aspects of sexuality immanent in the goddess Freyja and the god Frey, but is under the overall rulership of Heimdall and the element fire. It is associated with the Deal (Pine—*Pinus sylvestris*) and the Bilberry, Whortleberry, or Blaeberry *(Vaccinium myrtillus),* and its herb, the Cowslip *(Primula veris).* Ken has a female polarity.

Gyfu (*gebo*) is the seventh rune. It has the meaning of *gift* or *giving,* more specifically a gift of one's own ability or talent to the service of another. The talent itself can be seen as a gift from the gods. Gyfu therefore signifies unification through exchange. Gyfu expresses the essential unity between the donor and the person to whom the gift is given. Gyfu is personified in the Northern goddess Gefn, the bountiful giver. It has the qualities of linking seemingly separate parts of society, or the human with the divine. This interchange between people or humans and gods can also signify cooperation between two individuals. This may take the form of a common cause, a business partnership, or a magical working involving a voluntary sacrifice of one's resources. In *The Anglo-Saxon Rune Poem,* Gyfu's reading is: "To people, giving is an ornament of value, and to every outsider without any other, it is substance and honor."

The form of the rune Gyfu is the sacred *mark,* associated with both the Ash (*Fraxinus excelsior*) and the Wych Elm (*Ulmus glabra*). Its herb is the Wild Pansy (Heartsease, *Viola tricolor*), its element air, and its polarity both female and male. It is sacred to the goddess Gefn.

Wyn (**wunjo*) is the eighth rune, the last of the *ætt* of Frey and Freyja. It signifies joy, which is that elusive quality of being in a state of harmony within a largely disharmonious society, as expressed in *The Anglo-Saxon Rune Poem:* "Joy is for someone who knows little sorrow, without sorrow they will have bright fruits and happiness and houses enough." Wyn is a rune of balance, the midpoint between opposites necessary for a sane and happy existence, the removal of alienation either from shortage or excess. Wyn stands for the fulfilment of wishes and desires. This is accomplished by the establishment of necessary harmonies, the transformation of life for the better. It is a rune of fellowship, shared aims, and general well-being. The tree of Wyn is the Ash (*Fraxinus excelsior*), and its herb is Flax (*Linum usitatissimum*). Flax, the plant from which linen is made, was one of the gifts Frigg gave to human beings to start the process of civilization. The rune is thus sacred to both Frigg and Odin, and the element air. It is of male polarity.

Hagal (**haglaz*) or Hægl is at the beginning of the second *ætt,* which is ruled over by Heimdall, the Watcher of the Gods. Under the guise of Rig (Rígr), Heimdall is the organizer of traditional, agrarian-hunting society. The literal translation of the name Hagal is *hail,* frozen rain that falls from the sky. Hail is water transformed for a short while into ice, during which time it can fall from the sky and destroy crops or property. When it has done its damage, it melts, changing back into harmless, even beneficial, liquid water. Symbolically, Hagal is the icy primal seed of structure and transformation, patterned in accordance with the primal sacred geometry whose forms underlie the universe. In this manner, Hagal signifies the processes that are necessary for anything to be accomplished, and because of this it is sometimes interpreted as indicating or bringing a delay. Obviously, Hagal's element is ice, the fifth element in the Northern Tradition.

Fig. 2.3. The earlier form of the Mother Rune at the center of the mystic wheel of Hagal, emblematical of the three *ættir* of the Elder Futhark, and the eight festivals of the year. Starting at the top, going clockwise, they are: Yule, Brigantia, vernal equinox (Eostre), Beltane, midsummer solstice, Lammas, autumnal equinox, Samhain.

Hagal is a link between the upperworld and Middle Earth, upon which we live. It is the rune of the number nine, the most sacred number of the Northern Tradition, and, as such, is the *Mother Rune*. Hagal is associated with the guardian deities of the passages that link the world of human consciousness with other planes. These divinities are Heimdall, the watcher god who links Middle Earth on which we live with the upperworld by way of the Rainbow Bridge, Bifröst; and Modgud, the goddess who guards the bridge to the underworld. Ice crystals in the sky sometimes cause rainbow-hued haloes, such as those seen around the moon on icy nights. Similarly, the chilling bridge to the cold underworld is icy in nature. The rune is also associated with Urd, the eldest Norn, "that which was." Hagal is the rune of Samhain, the modern Hallowe'en.

Hagal's tree is the oldest-lived European species, the Yew (*Taxus baccata*), and its herb is Bryony (*Bryonia alba*). Both are associated with access to the underworld and upperworld through shamanism and death. Its sexual polarity is female. Hagal signifies patterns of energy originating in the past, which are active in and have an effect upon the present time. It manifests as Orlog influencing things in a powerful if subtle way. Accordingly, it represents the power of evolution within the framework of present existence. Hagal is the rune at the roots of things, both on a physical, material level, and in time. It is one of the major runes of Wyrd: those patterns of events in our past life that make the present what it is today.

Rune readers often regard the presence of Hagal in a shoat as a bad sign, signifying a disruption in life. The bad aspects of the rune may occur as the result of physical accidents or, more diffusely, as generally unforeseen "bad luck." But whatever they are, the events indicated by the rune may come suddenly and unexpectedly. In addition, they cannot be avoided, for these events are outside human control or intervention. However, they are not random, for they proceed according to established rules, such as in a court of law. So the outcome of the event will be impersonal and inexorable, not subject to human emotions or preferences. In this aspect, Hagal signifies the action of a mechanical process rather than the results of human creativity.

Hagal is the rune of the personal unconscious mind and of the formative process of thought. More specifically, it is a disruptive agency working in the unconscious, causing a much-needed change. Hagal tells us that these problems must be dealt with now if we are to progress. But, once recognized, this awareness is powerful. So Hagal is a protective sigil, the *lucky star,* which is drawn as arcs within a circle. It can be seen on many old buildings, still serving its protective function against bad weather. The ultimate effect of Hagal can be to cause us to alter our plans or to prepare ourselves for unavoidable transformative changes in the direction of our lives. Hagal shows us that the best way of living is to come into harmony with nature—with the natural cycles of the seasons, with our own true nature. Whatever happens to us, the way we deal with it is within our own free will. If we follow the traditional teaching, which tells us that the most important knowledge that we can acquire is knowledge of ourselves, then we can begin to live creatively within our own Wyrd.

Nyd (**naudiz*), or Not, is the tenth rune, with the literal meaning of *need*. This may accord with the common perception of need, the sort of need caused by absence or scarcity of something. This is the sort of need described in *The Anglo-Saxon Rune Poem:* "Need is a tight band across the chest, but often it can be transformed into a bringer of help, if attended to early." But, as expressed here, the rune also encompasses the more esoteric philosophical idea that the power to be released from need is found within the need itself. Nyd calls for caution in action, and the old adage "Know thyself" is particularly applicable to this rune. This can be seen as not striving against our Wyrd, but using it constructively. The shape of the rune is taken from the fire-bow and block, which was used customarily to ignite the needfire. In this way, the object is the mother of firelight. Naturally, the element of Nyd is fire. Its ruling deities are the goddess Nótt ("Night") and the future Norn Skuld. Nyd's trees are the Beech (*Fagus sylvatica*) and Rowan (*Sorbus acuparia*). Its herb is the Snakeroot (Bistort, *Polygonium bistorta*).

Is (pronounced *eess*; from **isaz/isan*) or Isa is the eleventh rune, the principle of static existence, as in *ice*. Ice is the result of a change in state from liquid to solid, as the result of a loss of energy. Fluid water becomes resistant ice. As the principle of inertia and entropy, it is the polar opposite of the rune Ken. But, according to the esoteric tradition of the North, in conflict with fire, ice brings forth matter. And within ice, there is the potential of melting, and again becoming fluid. It can also move, as in a glacier, exerting a force that is painfully slow-acting but nevertheless irresistible. As an iceberg, Is is deceptive, for only one-ninth of the true mass is visible above the surface. The rune Is thus signifies cessation of progress or the termination of a relationship, according to powerful, inexorable forces. *The Anglo-Saxon Rune*

Poem says: "Ice is very cold and slippery. It shines like glass, jewel-like. A frost-covered field is a beautiful sight." The tree of Is is the Alder (*Alnus glutinosa*), and its herb is Henbane (*Hyoscyamus niger*). Its polarity is female, and its element ice. It is under the rulership of the middle Norn, Verdandi, the present, or "that which is eternally becoming."

Jera (**jeran/jæran*), Jara, or Ger is the twelfth rune, with the meaning of *season*, or *year*. Jera expresses the essentially cyclic nature of time and the processes within time. Jera represents the fruition of right orderliness, the completion of the process immanent within Hagal. It is the successful harvest gained by correct husbandry, because if actions are carried out according to the correct principles, in harmony with the natural order, then the result will be beneficial, with "a bright abundance for both rich and poor." Jera is the rune of completion, and as such marks the winter solstice, the end of the old year and the beginning of the new. Its shape echoes its function, looking backward to the old year, and forward to the new, rather like the two-faced Roman god Janus.

A rune of Freyja and Frey, the form of Jera mirrors the mystic marriage between earth and the cosmos, or the transition through the seasons. Jera's tree is the Oak (*Quercus robur*), and its herb is Rosemary (*Rosemarinus officinalis*). It is of joint male-female polarity, and is of the element earth.

Eoh (**iwaz*) is the thirteenth rune, representing the Yew tree (*Taxus baccata*). *The Anglo-Saxon Rune Poem* describes it thus: "On the outside, the Yew is a rough tree, hard and fast in the Earth, guardian of the fire, a joy to the home." The Yew is the longest-lived of European trees. Sometimes, older trees that have died partially are regenerated by their own daughter trees growing inside them. There are also "bleeding" yews, where red resin flows like blood incessantly from a wound. Because of these characteristics, the Yew is a tree of death and rebirth, which is the reason it can be found today growing in many ancient churchyards, the site of former Pagan sacred enclosures. Customarily, the Yew possesses a dual function: that of protecting the dead, and that of giving access to the otherworld through very risky life-or-death shamanistic practices. A shaman's incense made from the resin or leaves of the Yew (very dangerous, perhaps lethal—do not make or use it!) has made Eoh the rune of death. It is no coincidence that Eoh is the traditionally unlucky number thirteen in the rune row.

Eoh is primarily the domain of the Norse god Ullr, dweller in Ýdalir, the "Valley of the Yews," but is also, during the summer period, ruled by Odin. Ullr presides over the season of Yule, the "yoke" between the old and new years. One of the major traditional uses of Yew wood is for the bow, which as a killer of animals in hunting and of humans in warfare, is a bringer of death. But in the days before firearms, to carry a bow was to warn off potential assailants, so Yew is magically defensive. Because of this, the rune Eoh can signify the magic runic staves made of Yew. Several of these survive from the heroic era of runemasters, such as the Britsum stave of the sixth century, and the Westeremden yew wand of around the year 800, both from Frisia. With these sacred objects, yew is a powerful magical wood used in banishing all harm, more specifically the powers of destruction and death. Therefore its power is affirmative of continuity and endurance. It is connected with the herb Mandrake (*Mandragora officinarum*), whose root has magical properties.* It is also allied with another tree, the Poplar (*Populus canescens*). In its polarity, Eoh is considered a male rune, ruling all five of the elements (earth, water, ice, air, and fire).

Peorth (**perþo?*) is the fourteenth rune, whose symbolism is the most contentious of any of the runes. One interpretation of it is the "dice cup," or a mechanism for casting lots. In a similar vein, it is also said to symbolize the pawn or game-piece, whose play upon the gameboard reflects the exigencies of human life. If Peorth is interpreted as a piece on a board game, then it reflects the interaction between conscious free will and the constraints of present conditions. In a game,

---

*See my *Pagan Magic of the Northern Tradition* (Pennick 2015), 204–6, for details of Mandrake lore in the Northern Tradition.

the pattern of movement of the game-pieces is already laid down in the rules and the design of the board itself. But, beyond these structural limitations, the actual movements in any game are not fixed. They are the result of the players' conscious skill and their interaction during the game. In life, too, we find ourselves in our own unique situation, but even there we have free will within our own Wyrd. Speaking of this rune, *The Anglo-Saxon Rune Poem* says: "A lively tune means laughter and play where brave people sit together in hall, beer-drinking warriors together." In her excellent intuitive analysis of the runes, *Leaves of Yggdrasil,* rune-mistress Freya Aswynn (1990, 67–69) has shown that the rune Peorth can mean the womb of the Great Goddess, All-Mother. In this aspect, Peorth is a bringer into existence, exposing those things that formerly were hidden. Thus, through all of the interpretations of the rune, Peorth signifies the potency of Wyrd functioning in the world, bringing forth the inherent patterns into manifestations. But, of course, this does not infer any sort of predestination, a concept that is alien to the Northern Tradition.

Peorth has two trees connected with it. Like Nyd, one tree of Peorth is the Beech (*Fagus sylvatica*). The other is the Aspen (*Populus tremula*). Its herb is the deadly Tyr's Helm (Monkshood or Aconite, *Aconitum napellus*). Its element is water, and it is sacred to Frigg. Interpreted, the rune can indicate initiation and hidden, inexplicable inner experiences.

Elhaz (**algiz*) or Eolh is the fifteenth rune. Its form represents the resistant power of the Elk, and the defensive "warding sign" of the splayed hand. In its Anglo-Saxon version, it also has the meaning of the Elk-Sedge (Elongated Sedge), a hardy and resistant fenland plant. According to *The Anglo-Saxon Rune Poem,* "Elk-Sedge grows mainly in fenland, flourishing in the water, grimly wounds, burning with the blood of anyone who tries to grip it." Both in its Elk and its Sedge forms, Elhaz is primarily a rune of protection. Elhaz signifies an optimistic protection and even offense against those forces or influences that are in conflict with ourselves. It is the power of intentioned and positive striving of the human toward divine qualities.

As with Hagal and Eoh, Elhaz has the Yew (*Taxus baccata*) as its sacred tree. But a second, rarer, sacred tree ascription is to the Wild Service Tree (*Sorbus torminalis*), another tree of protection against wild things. Elhaz is both female and male in polarity. Its herb is the Sedge (*Carex elongata*), whose habit echoes the rune's shape and its element is air. Elhaz, a defensive rune, is ruled by Heimdall, the watcher-god. It is the rune of the first spring festival of Imbolc or Brigantia.

Sigel (**sowilo*) or Sig is the sixteenth rune, symbolizing the power of the holy solar wheel, and the vital qualities of daylight. In *The Anglo-Saxon Rune Poem*, the poet describes Sigel as: "To seafarers, when they sail across the fishes' bath, the Sun always means hope, until the horse of the sea brings them to their haven." Sigel represents the stupendous power of the sun and its light, and the clear attainment of goals. This may be manifested on either the physical level, or the divine. Symbolically, Sigel is magical will acting beneficially throughout the world. It is that selfless spiritual quality that resists the forces of death and disintegration. Sigel is the herald of triumphant ascendancy of light over darkness, invoking the power of the sun for guidance and healing. Because of this, it is the rune of victory. The sacred trees of Sigel are the Bay (*Laurus nobilis*) and the Juniper (*Juniperus communis*), and its herb is the mystic semiparasite plant Mistletoe (*Viscum album*). Sigel's gender is male, its element is air, and it is ruled over by the goddess Sól and the god Balder (Baldr).

Tyr (**tiwaz*) is the seventeenth rune, and the first rune of the *ætt* of Tyr, the lord of justice. The name of the rune Tyr is from the archaic Germanic sky god Tiwaz, a designation just meaning "god." (*Tiwaz* in turn derives from the Indo-European term **deywos,* which is also the source for Latin *deus* and Sanskrit *deva,* both meaning "god," as well as the names of the Greek deity Zeus, and the Roman Jupiter.) Symbolically, Tyr is the rune of the courageous Æsir god Tyr, who gave his right hand to facilitate the binding of the destructive Fenris-Wolf that threatened the cosmic order. As the Anglo-Saxon Tiw, he is the patron god of the English places Tilsley, Hants; Tuesley, Surrey; Tysoe,

Warwickshire; and Tyesmere, Worcestershire. As the Continental Germanic Ziu, he also rules Tübingen and Augsburg in Germany (the latter city under its old name, Ziusburg). This rune is especially relevant at those places.

Tyr is described in *The Anglo-Saxon Rune Poem* (where the rune name appears at Tir) as "a special token which has the confidence of nobles. It is always under way and never fails in the darkness of the night." The northern divinity Tyr is paralleled with the Roman god Mars, ruler of Tuesday, whose name comes from the Anglo-Saxon deity Tiw. Tyr is a rune of positive regulation, manifested as the necessity that to rule justly one requires self-sacrifice. As the rune of Tyr, it signifies success tempered by sacrifice. The shape of the rune infers the targeting of assertive forces in the correct place for the greatest effect, the vault of the heavens over the cosmic pillar Irminsul. Tyr is a male rune, whose tree is the Oak *(Quercus robur)* and whose sacred herbs are the Sage *(Salvia officinalis)* and Tyr's Helm *(Aconitum napellus)*. It is ruled by the element air. The rune can signify a legal action, but the outcome will only be favorable if one is in the right. Miscarriages of justice, even if favorable to the querent, will not occur when Tyr rules.

Beorc (**berkanan*) or Bar is the eighteenth rune, representing the Birch tree *(Betula pendula)*. The Birch is symbolic of purity and purification, but Beorc is also the rune of mystery. As the first tree that recolonized the land after the retreat of the ice cap at the end of the last Ice Age, the Birch is symbolic of rebirth. *The Anglo-Saxon Rune Poem* describes it as: "The Birch bears no fruit, yet it shoots without seeding, has shining branches high in its ornamented helm, loaded with leaves, touching the sky." In its shape, the feminine rune Beorc echoes the breasts of the Earth Mother Goddess Nerthus. Naturally, Beorc's element is earth. As the eighteenth rune, Beorc's number is double the sacred nine of Hagal, signifying new beginnings on a higher, organic level. The number eighteen is one of the Northern numbers of completion, marking the point at which the primal laws have been defined, and the stage set for the play of life to begin in earnest. The rune is thus associated with the spring equinox. Beorc is ultimately connected with the first character of the Irish Ogham tree alphabet, *Beith,* the tree of the rebirth of the sun's vigor in springtime. It is the tree of purification, whose twigs form the brush part of the Wiccan besom, and also the Maypole. The herb corresponding to Beorc, sacred to the Mother Goddess, is Lady's Mantle (*Alchemilla xanthochlora*).

Ehwaz (**ehwaz*) or Eh is the nineteenth rune, with the literal meaning of a horse, one of the most sacred animals in the Elder Faith of northern Europe. *The Anglo-Saxon Rune Poem* states: "The horse is the joy of peers, stepping out with pride when talked about by wealthy riders all around, and to the restless, always a comfort." It is a rune of combination, associated with twins, brotherhood and sisterhood, and the (hopefully) inseparable bond between horse and rider. The quality signified by Ehwaz is the requirement of absolute trust and loyalty. Loyalty or faithfulness is a necessary quality for those who undertake a sacred journey, either in the form of a spiritual path or as a physical pilgrimage. Ehwaz signifies that movement necessary to undertake any task, more specifically, the task of life that our Wyrd has set us. Ehwaz symbolizes the beginning of a psychic journey or, more prosaically, a move of house or an alteration in lifestyle.

Ehwaz is ruled by the goddess Freyja. The element of earth is connected with Ehwaz, which has both polarities, feminine and masculine. Ehwaz has two sacred trees, the Oak (*Quercus robur*) and the Ash (*Fraxinus excelsior*). Its herb is the prolific yellow-flowered Ragwort (*Senecio jacobaea*).

Man (**mannaz*) is the twentieth rune. It stands for the basic reality of humanness, which is present in every person, whether they are male or female. It is the quality of the shared experience of every person's humanness. "A man in happiness is dear to his kindred, yet each must depart from one another, because the gods will commit their flesh to the ground," says *The Anglo-Saxon Rune Poem*. The form of the rune Man represents the archetypal human being as the reflection of all things: Man the Microcosm. As with Hagal, the divine attribute of the Man rune is the god Heimdall, under his byname of Rig, who was, according to legend, progenitor of the traditional classes of ancient European society. Man is thus the symbolic embodiment of the social order, without which the full potential of our humanness is not realizable. As with humans, there are both gender polarities in Man, and the secondary influences on the rune are from Odin and his consort, Frigg. Its sacred trees are the Alder (*Alnus glutinosa*), the Holly (*Ilex aquifolium*), and the Maple (*Acer campestre*). The herb of Man is the Madder (*Rubia tinctorum*).

Lagu (**laguz*) is the twenty-first rune, representing water in its many phases and moods. Lagu is preeminently the rune of fluidity, signifying the mutable uncertainties of existence. It is the rune of Beltane (May Day), the beginning of summer. Lagu symbolizes the life force inherent in matter, organic growth, and waxing force. It is the medium by which passage may be gained, but not without risk. For example, human life cannot continue without water, yet we also can be drowned in water. Growth proceeds in cycles, evident in the growth rings of seashells and tree-rings. This is manifested in Lagu as the ebb and flow of the tide. As *The Anglo-Saxon Rune Poem* says: "To landlubbers, water seems tedious if they go forth on a rocking ship, and the waves of the sea terrify them, and the horse of the sea ignores its bridle." This rune can signify any of a number of polar opposites, and appropriately, its deities are Nerthus and Njord (Njörðr), with some of the lunar influence of Máni. Its element is, naturally, water; its specific polarity is female, its tree the Osier (*Salix viminalis*), and its herb the Leek.

Ing (**ingwaz*) is the twenty-second rune, representing the god Ing, the male consort of the Earth Mother goddess of fertility and nurture, Nerthus. Ing is god of the hearth, the inglenook, and this rune has a protective quality for households. Ing is a symbol of light, firebrand, or beacon, transmitting a message far and wide. The god Ing is perceived as an aspect of Frey, with the byname Yngvi, whose ritual perambulations around his sacred enclosures in a consecrated wagon paralleled the ceremonies of Nerthus. *The Anglo-Saxon Rune Poem* relates: "At first, Ing was seen by the eastern Danes, departing over the waves with his wagon. Thus the Heardings named this champion." Ing stands for potential energy, with the capability of limitless extension reflected in the geometrical form of the rune itself. For this reason, it signifies the male orgasmic force and its consequences. It is that potential energy that must build up gradually for a period of accumulation before being released as a single burst of power. Ing's polarity is both masculine and feminine, and it is ruled by the elements of water and earth. Its sacred tree is the Apple (*Malus spp.*), and its herb is Selfheal (*Prunella vulgaris*).

Odal (*oþalan/oþilan*), Odil, Ethil, or Ethel is the twenty-third rune. It signifies the immutable ancestral property of the family—the homestead. In Frisian, the language spoken in the far northeast of Holland and the far northwest of the German Federal Republic, this rune is called *Eeyen-eerde*. This means "own earth" or "own land," an excellent expression of the qualities inherent in this rune, reflecting the element to which Odal belongs. *The Anglo-Saxon Rune Poem* says of Odal: "Home is loved by all human beings, if there they can peacefully prosper and enjoy frequent harvests." In its form as the enclosure necessary to delimit possession, Odal represents the qualities of belonging, togetherness, ancestral heritage, and the numinous qualities handed on from generation to generation. These qualities are sacred to Odin. Odal signifies innate qualities, material and spiritual heritage, which, as a rune of Odin, is expressed through the "odylic" force, *önd* (the Old Norse word for "soul" and "breath"). It resists the intrusion of the arbitrary rule of human governments: it is the wisdom of integrity, wise husbandry of resources, and the liberty of the individual and clan within the framework of natural law. The tree of Odal is the Hawthorn (*Crataegus monogyna*), and its herb is the White Clover (*Trifolium repens*).

Dag (*dagaz*) is the twenty-fourth, and final, rune of the Elder Futhark. *The Anglo-Saxon Rune Poem* says of it: "Day is the gods' messenger, the light means happiness and consolation to rich and poor alike." As the rune of midday, midsummer, and opening, Dag signifies day. It is a beneficial rune, of light, health, prosperity, and openings. On a more transcendent level, it signifies cosmic conscious-ness, light as the source of strength and joy. As a marker of the high point of the year, Dag expresses the seeming paradox of conjunction, the point at which apparent opposites are unified. It is a rune of catal-ysis in the cause of sudden change without itself being changed. It is the sort of change studied in catastrophe theory, where one appar-ently stable state "flips over" suddenly into another, quite different, yet steady, state.

Dag marks the end of one cycle, and preparation for the beginning of the next. In the runic circle, it is the rune of high noon and midsum-mer, opposite to the Bull's Noon (midnight) and midwinter rune, Jera. Dag is the rune equivalent of the Celtic Ogham tree alphabet character *Duir* (meaning "Oak"). In the Ogham tree calendar, it signifies mid-summer, the door between the rising half of the year and the declining half. The elements corresponding to Dag are fire and air.

The physical form of the Dag rune mirrors the balance between the polarities, especially light and darkness. It is directly related to the struc-ture of traditional looms, which, in turn, relate to a geometry derived from astronomical observation. One side of the Dag rune follows the path of the sun's light projected on the ground at the time of the winter solstice; the other reflects the sun's path at the summer solstice. The central cross marks the intersection of the diagonal axes of the solstice sunrises and sunsets. On a zero horizon, midwinter sunrise is opposite midsummer sunset, and midsummer sunrise opposes midwinter sunset. At the crossing point is the nowl, through which the Cosmic Axis runs, upward and downward. This pattern is archetypal, and of great antiq-uity in northern Europe. For example, the form of Dag is inherent in the Station Stone Rectangle at Stonehenge, which marked the solstice sunrises and sets, making it more than 4,000 years old. In some ways, Dag and Jera are opposite forms to one another. Dag is an outgoing rune, while Jera is an ingathering one. Dag is sacred to Heimdall, and has the Norway Spruce (*Picea abies*) as its tree. Its herb is Clary (*Salvia horminoides*).

Fig. 2.4. The summer quarter of the year, centered on the rune Dag,
represents the high point of the light, whether it is the day or the year,
the labyrinth here symbolizes the solar path through the year, aligned on a
horizon marker for the northernmost sunrise at the summer solstice. The
sacred color of this southern quarter is white.

RUNE ORDER IN THE ELDER FUTHARK

Just like the Roman alphabet, which begins A, B, C, D, and so forth, the order of the Elder Futhark is fixed. Because of the meanings and correspondences of the Elder Futhark runes, this order gives it a precise sequentiality related to the time cycle. The whole rune row forms an overall, coherent sequence. To alter the order would be to disrupt and render the pattern meaningless. The only exception to this fixed rune order can be found in the final two runes, Odal and Dag. Sometimes, these two are reversed, Dag coming before Odal, such as in one of the earliest known complete Futharks from a stone on the island of Gotland, Sweden, dated around the year 425 CE. However, there are good reasons why the rune row should end with Odal and Dag in that order. It is related to the runic cycles of the day and the year. Dag has the meaning of "day." More specifically, this refers to high noon, midday, the high point of the sun. As the high point of the solar year, the time when the law of the unity of opposites brings the beginning of the decline of the solar power, Dag is the most appropriate rune to mark this time period.

LATER ADDITIONS TO THE ELDER FUTHARK

Although the Elder Futhark had twenty-four runes, the people of Frisia found it necessary to add four new ones. This may have been partly because of linguistic changes, but also, perhaps because the Frisians were a maritime people having close connections with the lunar cycle. This twenty-eight-rune Futhark (or Futhork) is known to date from the period around 550–650 CE. Several Frisian runic staves have been found, including one dating from around 800, inscribed with a runic formula giving the owner power over the waves of the sea. When they reached England, the immigrant Angles, Saxons, and Jutes added a further rune to the Frisian Futhork, increasing it from twenty-eight to twenty-nine, perhaps a refinement of the lunar connection. An important survival of this twenty-nine-rune Futhork is engraved on a *scramasax* (short sword or ceremonial knife) now in the British Museum. It was found in the River Thames in 1857. It is most likely that it was thrown there as an offering to the sacred tidal river Thames. The twenty-nine runes on the Thames Scramasax are inlaid in silver, the metal associated with the moon.

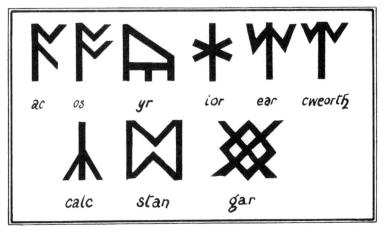

Fig. 2.5. Additional runic characters from
the Anglo-Saxon and Northumbrian Futhorks.

Like the Elder Futhark, the further nine runes of the Anglo-Saxon and Northumbrian rune rows have a specific order, which begins with **Ac,** the twenty-fifth rune. Ac is the first rune of the fourth *ætt:* the *ætt* of the gods, the Æsir. The literal meaning of Ac is "Oak," the sacred tree of Thunder Gods such as the Roman Jupiter, the Norse Thor, the Celtic Taranis, and the Balto-Slavic Perkunas. The acorn, fruit of the Oak, is symbolic of the cosmic egg, which contains inside it the primal potential of universal coming-into-being and growth. The meaning of Ac is therefore one of promising potential; powerful growth; and continued, unfailing support. Ac's polarity is male, its elemental correspondence fire, and its tutelary deity is Thor. Its herb is the Hemp (*Cannabis sativa*), formerly used for rope-making.

The next rune is **Os,** which, although here placed twenty-sixth, exchanges its place with the fourth rune of the 29- and 33-rune rows. The attributes of this rune have been discussed earlier. Not surprisingly, the meanings of As and Os are closely connected. This rune, Os, is specifically the rune of Odin in his mercurial aspect of god of eloquence. Os is the mouth from which comes the divine sound, the primal vibration of existence. Os signifies the creative power of words and thus wisdom itself. At a deeper level, it exemplifies information and its expression, which underlies the very processes of life. On a personal level, it is the core of human culture, expressed in song, saga, and literature. Os corresponds with the Ash tree (*Fraxinus excelsior*), and its "herb" is the hallucinogenic "magic mushroom." Its polarity is male, with the element air.

Yr is the twenty-seventh rune. It has the meaning of a bow. Traditionally made from the wood of the fateful Yew tree, the bow is an instrument of attack and divination. As Yr, the bow symbolizes the creative crafts, the combination of knowledgeable skills combined with materials from the physical world. Apart from its use as a deadly weapon, the bow is used in divination, both by studying the fall of an arrow, and in traditional rhabdomancy as a variety of dowsing rod. Yr thus signifies defense, protection at the expense of others, and correct location—being on target. Yr's herbal correspondences are with the Black-berried Bryony (*Bryonia alba*) and Mandrake (*Mandragora officinalis*), from whose roots the magical figures known as Alrauns are made. It is sacred to Odin, Frigg, and Vidar, who symbolize all of the elements together, and is both female and male in polarity.

Ior is the twenty-eighth rune, with the literal meaning of a sea animal. More specifically, this is a sea serpent, personified in Norse mythology as Jormungand, the World Serpent or Midgard Serpent (Miðgarðsormr). The rune has a form very close to the early Hagal. Here, it symbolizes the dual nature of matter, as in the amphibious habits of legendary wyrms and dragons. Northern mythology explains that while Jormungand is a dangerous beast, periodically threatening the stability of the world, it is a necessary part of the structure of the world. If it were possible, its removal would create a disaster far worse than its continued presence. Because of this, Ior is the embodiment of the necessary hardships and problems that must be accepted for life to continue tolerably. Jormungand, earth dragons, and the wolves are often shown not as threatening animals, but as beasts of protection. This is especially true when they are roof- or door-guardians, as on the medieval Norwegian stave churches. These beasts are representative of, or protectors of, certain forces in nature, so they are not killed. Instead, they are quelled and then integrated with the human and natural order. In the legend, Jormungand is caught by Thor, fishing for him with an ox-head representing the rune of strength, Ur. This is a foolhardy attempt by Thor to override the balance of nature. But before Thor can reel him in, Hymir (the giant with whom Thor is in the boat on the "serpent-fishing" expedition) cuts the rope, and the Midgard Serpent sinks back to the bottom of the Atlantic Ocean. Likewise, the Fenris-Wolf is not killed, but bound in the underworld. Both the sea serpent and the wolf, recognized as separate, are reintegrated with the chthonic powers of the earth. While dangerous, they are recognized nevertheless as essential to life, emphasizing the Northern Tradition's recognition of the law of the unity of opposites. The modern response to these dangerous forces is to attempt to destroy them. But as modern medical experience has shown, for example, when one disease is finally eliminated, then another disease—more virulent because it is new—evolves to fill the place vacated by the older one. The "trees" of Ior are the Linden (*Tilia platyphyllos*) and the Ivy (*Hedera helix*), while its "herb" is the seaweed known as Kelp (*Laminaria digitata*). Ior's element is water and its polarity feminine. Ior is ruled over by the deep-sea deity Njord.

Ear is the twenty-ninth rune. Literally, Ear is the dust, which interpreted symbolically means the grave. Ear is the termination of life. Yet without an end, there could never have been a beginning; there would have been no life in the first place. Ear signifies the unavoidable end of all things, more specifically, the inevitable return of living, individual, human beings to the undifferentiated material of which their bodies are made. Appropriately, Ear is the final stave of the Anglo-Saxon 29-rune row, and signifies the end of the lunar cycle, presaging the rebirth of the new, forthcoming, cycle. The tree of Ear is the Yew (*Taxus baccata*), and its herb is Hemlock (*Conium maculatum*). Its polarity is female; its element is earth. It is ruled over by Hel, the goddess of death and the lower world. It is the final rune of the Anglo-Saxon Futhork.

Finally, in Northumbria around the year 800, the Futhork was enlarged further to thirty-three characters, divided into four *eights* plus one central rune. Cweorth is the thirtieth rune, the first of the final four runes, which, added to the Anglo-Saxon Futhork, make up the Northumbrian Futhork. Again, they have a fixed order. Cweorth represents the climbing, swirling flames of the ritual fire. It can signify the fire of the Fire Festivals of the Elder Faith. Cweorth embodies the idea of a ritual cleansing by fire, the sacred hearth. It is usually connected with the feast fire of celebration and joy, the opposite to the needfire of the tenth rune, Nyd, kindled in hard times as an appeal for better days. Cweorth's trees are the Bay (*Laurus nobilis*) and the Beech (*Fagus sylvatica*). Its herb is the Rue (*Ruta graveolens*). The polarity of Cweorth is female; its element is fire. Its deity is Loki in his aspect as the god of fire.

Calc is the thirty-first rune. It has the meaning of an offering-cup or ritual container. The actual runic form is an inversion of the fifteenth rune, Elhaz, which may be taken as symbolic of the death of the individual. In this aspect it is the inverted, empty cup whose contents have been drained. As a sacred act, the contents may have been poured out on to the ground in a libation to the gods. If so, the contents have never been touched by human beings. Equally, Calc stands for our recall of absent friends or the departed in an act of remembrance. The esoteric mystery of Calc is of that which is full, yet empty. It is that aspect of the sacred that appears to be accessible, yet cannot be touched—the unattainable.

In medieval myth, it is the Holy Grail. Calc's trees are the Maple (*Acer campestris*), from which sacred cups were made in former times, and the Rowan (*Sorbus acuparia*). Its herb is the Yarrow or Milfoil

(*Achillea millefolium*). Its polarity is female, and its element earth. Calc is ruled over by the three Norns.

Stan is the thirty-second rune. It means "stone," in any of its many aspects. Stan can be the rocks in the ground, the "Bones of the Earth." It can be a "stone" or game-piece in a board game, for the rune is shaped like traditional forms of playing pieces used in Northern Tradition board games like the Welsh *tawlbort*. Stan may also signify a standing stone set up at a place of numinous power on the earth's surface, a megalithic marker of celestial and telluric influences. In all of these forms, the rune Stan is a link between human beings and earthly and heavenly powers. As a game-piece or a geomantic stone, Stan can provide protection, or act as a block to our progress. Stan's trees are the Blackthorn (*Prunus spinosa*) and the Witch Hazel (*Hamamellis mollis*), and its "herb" is the lichen Iceland moss (*Cetraria islandica*). Its element is earth and its polarity is male. It is ruled over by the goddess Nerthus.

Gar is the thirty-third and final rune in the Northumbrian system. Literally, it means spear, alluding specifically to *Gungnir,* the ash-handled spear belonging to Odin. Unlike the other thirty-two runes, Gar is not assigned to any of the four *ættir*, but acts as a central point to which all the other runes refer. As Odin's spear, it is an image of Yggdrassil, the central axletree of the runic wheel. So it takes no part in the runic time cycles. As the final stave, it is the rune of completion. But, as with all ending-points, Gar is also the beginning of a new order of things, encompassing all the other runes inside its sphere of influence. Gar's herb is the Garlic (*Allium sativum*), a powerful protection against infection. Its trees are the Ash (*Fraxinus excelsior*) and the Spindle Tree (*Euonymus europaea*). It has a masculine polarity, and refers to all of the elements. It is ruled by Odin.

At thirty-three runes, the Northumbrian rune row was the longest. In England, with the institution of Roman-style education by King Alfred the Great, the runes went out of use except as individual magical sigils and in house protection. But in Scandinavia, where the runes flourished for all types of writing, sacred and secular, the Futhark was

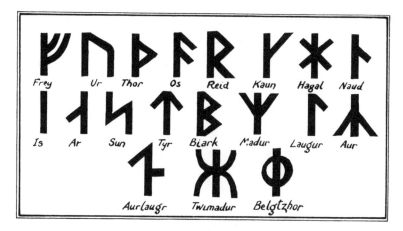

Fig. 2.6. The "calendar runes" of the extended Younger Futhark,
as used in late Norse almanacs.

reduced, not enlarged. Eight of the original twenty-four runes of the
Elder Futhark were abandoned, reducing the row to sixteen characters.
But on the Swedish wooden calendars known as runestocks (*runstav*),
three new runes (actually "bind-runes" composed of two ligatured
runes) were added to bring the number up to nineteen, to mark the
number of years in cycles of sun and moon.

These Swedish calendar runes, which remained in everyday practical use until the late eighteenth century, have a slightly different order
from that of the Elder Futhark and its extensions. The calendar runes
are sometimes attested with slightly different names, depending on
when and in what Scandinavian language they were recorded, but they
are clearly derived from the Younger Futhark runes and names that I
will give here (the equivalent runes in the Elder Futhark–based system
I am using follow in brackets): Fé (Feoh); Úr (Ur); Thurs (Thorn); Óss
(As); Reið (Rad); Kaun (Ken); Hagall (Hagal); Nauð (Nyd); Ís (Is);
Ár (Jera); Sól (Sigel); Týr (Tyr); Bjarkan (Beorc); Lögr/Laugr (Lagu);
Maðr/Madur (Man); Ýr (Yr); Árlögr/Arlaugr (bind-rune of Ár and
Lögr/Laugr); Tvímaðr/Tvimadur (bind-rune of Maðr and Ýr); and
Belgthor (a mirrored Thurs rune).

3

CYCLES OF SPACE AND TIME

Think not thy time short in this World since the World itself is not long. The created World is but a small parenthesis in Eternity, and a short interposition for a time between such a state of duration, as was before it and may be after it.

SIR THOMAS BROWNE, *CHRISTIAN MORALS* (1716)

ÆTTCUNNING:
THE FOURFOLD AND THE EIGHTFOLD

To us as human beings, the natural division of the horizon circle seems to be into four parts, which correspond with the four seasons of the year and the apparent motion of the sun and moon. But when this division into four is looked at practically in detail, it is clear that in relation to the cardinal points, there are two ways of dividing the circle. Firstly, it can be divided by lines running from the center to the four "directions" or cardinal points, North, East, South, and West. This is the basic arrangement according to Northern Tradition myth, where the four "corners" of the cosmos are upheld by four guardian dwarves called Norðri (Northern One), Austri (Eastern One), Suðri (Southern One), and Vestri (Western

One). The cosmological concept of these dwarves of the quarters was widespread in northern Europe and can still be found in medieval church architecture. There is a remarkable example in the Chapel of the Cross at the monastery of Mont Sainte Odile, the holy mountain of Alsace, France. The Romanesque chapel has a central pillar, at the base of which are carved four pairs of hands. These hands are at the four corners of the pillar's square plinth, tied together as if the left hand of one person were tied to the right hand of another, and so on. It is as though four humans were buried beneath the floor with only their hands left showing. The hands can be explained as the only visible part of the dwarves Norðri, Austri, Suðri, and Vestri, pinned down as the sacrificial foundation of the world, or at least the church (Fig. 3.1). In England, too, many Romanesque church fonts have representations of these dwarves, or their derivatives, supporting the water container.

Fig. 3.1. The central pillar of the Chapel of the Cross in the sacred mountain convent of Mont Sainte Odile, Alsace, France. At the base of the pillar are carved four pairs of hands, tied together as if sacrificed foundation victims.

The second possible division is along lines running to the inter-cardinal directions, Northeast, Southeast, Southwest, and Northwest. This makes the quarters face the cardinal direction, as does a person or rectangular building when oriented. The northern quarter runs from Northwest to Northeast; the eastern quarter from Northeast to Southeast; the southern quarter from Southeast to Southwest, and the western quarter from Southwest to Northwest. This is the basic *foursquare* pattern upon which rectilinear "civilized" architecture is patterned. In traditional land division, this fourfold concept is wide-spread, having both a physical and a magical dimension. The Northern Tradition ascribes various divinities to be guardians of the quarters. The northern quarter can be allotted to Odin and the three Norns; the eastern to Frigg and Tyr; the southern to Thor and Iduna (Iðunn); and the western sector to Freyja and Njord. Each of these quarters has an associated power object for each deity: Odin's spear and the Norns' threads; Frigg's distaff and Tyr's sword; Thor's hammer and Iduna's apples of immortality; Freyja's necklace and Njord's axe. Each of the quarters is ruled by a central rune, and contains the whole of five runes, and half of two others. The central rune of the northern quarter is Jera; that of the east is the "goddess rune," Beorc; to the south is Dag; and to the west is Ken. The other runes are arranged in sequence relative to these. This is the spatial basis of every runic time cycle, whether they be that of the hour, the day, the season, the solar year, or the Great Year. These are dealt with in detail in later chapters.

Magically, there are also four supernatural beasts that act as guard-ians of the directions in the Northern Tradition. They are recorded in a tale about Harald Gormsson, a medieval king of Norway, who wanted to mount an attack on Iceland. But before he could launch his expedi-tionary force to the island, he had to send a reconnaissance mission. But so as not to arouse suspicion among the Icelanders, Harald Gormsson sent only his personal *vitki* (sorcerer). The sorcerer did not sail to Iceland, but did *hamfar,* which means he traveled in shape-shifted ani-mal form—in this case, that of a whale. When the whale-wizard finally

Fig. 3.2. The runic wheel of the gods. In the north, the quarter
is ruled by Odin and the Norns, the east is ruled by Frigg and Tyr,
the south by Thor and Iduna, and the west by Freyja and Njord.
There is a direct mystic link between these attributes, the wheel
of the runes, and the corresponding times of the year.

reached Iceland, he was repulsed magically by four guardian beings. At
Vopnafjörður on the northeast coast of the island, the *vitki* encountered
a dragon; at Eyjafjörður in the west a huge eaglelike bird attacked him;
at Breiðafjörður in the southwest, a powerful bull patrolled the shore;
and at Reykjanes Peninsula to the south, a rock-giant brandishing an
iron-staff warded him off. When the sorcerer reported his encounter
with these magical guardians of the quarters to the Norwegian mon-
arch, the prospective invasion of Iceland was postponed indefinitely!

Relics of this geomantic system from the Northern Tradition can
be found in many places, often laid out around a fifth "quarter," a central point of some kind. The best-known example, which still exists
in its essentials, is the division of Ireland. The island is divided into
four provinces: Leinster in the east, Munster in the south, Connacht in
the west, and Ulster in the north. Leinster had the appellation *Bláth,*

meaning "prosperity," and a whole string of direction attributes including supplies, abundance, many treasures, dignity, feats of arms, wonders, good custom, good manners, hospitality, and many arts. Munster, the south, had the attribute of *Seis,* "music." Its qualities included fairs, musicianship, minstrelsy, learning, *fidchell*-playing, poetry, advocacy, fertility, and modesty. In the west, Connacht had the attribute of *Fis,* "learning." It also contained teaching, judgment, history, stories, eloquence, comeliness, abundance, and wealth. Finally, in the north of Ireland, Ulster stood for "battle" (*Cath*), bringing conflict, strife, haughtiness, pride, assaults, wars, bad places, and unprofitableness. The central point of this Irish division was the fifth province, Meath, whose capital was Tara. Its directional attributes were stability, establishment, kingship, military prowess, fame, and prosperity.

Iceland, colonized in the 900s, was divided similarly into four quarters or "farthings": Austfirðingafjórðungr (the farthing of the Eastfjorders), Sunnlendingafjórðungr (the farthing of the Southlanders), Vestfirðingafjórðungr (the farthing of the Westfjorders), and Norðlendingafjórðungr (the farthing of the Northlanders). As a democratic republic, ancient Iceland had a parliament that was held each midsummer. There, an encampment was set out around the moot-place, which reflected the layout of the whole island, being divided into four quarters. From these quarters came the corresponding magistrates and *Gothar* (high priests), twelve of each. In the Baltic, the island of Bornholm was divided similarly to Ireland and Iceland into the quarters of Østre herred (Eastern Shire), Søndre herred (Southern Shire), Vestre herred (Western Shire), and Nørre herred (Northern Shire). Lawgiving in Scandinavia and Britain was associated with these central points. The Irish laws were enacted at Tara, when the *Ardrí* (High King) called together the kings of the four provinces and their leading people at the festival of Samhain (1 November), the Celtic New Year. Similarly, the tin-miners' parliament in Cornwall, the Stannary, met at Crockern Tor. The moots consisted of 96 representatives, 24 from each quarter of the nation, whose flag is a black one quartered by a white cross.

This geomantic parliamentary principle is still adhered to on the Isle of Man. There, each midsummer, as in ancient Iceland, the Manx parliament known as the Tynwald (the first element of the name, *tyn-*, corresponds to the Norse word *þing*, "assembly") meets at the central point, Tynwald Hill, a direct parallel of the Icelandic Thingvellir. This is a moot-hill in the seventeenth and central parish. As a microcosm of the Isle of Man, Tynwald Hill is composed of earth taken from the other sixteen parishes of the island. Its form imitates the traditional pattern of the Cosmic Axis, being composed of three "steps." When the parliamentary ceremony is enacted, the governor and council occupy the top of the mound, the members of the House of Keys (corresponding to the old Norse legislature, the *lögretta*) occupy the second step, and the clergy occupy the lower step. Around this, the sacred enclosure (in Norse, *vébönd*) was demarcated, consisting of posts joined together by rope. Thus, on the Isle of Man, an appropriate spatial arrangement of society, mimicking the traditional cosmic order, is brought into being at the right place and the right time so that the island will continue to prosper in accordance with natural law.

This principle of four quarters or divisions is very widespread in traditional administration. It exists in many medieval towns, where the area within the walls was divided into four quarters, usually administrative wards and ecclesiastical parishes, but sometimes also according to trades. At the center was the marketplace or a crossroads, usually marked by a stone or a perron. But the fourfold division also existed on a much larger scale, too. In Scotland, the area known as the Lothians was composed of East-, Mid- and West-Lothian, to the north of which was Fife, and to the south, the Borders region. The Saxon area around London (itself the original capital of Essex) consisted of Essex, Middlesex, Wessex, and Sussex. East Anglia was divided into Norfolk and Suffolk, each divided again into east and west shires. The fourfold/fivefold division of Ireland and Wales was retained and continued by the Celtic Church when deciding on the sites for their controlling cathedrals. In Ireland, there were four cathedrals that ruled ecclesiastical provinces. They were Dublinensis, ruled from Dublin; Cassiliensis, under Cashel; Tuamensis, ruled by Tuam; and Ardnamachana, under Armagh. All of these cathedrals were built on former sites of sanctity of the Elder Faith, and the divisions may well have continued former Pagan religious constituencies. In medieval Wales, the four bishoprics were located at Llandaff in the southeast, St. David's in the southwest, Bangor in the northwest, and St. Asaph in the northeast. The central point was the holy mountain of Pumlumon, which means "Five Peaks."

In the Northern Tradition, the four quarters of the earth and heavens, and the central point, are assigned certain distinct qualities and corresponding runes:

QUARTER	COLOR	SEASON	WEATHER	ELEMENT	RULING RUNE
East	Red	Spring	Windy	Air	Beorc
South	White	Summer	Sunny	Fire	Dag
West	Brown	Autumn	Rainy	Water	Ken
North	Black	Winter	Cold	Ice	Jera
Center	Blue	All/No time	Still	Earth	Gar

These qualities are inherent in the regions to which they correspond, which retain a mystic link with their elemental and runic qualities, even if they are recognized no longer. A traditional Danish folk ballad, "The Avenging Sword," gives another customary version of the directions' solar qualities. In it, the hero, Sir Peter, seeks to avenge his father's murder. So far unsuccessful in his quest, he bewails his travels:

> *Oh, I ha' been so southerly*
> *Until the sun bowed down to me.*
> *And I ha' been so westerly*
> *Until the sun sank near to me.*
> *And I ha' been so northerly*

Until the frost was frore [frozen] to see.
And I ha' been so easterly
Until the day was fair to see.
                                        (SMITH-DAMPIER 1920, 109–110)

Seemingly, Sir Peter had visited the "four corners of the Earth." We will see later how *Saint* Peter has a curiously similar connection with the sun and its relationship to the directions.

Except in special circumstances, however, this basic fourfold division is not of much practical use as it stands, so a more developed system lies at the base of Northern Tradition measurement of direction and time. This is based upon the fourfold system divided intercardinally, with the sides of the figure facing the directions, but with eight instead of four. At the middle of each eighth is the cardinal or intercardinal direction, the *ætting*. This principle applies also to the twenty-four runic time-directions.

The division into eight comes from the amalgamation of lines to the cardinal and to the intercardinal directions. These divide the square

Fig. 3.3. The runic wheel of the eight festivals, drawn according to the ancient Irish tradition of *Fionn's Shield*. Fionn's Shield is a traditional Irish form of arranging the Ogham characters.

into eight equal triangular divisions, or a circle into eight equal sectors. However it is defined geometrically, eightfoldness is fundamental to human traditions all over the world. The Norse word *ætt* can mean a "group of eight," as in the directions or a rubric of eight runes. It also has the meaning of a "region of the sky," a "direction," and a "family." From this comes the word signifying one's extraction, *ætterni,* meaning "descent, extraction; belonging by birth or family to a place," and *ættmaðr,* a "relative or kinsperson." As a universal system, this division into eight is the basis of the traditional year cycle. Here, there are eight festivals, based upon the equinoxes and solstices and the harvest cycle. In the Northern Tradition, they are the autumnal equinox (23 September); Samhain (1 November); midwinter (Yule—21–25 December); Brigantia (1 February); vernal equinox (21 March); Beltane (May Day—1 May); summer solstice (21 June); and Lammas (1 August). These are the eight "fire festivals" observed today in modern British Paganism.*

The eightfold division of space is enshrined in the Noble Eightfold Path of the Buddhists, and the "Four Royal Roads of Britain" recounted in *The History of the Kings of Britain* by Geoffrey of Monmouth. In Tibet, each of the eight directions was under the hereditary guardianship of a specific family, a tradition that was paralleled in Inca Peru and in ancient Celtic Britain. Eight Noble Families were recognized in ancient Britain, from which all of the kings and saints of the Celtic Church were drawn. The octagon and its sixteenfold derivative underlies much medieval Gothic architecture, including the fine pavement labyrinths in France at Amiens and Saint-Quentin.

Once the basic fourfold land division had been made, then it was usual to subdivide each of the quarters once more in some way. Often they were split into three "thirdings" or "ridings." The Icelandic division followed this pattern. Around the coast, as nearly equidistant from one another as possible, were twelve courts, one for each of the divisions

---

*The whole system is explained in more detail in my book *Practical Magic in the Northern Tradition* (Pennick 1989), 33–41.

Fig. 3.4. The octagonal pavement labyrinth, designed by Regnault de Cormont, and constructed in the year 1288 in the Cathedral of Notre-Dame at Amiens, France. At the center is a plaque, aligned to the cardinal directions, which shows that the labyrinth is orientated according to its diagonals.

of the island—three in each quarter. This produces the classic dode-cagonal "clock-face" pattern, once extant as a turf labyrinth near the village of Marfleet in the Holderness district of Northumbria (now North Humberside). However, the eightfold division is the most commonly used geomantic division, reflecting the eightfold year.

The eightfold division of things is the basis of the natural measure of the north. It is a natural division, obtained by halving anything, then halving again, and halving for a third time. It works well with anything and can be achieved by comparison without measurement. In this way, it is an analogue system that can be applied anywhere on any scale. Fixed measures are far less universal in application. Although the metric system has largely destroyed it now, there are still a few fragments in use of the once-universal system. In the Viking Age, the system of weights was arranged as follows, based on an 8/30 division:

1 *mörk* (mark) = 8 *aurar*
8 *aurar* = 24 *ørtogar*
24 *ørtogar* = 240 *penningar*

The *eyrir* (the singular unit of *aurar*) was approximately equivalent in weight to the modern ounce. The *ørtog* was thus ⅓ of an ounce, approximately. Until decimalization in 1971, the British pound sterling was divided by this 8/30 system, consisting of 240 pence (8 × 30) to the pound. This was divided intermediately into the shilling of 12 pence, a score of which made a pound. The present pound avoirdupois consists of 16 ounces. This eightfold division is still used in liquid measure, where the gallon is halved and halved again. Half a gallon is a pottle, half a pottle is a quart, and half a quart is a pint. Thus, eight pints make a gallon. This principle was also applied to time, as we will see later.

But often the division into eight was only part of the way toward a greater subdivision. In the Isle of Man, this takes the form of a sixteenfold division, by a twofold division of each of the eights. The threefold or *triadic* division of each of the eighths of the circle, however, produces 24 sectors, each of which corresponds to one of the runes of the Elder Futhark. This is the basic twenty four-fold division of the "day" into 24 hours. In former times, sometimes this twenty four-fold division of the circle was laid down in physical form as stone circles. The famous Domsteinane stone circle near Sola in Norway is a perfect example of this concept. This consisted of a circle of 24 megaliths between which were arranged regularly 72 smaller stones. The larger megaliths symbolized and marked the 24 hours of the day, and the 24 runic half-months of the year. At the center of the circle was a wooden building in which *Things* (council meetings) of eight local districts were held. From the center to the circumference ran eight radial rows of small stones.

When used in geomancy or astrologically, the twenty-four runic sectors or "houses" can be defined in geometrical terms. Each rune is allocated one twenty-fourth part of the circle, orientated according to the eight directions. Each sector or house thus occupies fifteen degrees of the whole circle. The runic sectors are arranged so that each of the eight directions or *ættings* are at the center of a sector. This means that the 24-rune circle begins at one forty-eighth of a circle to the west of south (7° 30'). Taking due north as zero degrees, and traveling *deiseal* (clockwise) round the circle, the runic sectors are as follows:

Feoh	187° 30' to 202° 30'	Eoh	7° 30' to 22° 30'
Ur	202° 30' to 217° 30'	Peorth	22° 30' to 37° 30'
Thorn	217° 30' to 232° 30'	Elhaz	37° 30' to 52° 30'
As	232° 30' to 247° 30'	Sigel	50° 30' to 67° 30'
Rad	247° 30' to 262° 30'	Tyr	67° 30' to 82° 30'
Ken	262° 30' to 277° 30'	Beorc	82° 30' to 97° 30'
Gyfu	277° 30' to 292° 30'	Ehwaz	97° 30' to 112° 30'
Wyn	292° 30' to 307° 30'	Man	112° 30' to 127° 30'
Hagal	307° 30' to 322° 30'	Lagu	127° 30' to 142° 30'
Nyd	322° 30' to 337° 30'	Ing	142° 30' to 157° 30'
Is	337° 30' to 352° 30'	Odal	157° 30' to 172° 30'
Jera	352° 30' to 7° 30'	Dag	172° 30' to 187° 30'

From the above it can be seen that the direction of north is in the runic sector of Jera; northeast in Elhaz; east in Beorc; southeast in Lagu; and south in Dag. Southwest is in the "house" of Thorn; west in Ken, and northwest in Hagal. These directions, and their appropriate runes, relate to the corresponding times of day and seasons. These are the basic roots of the runic time cycles. It is possible to subdivide the 24 sectors again; a tenfold division seems traditionally the most appropriate, making a 240-fold division of the circle, using the 8 × 30 numerology of northern Natural Measure. Here, each division will measure 1° 30'. But for practical purposes, the twofold division (marked by a centerline) or a threefold division (creating a beginning, a middle, and an end), are most useful.

THE TRIADIC STRUCTURE OF THINGS

In the Northern Tradition, everything is recognized as being composed of three aspects. Most fundamentally, this triplicity can be seen in the fact that everything has a beginning, a middle, and an end. Everything that exists in time is subject to this triadic law. We, as humans, must experience birth, life, and death. In life, there is a threefold structure of youth, maturity, and old age. The cycle of the day can be seen as three-fold, starting with sunrise, culminating at midday, and ending with sunset. Less precise, but nevertheless triadic, is the common division of the daylight hours into morning, midday, and afternoon. Similarly, the evening, midnight, and sunrise. During the year, sunrise and sun-set points each have a threefold nature. At the midwinter solstice, the sun rises at its most southerly point and sets at its most southerly; at the two equinoxes, it rises and sets due east and west respectively; and at midsummer, the most northerly points of rise and set are reached. Consequently, from any viewpoint, there are three sightlines marking each of the notable positions of sunrise and sunset. Likewise, the moon has three light phases: First Quarter, Full Moon, and Last Quarter. Like everything else, these three lunar phases follow the triadic form of increase, maximum, and decline.

This triadic nature of things is recognized in the Threefold Goddess of the Wiccans, who goes under various names depending on the tra-dition. She exists simultaneously as the virgin, the mother, and the old woman: Diana, Selene, and Hecate, who may be seen in terms of the three phases of the moon. In the Northern Tradition, there are the three Norns: Urd, Verdandi, and Skuld, the fates who represent respectively the past, present, and future. In Celto-Germanic tradition, there were three similar goddesses, the Matrones (Mothers), who watched over human-kind. In his studies of the threefold goddess of northern Germany (*Die Drei Ewigen*), Hans Christoph Scholl wrote of the remains of the ancient tradition that saw these "Three Eternal Ones" as the Earth, Sun, and Moon. Often, they are shown as three goddesses: the Earth is represented by Nerthus or Nehalennia, holding an ear of corn; the Sun is the god-dess Sól or Sunna, with her radiant headdress; and the Moon goddess appears with her headdress of hares' ears and lunar crescent.* Sometimes, this threefold nature was incorporated as a triplicity-in-one. Among the

---

*But note that in the Norse tradition, the Moon is a male deity, Máni.

divinities of the elder faith of the Baltic lands was a threefold god, Triglav, who was represented with three faces. At the present day, the Christian religion asserts that the godhead is three-in-one: God the Father, God the Son, and God the Holy Ghost.

The Bardic tradition of ancient Celtic lands did much of its teaching by means of the *triad*—three-line groupings of information or wisdom. Bardic cosmology itself is based on an eternal threefold. Existence is triadic: "The three materials of every being and existence: *calas,* and hence every motionless body and solidity, and every hardness and concretion; fluidity, and hence every cessation, migration, and return; and *nwyvre,* hence every animation and life, and every strength, understanding, and knowledge" (Morgannwg 1862, 372–73). *Nwyvre* is the Celtic equivalent of the Norse *önd,* the cosmic "breath of life" that many equate with an all-pervading divine principle. Today, the mythological beast known as the Wyvern remains as a personification of this mysterious life force. Likewise, the states of being accessible to humans are threefold: we live at the midpoint of the cosmic axis, Middle Earth (the Norse Midgard or Welsh Abred). Spiritually above Abred is Gwynvyd, the White Land, place of divine beings and humans who are spiritually ascended. This is equivalent to the Norse Asgard, abode of the gods. Below Abred is the Abyss, known in triadic terms as Annwn. Here is the incorporeal netherworld, from which come lower spiritual forms, and into which the unrighteous must descend for repurification and rebirth into Abred. Above or external to this triad of "circles of existence" is Ceugant, the place of the unknowable and ineffable One.

Clearly, the triadic form is admirable for classifying and understanding the universe. In Bardic tradition, even the way one may die is categorizable in triadic form, for there are *three accelerations* of the end of Abred (a human being's existence in this world). These are diseases, fighting, and becoming *eneidvaddeu.**

---

*This is a Welsh word with a meaning similar to "reparation." When used in the triads, it means being executed.

Anglo-Saxon tradition, too, has a triadic structure. The three mystic crowns sacred in the kingdom of East Anglia symbolized this very principle. When applied to the runelore, this triadic structure underlies the basic runic division of each of the eighths into a twenty-fourth. Each group of three, while distinct, has a natural affinity. In the runic day cycle, each three is composed of a rune for the *ætting* time-division, such as Dag for midday, flanked on either side by the preceding and succeeding runes. So, for instance, the midday three are Odal, Dag, and Feoh. Similarly, in the year cycle, three runes cluster around each marker. Lagu marks Beltane (May Day), and it is preceded by the rune Man and followed by the rune Ing. Dag marks midsummer, flanked by Odal and Feoh; Lammas is marked by Thorn, on either side of which are Ur and As; and so on, round the year circle. One rune can be thought of as a precursor, and the other as a terminator, of the definitive rune of the festival.

KING ARTHUR'S ROUND TABLE: THE ZODIAC, AND MUCH MORE

This famous table is another symbolic form of the division of the world and the horizon. The wizard Merlin is said to have made the table in token of the world's roundness. According to the esoteric tradition preserved at King Arthur's Hall in Tintagel, it is supposed to have been divided originally into thirteen equal sectors. Each of these sectors was allocated to a knight or King Arthur himself. At the beginning, one seat, the *Siege Perilous,* remained unoccupied, awaiting the knight, then unknown, who had lived an absolutely pure life. The lunar quality of the Round Table is apparent from its thirteenfold division, representing the thirteen Full Moons that fall in each solar year. Before the arrival of the absolutely pure knight, Sir Galahad, only twelve people actually sat at the table, representing the twelve solar divisions of the year. In recent times, a number of esoteric writers have taken the table as having a twelvefold form, signifying the circle of the twelve signs of the zodiac. Here, each of twelve knights is ascribed correspondences with appropriate zodiacal signs. The four quarters are ascribed to Sir Percival for winter (Aquarius); Sir Gawaine for spring (Aries); Sir Launcelot for summer (Leo); and King Arthur for autumn (Sagittarius). The other zodiacal signs have been ascribed as follows: Sir Ector, Taurus; Sir Galahad, Gemini; Sir Tristram, Cancer; Sir Kay, Virgo; Sir Bedivere, Libra; Sir Mordred, Scorpio; Sir Balin, Capricorn; Sir Bors, Pisces. In the 1920s, Katharine Maltwood, sculptor and landscape mystic, claimed that the countryside around Glastonbury was an image of the Round Table as the signs of the zodiac. Whatever the truth of her claims, as a 12/13 system, the Round Table can be seen as reconciling the twelve-fold and thirteenfold solar and lunar years. According to tradition, the Round Table was set in a round hall, but also, paradoxically, it was taken around the country during the king's progress and used ceremonially at the lunar festival of Easter. But in Malory's *Le Morte d'Arthur* (III, 1), the Round Table "when it is full complete, there is an hundred knights and fifty." At first Arthur cannot find 150 knights and settles for 50. The king's wizard is sent out to find them, and "Within short time Merlin had found such knights that should fulfil twenty and eight knights, but no more could he find." Again, another lunar-astrological number, 28, is connected with the Round Table.

In Arthurian legend, the Round Table is connected overtly with the Wheel of Fortune, which symbolizes the recurring cycles of time and their effect upon us all. One story tells of a dream that King Arthur had, in which he thought he was riding the Wheel of Fortune. One moment, he was on top of it, lord of all things, but in a trice, the wheel turned, and Arthur was at the bottom, smothered in a pit of venomous serpents. This is yet another aspect of the cycle of being symbolized by the Round Table and the circle of the runes. Traditionally, Lady Luck, the Roman goddess Fortuna, is depicted carrying this Wheel of Fortune. In the Northern Tradition, she can be seen as the goddess Frigg, ruler of the starry heavens, with her spindle and distaff.

The 18-foot-diameter medieval Arthurian Round Table preserved at

Fig. 3.5. The Round Table of King Arthur, after the medieval
tabletop preserved at Winchester.

Castle Hall in Winchester has a closer connection to the runic circle of
the Elder Futhark. Of course, the table does not actually date from the
time of Arthur, the early sixth century CE. But it has been dated scientifically by examination of the tree rings of the oak from which it is made
to the time of the chivalric King Edward III around the year 1340, so it
is still a repository of ancient esoteric lore. It is painted in alternate segments, green and white, the traditional royal colors of the kings of Britain.
There are twenty-four segments, allocated to the knights whose names are
written in Gothic characters around the circumference. Overlapping two
of them is an image of King Arthur himself. This repainting was done in
1522, and it was repainted once more in 1789, when the design remained
unaltered. Originally, the table, which now hangs on a wall, had twelve
legs. The Winchester table has a direct connection to the runic circle,

being twenty-four-fold, although this is modified geometrically to allow the overpainting of King Arthur's depiction.

SYMBOLIC NUMBERS OF DIVISION

In the runic time cycles, the most important numerical divisions expressed in the various rune rows are 19, 24, 28, 29, and 33. They are ascribed in detail below. Nineteen is a number connected with the cycles of sun and moon (see chapter 6). Twenty-four marks the division of the circle into runic sectors, the day into hours, and the year into half-months. Twenty-eight is the number of the Lunar Seles (Mansions of the Moon) and 29 the lunar month. The longest rune row, the Northumbrian, has 33 runes, which relates both to the division of the circle as the 32-fold compass rose (plus the center), and the longest human biorhythmic cycle. This number, 33, is very important in Indo-European myths and histories, being a number of completion *par excellence.* Because of this, it occurs throughout myth and history. The Hindus of Vedic India knew of 33 major divinities, known as *viśve-devāḥ,* meaning "all the gods." Pagan Roman officialdom consisted of 30 Lictors who operated with 3 Augurs, making 33 officers in all. After war was declared by the Romans, 33 days known as *dies justi* had to elapse before the departure of the fully equipped army. The Irish legends of the two battles of Mag Tuired have 33 leaders of the Tuatha Dé Danann named in the first (32 plus the god Lugh), and the Fomoire have 33 leaders in the second battle (32 plus their *Ardrí,* or High King). In the Arthurian saga *Perlesvaus,* 33 men sit at tables in the island castle in the otherworld. The Irish hero Cú Chulainn killed 33 opponents of Labraid. In ancient Welsh literature, some versions of Nennius's *Historia* state that there are 33 cities in Britain (others cite 28—another key number in the runic rows derived from the Elder Futhark). In Anglo-Saxon England, King Alfred the Great founded 33 new *Burghs* (defended towns) in his wars against the Danes. Charlemagne's crusade against the Saxons lasted for 33 years. Finally, both Jesus and Alexander the Great died at the symbolic age of 33. The significant symbolic numbers found in the runes and myth are also found in a strange place: the geared calendars of ancient Rome and medieval Islam. Around the year 1000 CE, the astronomer-mathematician Al-Biruni wrote two treatises on the use of the Astrolabe. He describes a mechanical instrument that showed the phases of the moon and its age in days, and the relative motions of the sun and the moon in the zodiac (the day of the year and the lunar mansion). The device was driven by hand, through an arbor, moved one day at a time. The motion is transmitted to the displays by means of gearing. In many ways, these instruments were forerunners of mechanical clocks. Many seventeeth- and eighteenth-century European longcase clocks show the appropriate phase of the moon and its age in days, just as Al-Biruni's mechanism did.

Of interest to time cycles, and numerological correspondences, are the number of teeth on the gears in the gear trains (see Fig. 3.6). The numbers involved are 7, 10, 19, 24, 40, 48, and 59. The numbers used in this gear train are some of the most commonly encountered symbolic

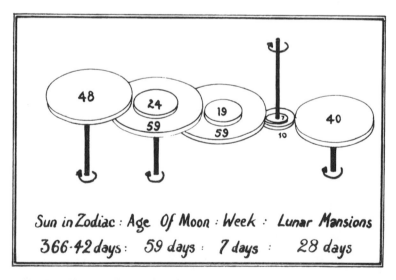

Fig. 3.6. The numbers of teeth of the gear train as described by the medieval astronomer Al-Biruni for use in an astronomical calculator, ca. 1000 CE.

numbers. J. V. Field and M. T. Wright, researchers at London's Science Museum, have shown that comparable mathematical gearing existed much earlier in the Byzantine era. In Al-Biruni's mechanism, these numbers, when in the appropriate combination, show the day of the year, the age of the moon, and the lunar mansion. However, being based on mechanical gears, each of which must have a whole number of teeth, these numbers are not completely accurate. But they are good approximators. Using this system, the year is 366.42 days long, the age of the moon is based on the two-monthly approximation of 59 days, and the lunar mansion cycle is of 28 days' duration. There may well be further connections between mechanical representations of celestial phenomena and magical numerology. Wherever they occur, they have one thing in common: like the gear wheels, they are cyclic, and, however long they may take to realign, eventually the conditions prevailing at the beginning prevail once more.

4

SOLAR RUNEPOWER

Time and tide wait for no man.

Traditional adage

THE DAY WHEEL

The very way our consciousness works, makes us, as human beings, perceive the world in a certain way. Our bodily arrangement, with a front and back, left and right sides, makes us think of the world similarly divided into four corresponding parts. When drawn, this pattern is the quartered circle, which, according to Jung, is the archetypal symbol of completion and thus of wholeness. However, as shown in the preceding chapter, this orientation of quartering is not the only possible one. There is another fourfold division, based upon facing the four directions, with the dividing lines at 45° to the first one. When taken in combination with the first fourfold division, this produces an eightfold pattern. The *airt* lines or *ættings* produced by defining the intercardinal directions mark the four quarters of the earth and heavens. These lines, and the others marking the cardinal directions, are the center-points of the sectors of the day wheel from which the customary division of the time known as the eight *Tides of the Day* are defined.

THE TIDES OF THE DAY

Like all traditional systems of time, the Tides of the Day are based upon the apparent motion of the sun and not on an artificial, mechanical, arbitrary clock system. During any specific hour of daylight, the sun is in a definite place when viewed from any designated point. Likewise, at night, although invisible "beneath the earth," the sun is also in a precise specific direction from any designated point. So, concurrent with the eightfold division of the circle of the horizon into its *airts,* we also have an eightfold division of the daily solar circle. In the Northern Tradition these eight *airts* mark the Eight Tides of the day. They overlap the four quarters. Four of the eight are wholly in a corresponding quarter, and four are each at the junction of two quarters. Of course, these Tides of the Day have no connection with the tidal ebb and flow of the sea, which obey a different cycle controlled by the interaction of the moon, the earth and the sun. Because the 24-hour day is divided by eight, each of the Tides of the Day lasts three hours. The cardinal or intercardinal direction, known as the *ætting,* lies at the exact middle of each tide. Noon, for example,

Fig. 4.1. The wheel of the Tides of the Day, compared with the runic wheel and the eight directions of the compass rose.

falls at the middle of Noontide or High Day, due south; opposite this, Midnight, 12 p.m., falls at the center of the Tide of Midnight, with a direction of due north. Esoterically, these eight *ættings* are special times, for people born at these tidal center-points (known also as the Chime Hours) have always been thought of as having psychic abilities. In the 24-hour clock, these Chime Hours are 03:00, 06:00, 09:00, 12:00, 15:00, 18:00, 21:00, and 24:00 hours.

Each Tide of the Day has its own correspondences to the directions, times of the year, certain runes, and other magical qualities. These may be summarized as follows:

CLOCK TIMES	ENGLISH	ANGLO-SAXON NAME	QUALITIES
04:30–07:30	Morntide	*morgen*	Arousing, awakening, fertility, life
07:30–10:30	Daytide, Undernoon	*dægmæl, dægtid*	Gentleness, earning, gain, money
10:30–13:30	Midday, Noontide	*middæg*	Sustenance, personal will, continuance
13:30–16:30	Afternoon, Undorne	*ofernon*	Receptiveness, transformation, parenting
16:30–19:30	Eventide	*æfentid*	Joyousness, spirituality, family, children
19:30–22:30	Nighttide	*niht*	Creativeness, teaching
22:30–01:30	Midnight	*midniht*	Staticity, healing, regeneration
01:30–04:30	Uht	*uht, uhtantid*	Stillness, sleep, death

In addition to the Tides themselves are several important marks, some of which designate the beginning and end of Tides, and others which are in the middle of Tides, are shown in the table on facing page 91.

TIME	MODERN ENGLISH NAME	ANGLO-SAXON NAME	AZIMUTH	COMPASS POINT
00:00	Midnight (Bull's Noon or Low Noon)	*midnight*	0°	Due North
04:30	Rising	*dægred* (dawn)	67° 30'	ENE
07:30	Daymark	*dægmæl*	112° 30'	ESE
12:00	Noon (High Noon)	*non*	180°	Due South
16:30	Eykt	—	247° 30'	WSW
19:30	Suppertime	—	292° 30'	WNW

TRADITIONAL DIVISIONS ON ANCIENT SUNDIALS

There are many possible ways of marking the passing of time, all of them appropriate under certain conditions, and inappropriate in others. The division systems are taken from the basic geometry of the circle, being either the fourfold or sixfold division with their corresponding subdivisions. The Romans divided the day into twelve parts from sunrise to sunset, a system that works better the nearer to the Equator one gets. The farther away from the Equator one is, the greater the difference in day length between winter and summer, and the greater the difference in length of the twelve "hours." The Northern Tradition day-division is based on quite a different principle, being determined by solar position with regard to the horizon, divided eightfold. The 24-hour system, in use today, goes some way to reconciling the two systems. Even today, surviving ancient sundials may be found on certain Norman or pre-Conquest churches in England, and of churches of similar date in Ireland, Scotland, and mainland Europe. These are known by several names: sexton's wheel, scratch dial, mass-clock, and plain sundial being the most common. Perhaps the Anglo-Saxon name of "sun markers" is best. Their specific function, other than generally telling the time, is not known, but many experts agree that their occurrence on churches indicates that they were used for showing the times of religious services. This is why the name "mass-clock" is used. Usually, they are composed of just a few lines scratched into the ashlar stone surround of a door or window, but in a few cases they are fully carved dials with inscriptions. They are arranged vertically, unlike the better-known modern dials, which are usually erected on a pedestal as a garden ornament.

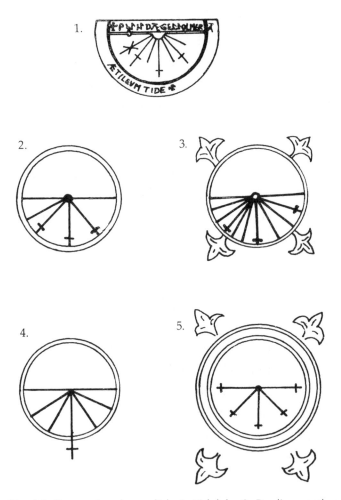

Fig. 4.2. Saxon church sundials. 1. Kirkdale; 2. Daglingworth;
3. St. Michael's, Winchester; 4. Sherborne St. John; 5. Warnford.

The earliest dateable sun markers have a fourfold division of the day, while later ones tend to reconcile the eightfold with the twelvefold division. In Ireland, the earliest sun markers incised on upright stone slabs divide the day into four. They date from the seventh century onward. One can still be seen in the churchyard at Kells, and another at Monasterboice. A seventh-century sundial at the church at Escombe, Durham, England is a simple fourfold division. It is probably one of the oldest still *in situ*. Similar Saxon dials divided into four tides exist on the churches at Warnford and Corhampton in Hampshire, and at Darlingworth in Gloucestershire. The Bewcastle cross in Cumbria, which is dated at around 675 CE, has a fourfold division marked by bold lines, each area of which is divided into three sections by lighter lines. A sun marker dated from between 1056 and 1066 exists at Kirkdale, Yorkshire. On the south side of the church is a stone more than two meters long that has a dial at the center of an inscription in Anglo-Saxon. The dial is divided by lines into eight subdivisions, three marked with a cross line at right angles, and one with an elder form Hagal rune. Part of the inscription reads: *þis is dæges solmerca æt ilcum tide*—"This is the day's sun-marker at every tide." Connected with important sundials were professional sundial-readers with the title of *dægmælsceawere* (daymark-shewer) or *tid-sceawere* (tide-shewer), according to the Anglo-Saxon grammarian Ælfric (ca. 950–1021). These names describe a time-announcer, whose duty it was to observe the dial and tell the tides to local people. The skills associated with making sundials, like all skills, are acquired only with tuition, which infers that some kind of network of practical knowledge concerning natural time-telling, which was Pagan in origin, continued in official use (by the Church in England) until the Norman Conquest. The source of their knowledge in the Northern Tradition is made clear by their use of the eightfold system. In his book *A History of the Church of the Holy Sepulchre, Northampton,* the Victorian researcher J. Charles Cox wrote:

The Greek and Latin method of dividing a day and night into twenty-four hours, though doubtless introduced into Britain during the centuries that it was a Roman province, seems for the most part to have died out with the departure of our rulers.

The invading tribes that subsequently settled in England, knew little or nothing of the more civilised system, and whether Angles or Norsemen were accustomed to the octaval division of day-night, with its sub-division into sixteen, which still exists in Iceland and the Faroe Islands. (Cox 1897, 28)

In northern latitudes, the eightfold division is far more practical for dividing the day than is the duodecimal system. The variation in the length of summer and winter days, and hence their subdivisions, is too great for a twelvefold system to work well. The traditional eightfold system was abandoned gradually after the Norman Conquest, when the southern European system of twelvefold division became official. It was this system that was adopted for mechanical clocks when they were invented.

Some of the ancient dials that still survive seem to be an attempt to reconcile the eightfold division of the horizon with the "time of day"—the regular division of the period of light. The *Dægmæl* Point, at 7:30 a.m., the beginning of the workday in the winter half of the year, is often marked on ancient sundials, as it was in the Anglo-Saxon countryside as a horizon-marker, the *dægmælspilu* (daymark's stake). This is marked by an elder form Hagal rune on some dials, or by a swastika, as at Aldborough, Yorkshire. Hagal is the rune of the watcher-god, Heimdall, who would have been the patronal deity of the *Dægmæl* Shewer. It is also possible that the apocryphal Celtic Saint, Dogmael, whose feast day was celebrated in Wales and Cornwall on 14 June, was a sanctification of the office of *Dægmæl* Shewer, or even a canonization of the *ætting* of *dægmæl*!

Because they were superseded by mechanical clocks and watches, the great number of carved sun markers that once existed has been reduced to a few meager survivals. It is likely that whole types or classes of sundial tht once were in general use have been completely destroyed and are only hinted at in surviving literature. These sophisticated instruments were the heir of twin traditions: one from northern and one from southern Europe. Their northern European heritage was from the ancient tradition of direct observation of the sun and moon, as recoverable from the alignments of stone circles and incorporated later in the structure of ancient churches. The southern European or Mediterranean heritage was from the divisions of the circle and their attributes, enshrined in the ancient dials and geared calculating machines of ancient Greek science, which continued through the medieval period at Constantinople. These dials, of which a few survive, were sophisticated calculating machines that enabled the user to calculate forthcoming astronomical events such as on which days the phases of the moon would fall. The best-preserved of these is the so-called Antikythera Mechanism, discovered in a shipwreck almost a century ago, and dated at around 80 BCE. Several other, less complex, geared calculator-sundials are known that date from then to about 500 CE. In their geared mechanisms, they were the direct forerunners of powered mechanical clocks.

In the early runic period, then, there was known technology not only of accurate sun markers and calendar making, but also of geared mechanisms. The sundial-making and astronomical knowledge of the Mediterranean region was developed, after the fall of the western Roman Empire, for the use of the Church, and was finally amalgamated with the indigenous eightfold dialing of northern Europe. Although surviving examples are few—and often restricted to a few scratches on stones, on perrons, or in churches—they show a complexity that demonstrates the considerable knowledge of their markers. In the last century, a rare survival of one such sundial with geomantic applications was in the possession of a Free Church minister at Kinneff, Kincardineshire, Scotland. Dated 22 September 1632, it was a polar equinoctial dial made from a slab of slate by John Bonar, a schoolmaster of Ayr. It is an example of a class of sundials where a slab with inscriptions is set in the plane of the equator at the angle of the degree of latitude. The Scottish

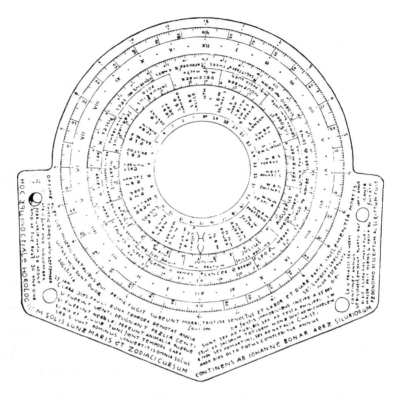

Fig. 4.3. Bonar's 1632 equinoctial dial, a rare survival
of ancient Scots technology.

dial bore many divisions and inscriptions, the most significant of which
is a poem in the old Scots language:

> The Oreades that hants on Mearocks Mote
> And Satyres tripping aye from Hill to Hill
> Admiring Phœbus couirs and Phœbes lote |
> The edub cauld: quhair ofe they hade no skill
> Then all agreeing with teares that did distill
> Out our | thair cheeks to mak a bullerand strand:
> The earth to breack; as they were warned till
> Be arladge | Voice: At Keyloche they me fand
> Out throwe my center a gnomon they made stand. |

At morning noon and euen of an lengthe
The Zodiack signs weel till | wnderstand
With œquinox and solstices the strengthe
Sen Phœbus | heer brings trouble caire and toyll
Praye vnto God to send | an better soyll

(CALLANDER 1910, 177)

This inscription contains within it a traditional cosmology expressed in the mixture of indigenous and classical allusion typical of Scottish tradition at that period. The *Oreades* are mountain sprites; *bullerand strand,* a bubbling stream; *arladge,* a clock; and *Phœbus,* as in East Anglian dialect, the sun. The inscription refers to the spirits of the place and the course of the sun across the heavens. In addition to the compass rose, it bore important places on lines radiating from the point of the gnomon, for it was designed to operate in a specific place, Mearock's Mote, probably Merrick Hill in Kircudbrightshire. The combination of the signs of the zodiac and their bodily correspondences, place-names, quadrants, and other geometrical divisions of the circle makes this sundial the only recorded indigenous British example of a system that might have been widespread at one time, but which succumbed to the advance of mechanical clocks and watches.

PERRONS

In many parts of northern Europe, *perrons* can be found. In England, these are often called "market crosses" or "butter crosses," but more often than not, they have no sign of being crosses at all. Their main feature is a small "pyramid" of steps, usually square in plan, but sometimes octagonal. From this "pyramid" comes an upright stone, which is often topped with a ball. Sometimes, this ball bears a sundial. This topmost orb signifies the solar sphere. The smallest number of steps on a perron is three. When there are only three, these steps represent the three heights of the sun: the highest point at the summer solstice, the midpoint at the equinoxes, and the low point at the midwinter solstice. The perron structure is almost identical with the three-stepped tiers of the Tynwald moot-hill on the Isle of Man, complete with central flag-pole. The old cross at Cricklade—an important geomantic place—had three, as did many others, including one at Bitterley in Shropshire. Sometimes, perrons have more than three steps. Hempsted Cross, in Gloucestershire, had four. The one at Bromborough, Cheshire, has seven plus the shaft's base, which may be considered to be eight steps, while the famous perron at the former Pictish capital of Caledonia (Scotland), Clackmannan, which stands close to an archaic phallic-shaped megalith, has the same number—seven, plus a cross base (Fig. 4.4). This number of steps existed beneath the stone cross at Lydney in Gloucestershire. Beneath the Whitefriars' Cross in Hereford were seven. There are many more examples, even today, though most of England's perrons have suffered deliberate demolition. Alfred Rimmer, the mid-nineteenth-century expert on stone crosses wrote (1875, 15): "There were probably not fewer than five thousand crosses in England . . . at the time of the Reformation." But today, more often than not, the memory of these markers survives only in place-names. The structures themselves were victims of "the general destruction of crosses, when the Cromwellites . . . warred against these objects of beauty" (Rimmer 1875, 6). Irish high crosses, such as those extant at Kells, Monasterboice, Clonmacnois, and so on, are set in a large socket-stone, which usually has the form of a truncated square pyramid. This represents the world mountain. Unlike the perrons, however, the Irish high crosses have a full cruciform super-structure, based on the sunwheel-form Celtic Cross. A similar, though less ornate, Celtic cross on Iona has three steps. The later, thirteenth-century Eleanor Crosses of England, though fully architectural monuments, still preserved the stepped base. The original Charing Cross had four steps, while the hexagonal-triangular cross at Geddington, Northamptonshire, was raised on seven steps, as was the monument at Waltham Cross.

The name *perron* comes ultimately from the Greek word πέτρος, a

Fig. 4.4. Phallic megalith and perron at Clackmannan, Scotland, former site of the proclamation of the Kings of the Picts.

stone, indicating that it was the base and not the upper part which was considered important. From some surviving relics, it is clear that these perrons originated in the time of the Elder Faith, and that, where they bore Christian imagery, this was secondary to their real function as a geomantic marker linking a specific place on the earth with the phenomena of the heavens. Such a perron, based on an almost unworked megalith, existed at the crossing of the Icknield Way and Ermine Street, two of the Royal Roads of Britain, at Royston in Hertfordshire. The megalithic stone, complete with socket, after which the town is named, now stands on a new plinth close to its original site. Its location at a major crossroads is typical of such representations of the cosmic axis at the center of the world. It is believed that the Royston perron was a wooden post slotted into the megalith. Another existed at Dunstable, where the Icknield Way crosses Watling Street, another of the Four Royal Roads of Britain. The earlier place-name element in Dunstable, *staple,* refers to a wooden post that existed once at the crossing, as at Royston. The third crossing-point of the Royal Roads is at High Cross, near Leicester, where the Fosse Way and Watling Street intersect. There, as the name implies, was another perron. Cirencester, the fourth and final crossing-point of the Royal Roads (the Icknield Way and the Fosse Way) was noted in Romano-British times for its sacred pillar dedicated to Jupiter, and a later medieval perron.

The customary ceremonies associated with perrons involve sun-wise perambulations, in imitation of the sun's path around the upright. This upright shaft of the perron is a veritable gnomon, which will cast a shadow on the ground on sunny days. The steps around it can be used as a calibration, both for the direction of the shadow, and for the sun's height, showing that a major function of the perron was as a day marker. The turf labyrinth at Hilton (Cambridgeshire, formerly Huntingdonshire) has an early eighteenth-century stone monument surmounted by a ball at its center. It bears a sundial whose gnomon fell out in 1982. The gyres of the turf labyrinth seem to be similar in function to the steps of a perron, linked directly with perron peram-bulations, and thus with the apparent motion of the sun. The perron was the nowl of the town, the place at which public announcements were made, laws promulgated, justice meted out, weights and measures assized, and general commerce enacted. The principle of observing the sun from a specific point is obvious. In the Northern Tradition, outside the house lay the "house stone," onto which an observer had to step to tell the correct time from the sun's position over known horizon markers. At the Icelandic Althing, this was done at the lawspeaker's seat. In a town, the appropriate point for viewing the sun was the perron, usually set at the crossroads, whose orientation was plain to see.

SOLAR AND LOCAL TIME

In the natural world, the horizon around us can be seen as forming a 360° circle, with us at the center. Each direction-point on the horizon relates directly to a time of day, which is the time when the sun appears to be present there. It is the direction from which the light comes. Even during the hours of darkness, the sun is still in the appropriate time-direction, but "beneath the earth." As I have shown above, owing to the apparent daily motion of the sun, the eight basic directions also correspond to times of day. When we tell the time by the sun, as our ancestors did, we do so noting the direction of the sun. This can be done either directly, by observing the sun's position, or indirectly, by inspecting the shadow cast by the gnomon of a sundial. In the northern hemisphere, the most basic observation is that when the apparent position of the sun is due south, then it is noon or midday. Irrespective of the season of the year, the noonday sun always stands due south of the observer. This is almost exactly halfway between the azimuths of sunrise and sunset.

However, these sunrise and sunset azimuths vary with the seasons. At the vernal and autumnal equinoxes, when the length of day and night are equal, the sun rises in the due east and sets in the due west. This makes the length of daylight on these two days in the year exactly half of the 24-hour cycle. At the midsummer solstice, the longest day, both sunrise and sunset are at their most northerly azimuths. At the other end of the year, Yule, the winter solstice, day length is shortest. Both sunrise and sunset at midwinter are at their most southerly azimuths. The midwinter sunrise–sunset line is as many degrees south of the east–west line as the summer solstices are north of it. After the winter solstice, the sun rises and sets progressively northward until the summer solstice is reached. After this, rises and sets occur progressively southward until the winter solstice is reached again, and so the cycle continues. Halfway between the two solstices lie the equinoxes.

In former times, the time of day was told by observing the azimuth of the sun, whose direction indicated the Tide or hour of the day. This was easily accomplished by reference to physical landmarks visible from a central viewing place. Prominent features were used as day markers. In the main, they were natural elements of the landscape, such as mountain peaks, hilltops, headlands, and sea-stacks. These were augmented where necessary by artificial markers like cairns, standing stones, artificial notches in the horizon, and specially planted trees. When the sun rose, set, or stood over them, local people knew that it was then the corresponding time of day. In the parts of northern and central Europe where this system was used, the markers were variously known as a "day mark," "*eykt* mark," *dægmælspilu,* Ward Hill, or Pointe-du-Jour. Although none of them are in use for these functions today, many of these ancient markers do still exist, waiting to be rediscovered by those who go looking for them. In some districts, the names of prominent features still recall their time-telling function. Where this system existed fully, the whole landscape was a means of time-telling, not only of the time of day, but of the season and even special days, too. Because sunrises and sunsets occur at certain places corresponding with the time of year, these horizon markers also served as indicators of the seasons and festivals.

In his research into the ancient straight trackways he called leys, Alfred Watkins (1855–1935) noted that straight tracks had a traditional connection with solar observation. In Welsh, he explained, there is an etymological complex that throws significant light upon several ancient practices connected with tracks. The Welsh word *llwybr* means a "path" or "track"; *llwybro,* "to go a course, to travel"; *wybwr,* an "astronomer"; *gole,* "light, splendor"; and *golwybro,* "to make a track or path." The inescapable conclusion of looking at this word complex is that trackways were connected in an intimate way with astronomical observation. Laying out straight tracks like this toward significant sunrise points on

Fig. 4.5. Eighteenth-century Swedish emblematical engraving of Saami
time-marking. Below it is the full nineteen-rune Golden Number row,
numerical bindrunes, and the "St. Peter's Game" sequence.

the horizon is precisely what was done in the Etruscan Discipline. A
series of straight lines, conceptual or physical, can radiate from a central point to the markers of the Tides of the Day or the hour lines that
lie at the center of each runic hour. The Domsteinane standing-stone

"wheel" at Sola, Norway, was a perfect example of this. Markers of the sun's position, chairs or stations of the sun, can be many things. In Homer's *Odyssey* (bk. XV), Eumaeus mentions an island where "the Sun turned." It marked a solsticial sunrise. Archaeoastronomers have noted mountain peaks, isolated rocks, and artificial mounds as markers. Often such points are marked by stones, such as the twin peaks shown in the engraving of eighteenth-century Saami cosmological tradition (Fig. 4.5). Recent discoveries at Stonehenge have shown that toward the midsummer sunrise direction, outside the ring of trilithons, there were *two* Heelstones, between which the sun would rise at its most northerly point at the solstice. When the sun rose between these double features, that was the solstice. In the landscape, any ley, solar line, or spirit path running to the horizon from a sacred nowl (*omphalos*) will magically draw in the appropriate runic quality of the direction, especially at the corresponding *sele* (see below).

THE RUNIC HOURS

As defined by the sun's position, due south is noon, and due north is midnight. Halfway between midday and midnight, due east, is 6 a.m., and correspondingly, due west is 6 p.m., 18:00 hours. Consequently, every direction corresponds with its own time of day. When the twenty-four runes of the Elder Futhark are arranged in their proper order around this horizon circle, each rune can be seen to correspond significantly with a certain time of day. Because there are twenty-four runes in the Elder Futhark, the runic horizon is divided into twenty-four equal sections, each of which corresponds to some major quality of its ruling rune. Consequently, each hour of the day is ruled by its own corresponding rune. Each rune rules its specific hour of the day, beginning at the half-hour preceding the hour to the half-hour that follows it. The runes are arranged in their customary sequence. The first runic hour begins with Feoh. It starts at 12:30 p.m. and ends at 1:30 p.m. Ur begins at 1:30 p.m. and ends at 2:30 p.m., and so on, around the clock.

The twenty-fourth and final rune, Dag, completes the day circle, occupying the hour of Noon, from 11:30 a.m. until 12:30 p.m.

Even though we measure it, time is really continuous and unbroken, so the Tides of the Day have no beginning-point. But in the runic time-cycle system, which must start somewhere, the first rune, Feoh, begins at 12:30, at the end of Midday, or Noontide. At 1:30 p.m. begins the Tide called Afternoon or Undorne, which contains the runes Ur,

Fig. 4.6. A chart of the tides of day from Stefán Björnsson's *Rymbegla* (1780), an edition of the early seventeenth-century Icelandic computational and calendrical treatise *Rímbegla*.

Thorn, and As. Afternoon ends at a time called *eykt* by the Norse, 4:30 p.m. In the summer half of the year, this is the customary time when work ends. At *eykt*, the Tide of Eventide begins, passing mid-evening at 6 p.m. and ending at 7:30. It contains the runes, Rad, Ken, and Gyfu. After Eventide comes the Tide of Night, or Nighttide. It lasts the final three hours until the Tide of Midnight commences at 10:30 p.m. Nighttide contains the runes Wyn, Hagal, and Nyd. Next, Midnight runs from 10:30 p.m. until 1:30 a.m., containing Is, Jera, and Eoh. The next Tide, Uht, covers the runes Peorth, Elhaz, and Sigel. It runs from 1:30 to 4:30 p.m., 4:30 being the time called *rismál*, "rising time." It is followed by Morntide, with the runes Tyr, Beorc, and Eh, running from 4:30 until 7:30, a time that is known as the "day mark" (*dægmæl*). Next comes Daytide, or Undernoon, from 7:30 until 10:30, with the runes Man, Lagu, and Ing. Finally, back to Midday, or Noontide, which contains the final runes, Odal and Dag, and the first rune, Feoh.

At any time during daylight, then, when the sun is in its corresponding time-direction, the power of the appropriate hour-rune can be visualized as being energized by the rays of sunlight streaming through it toward us. Of course, in every 24-hour cycle, each rune is energized by the sun for one hour. The maximum effect of any rune is present at the whole hour itself (one o'clock for Feoh, two o'clock for Ur, and so on). As each rune has a specific meaning, quality, and effect, that hour of the day is pervaded by that property. The Northern Tradition term for an appropriate or corresponding time is *sele*. This comes from East Anglian custom, which, in turn, is from the identical Anglo-Saxon word *sele*, which means a "hall," here with the meaning of a "mansion" of the sun in the corresponding rune. It is from the direction of the sun that the *önd* can be felt to emanate. Because each time has a ruling rune, this knowledge can be used to carry out acts at the time corresponding with the most favorable rune, when its qualities are at their maximum effectiveness. In each runic hour, the sun is actually in that direction from us, and so the power inherent in the rune is augmented by the solar power coming from that direction. It can be visualized as the sun shining brightly through a stained-glass window on which the rune and its attributes are depicted, bringing illumination. Esoterically, as the sun's power flows toward us, another telluric power is said to flow back toward the sun. It is this power, some runecasters believe, that is the driving force of runic divination.

REAL TIME

It is vitally important to note that *all* runic times are expressed only in real time, that is time determined by the actual visible position of the sun at any one point on the Earth's surface. More specifically, this is defined by taking midday (high noon) as a reference point. Midday is defined as *sun due south* (local apparent noon). There is an important reason for using real time instead of clock time: if we were to use local clock time, the chances are that it will have only a tenuous connection with solar time. Standard times, arranged in zones, from which our clock time is taken, were set up for the convenience of transport, commerce, and politics. Rarely do they correspond with local time.

Because the Earth is rotating, when we tell the time by the sun we are seeing its apparent position in relation to our viewing-point. So the kind of time that we use in runic time cycles is known technically as Local Apparent Time (LAT) or True Local Time (TLT), and colloquially as "real time." This is the sort of time that is shown by the traditional sundial. Because any one time is localized to a specific meridian, two places that are not on the same meridian will not have the same LAT. A meridian is any imaginary line that runs in a direct north–south line from the north pole to the south pole. When the sun is above a meridian, the time at any place along it is noon. Places to the east of the meridian are in afternoon, and to its west in the forenoon. All places along the meridian are at noon. It follows that only the sites on the meridian, places with the same longitude, are at the mean time of the time zone that defines the meridian. Places east or west of the meridian must have different times. A place 15° east or west will be one hour behind or in front, respectively, of any specific meridian. Depending on latitude, the actual physical distance varies. But even a relatively small distance east or west of a meridian really makes a significant difference. In the Northern Hemisphere, the further north one goes, the shorter the distance. At latitude 30°, the east–west distance that makes a time-difference of one second is 401 meters (1,316 feet); at latitude 35°, it is 380 meters (1,245 feet); for latitude 45°, the distance is 328 meters (1,075 feet); at latitude 50°, it is 299 meters (977 feet); and for latitude 55°, 266 meters (872 feet).

Clocks, being mechanical systems based upon gear ratios and with constant speed escapements to regulate them, are made to run at a precisely fixed rate. Because of this, we tend to think of all time measurement as proceeding precisely like a clock. But because the Earth is part of nature and not a rigid, human-made, mechanical structure, days measured by the sun vary in length at different times of the year when compared to regular clock time. Around the autumnal equinox, days are about 20 seconds shorter than the average, and at Yule about 30 seconds longer. In mid-February, around St. Oswy's Day, the sun stands on the meridional line nearly 14½ minutes later than an averaged day. In late October and early November, around Samhain, the sun is at the meridian 16½ minutes earlier than an averaged day. This apparent solar motion is irregular when measured according to human mechanistic ways of metrology. Because of this, official time is reckoned from a hypothetical "accurate" Sun, which moves at a constant speed along the Celestial Equator. This produces an averaged day, compared with which the sun sometimes runs ahead, and at other times runs behind. Only on 16 April (St. Padarn's Day), 14 June (St. Dogmael's), 2 September (St. Sulien's), and 25 December (Yule/Christmas), do real time and the fictitious averaged time coincide. This fictitious hypothetical averaged day is actually the basis of clock time, *mean time,* used almost everywhere, which has a mechanically (or electronically) derived basis. The accompanying diagrams show the equation of time and the precise relevant dates (Fig. 4.7).

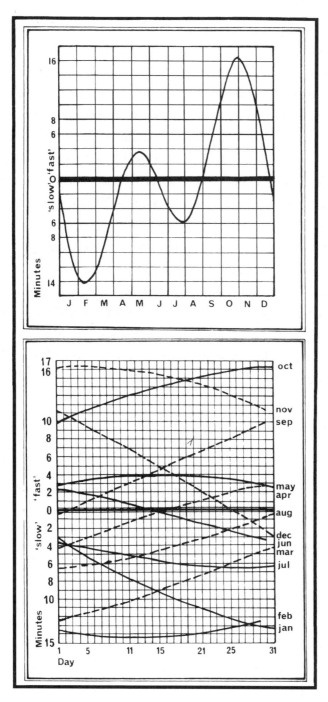

Fig. 4.7. Upper: graph of the *equation of time*. Lower: solar time (LAT) at any time of the year as compared with local mean time.

Using the graphs, it is easy to calculate the difference between real time (LAT), upon which the runic hours are based, and mean time, which is the time shown on the clocks. The runic hours then run from the real time half-hour to the next half-hour. But if it is not possible to calculate local apparent time, then it is possible to use a rule of thumb that enables one to gauge approximately the runic hour. In practice, "on the hour" will be within the runic hour so long as it is adjusted for daylight saving time, that is so that mean time high noon is when the sun is approximately due south. Then, if it is not possible to judge the difference between real time (LAT) and mean time by using the equation of time, the following will give a reasonable approximation. However, it restricts the use of the runic hour to a 40-minute period either side of the clock hour. Thus, the rule-of-thumb times for the hour of Feoh will be from 12:40 until 13:20; for Ur from 13:40 until 14:20; for Thorn from 14:40 until 15:20; and so on, from the 20 minutes before the hour until the 20-minute-marker after the hour. Clearly, this is not as satisfactory as determining the real time at the place where the runic hour is required to be known.

The abandonment of real time is a major symptom of the alienation from the natural world, which characterizes modern society. Like everything in the world, this was not sudden, but the result of a long process. The first deviation from the use of real time came with the invention of weight-driven mechanical clocks. From these came the concepts of mean time and then Standard Time. From this came the concept of Local Mean Time, where the apparent motion of the sun was replaced by a mechanically regulated and regularized timekeeping that removed direct observation and rendered sundials—which measured the *actual* basis of time—inaccurate! Then, with the advent of railways and centralized government control, time-zones were instituted, often based on the mean time calculated at company headquarters or the meridian of the capital city. No longer could local time be used when trains started running to a timetable. Some of the earliest instances came in the 1840s, when the first long-distance railway lines opened between London and Southampton and London and Bristol. Because of these new timetabled transport links,

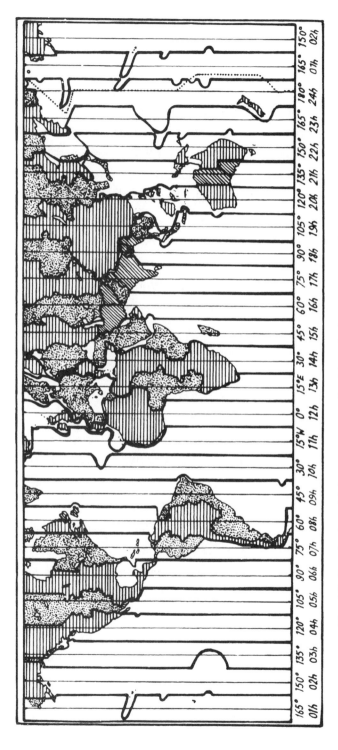

Fig. 4.8. Standard world time zones as of 1989, with their corresponding hour for midday Greenwich Mean Time. Heavy lines are time-zone boundaries; light lines represent the meridians at the middle of each zone, theoretically defining the hour of the zone.

the inhabitants of those ports abandoned the use of local time and started to use London time instead. Eventually, the mean time on the London meridian, London Mean Time (otherwise known as "Railway Time" or "Parliament Time"), was made compulsory throughout Britain, and local time ceased to be recognized.

Finally, with the establishment of the Greenwich Meridian in 1886, a worldwide system of zones was set up. It was based around the zero meridian of Britain, located at the Royal Observatory at Greenwich in southeast London. From the Greenwich Meridian, further meridians at 15° and multiples of 15° from it were defined. According to this new system, every place within that time zone, stretching for 7° 30' on either side of any designated meridian, had the same mean time. This means that places near zonal boundaries have a standard time that has little connection with real time as told from the position of the sun. Places 7° 30' east of the meridian are half an hour in front of meridional mean time, and those 7° 30' west are half an hour behind. Added to this, time zones are now determined by political boundaries and other similar factors, and so may be up to two hours different from actual solar time, and three hours when so-called Daylight Saving Time is implemented in summertime.

Over the years, an unfortunate tendency has been to "iron out" relatively correct local time-zones into increasingly inappropriate large ones. This has usually taken place as the result of war or economic union. For example, Dublin, 6° 15' west of London, had a time 25 minutes behind London until 1 October 1916, when (along with the rest of Ireland), it was "brought into line" with London. Until then, although part of the United Kingdom, all of Ireland had used Dublin time since the advent of railways. The Netherlands used an even more accurate time zone 19 minutes 32.1 seconds fast of Greenwich Time until 1940, when it was "rounded up" to 20 minutes. It was finally abolished in 1950, when Central European Time was imposed. When it was part of the British Empire, Aden, in south Arabia, had a time 2 hours, 29 minutes, and 54 seconds in front of that at Greenwich. Most large countries, however, are divided into several separate time zones. The United States has four major zones, set up in 1883 by an agreement between the railroad companies, who devised the idea of adjacent zones with one hour's difference in time from one another. The USSR has eleven time zones, but China has only one, although it runs from around 75° E to around 125° E, over three hours difference in Real Time. At the time of writing, Western Europe, excepting Portugal and the British Isles, is in a time zone that is actually based on mean time calculated on the meridian of 15° E—some miles to the east of Prague in Czechoslovakia, so the clocks there can be giving a reading that is over an hour in front of the real time. Moreover, as another consequence of world wars, additional alterations have been made

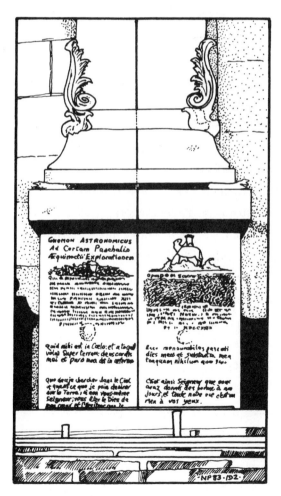

Fig. 4.9. The Meridian of France in the Church of Saint-Sulpice, Paris. Until 1886, when the Greenwich Meridian was adopted universally as the prime meridian, this marker served as the prime meridian for the French.

to timekeeping. Known variously as "Summer Time," "Daylight Saving Time" and "War Time," this has been created by "putting the clock forward," that is, calling midnight 1 a.m. and so on. The argument for this was to make the working day start an hour earlier and end an hour earlier to utilize daylight better and thus save energy in lighting. Implicit in this is the assumption that people would refuse to go to work an hour earlier in the summer and keep the clock the same. In that, it is a monumental confidence trick and an insult to the intelligence of the populace at large. Universal time is yet another convention, based upon Greenwich Mean Time, and applied to the whole planet to give a frame of reference for international events.

But all of these are profane times, which are separated irrevocably now both from the physical reality of the world and the realm of the sacred. The observance of sacred times, which exists to bring us into harmony with nature, is at odds with modern commercial timekeeping. If they are to have any effect, sacred times must be related directly to local time, not the artificial time zones of reductionist science and politico-fiscal systems. So, when working with the runes, planetary hours, or the Tides of the Day, we must use LAT, or our actions will be out of step with the inherent natural qualities of time. To do otherwise is to deny the special qualities of those times that these systems claim to observe.

5

THE EIGHTFOLD WAY—
THE YEAR CYCLE

Every moment begins existence, around every "here" rolls the ball "there." The middle is everywhere.

NIETZSCHE, *THUS SPAKE ZARATHUSTRA*
(TRANS. COMMON)

THE WHEEL OF THE YEAR

It is possible to divide up the year in at least eight significant ways, based on two perceptions of the annual cyclic round. The first—and possibly the older—of these perceptions is based on the cycle of vegetation: the "Flower Year," which begins in November, with May at its center, ending again in November. If this year is begun in May, then it runs from May to November and on to the next May. The vegetation year can also take the harvest as the marker. In this case, it can start in August, with February as the center-point, ending the next August. Conversely, if the year is taken to begin in February, it runs from February to August and on to the following February. Customarily, the key days of the Vegetation Years are marked by times of celebration, which are the major ancient festivals of the Northern Tradition.

Although their time of year have remained constant, these celebrations have gone under many names over their long existence. The Celtic tradition knows the November festival at the beginning of the year as *Samhain*. The February festival is *Imbolc* or *Brigantia*. May Day, the beginning of Summer, is *Beltane,* while the August grain harvest festival is *Lughnassadh*. These names are the most commonly used today in modern practice. In the times when Celtic Paganism was the official religion, the seasons' beginnings were defined by the festivals: winter began at Samhain, spring at Imbolc, summer at Beltane, and autumn at Lughnassadh. To the Saxons and Norse, the year was divided into winter and summer halves. Winter began on 14 October, at the beginning of the half-month of Wyn, and summer on 14 April, the beginning of the half-month of Man. But wherever the year is deemed to begin, to an agricultural society, the most important aspect of the vegetation year is the harvest cycle, which culminates in the autumn. The passing of this "back-end of the year" is threefold, being marked by the *Three Harvests*. Lammas is the first harvest. At Lammas, the ripe grain is cut. The autumnal equinox marks the second harvest, when the fruits are ripening and ready for picking. The third and final harvest is Samhain, when it was customary to slaughter most of the farm animals to prepare preserved meat for hard times in the coming winter. As they were an integral part of life, and could not be abolished, the Christian Church absorbed these Pagan festivals, as was its custom. They were renamed then: Samhain became All Saints' Day (1 November) and the February festival became Candlemas (2 February). Because of the power of the Pagan festival of Beltane, it was never Christianized as a major festival of the year, only being ascribed the attributes of minor saints. In the Church calendar, it is the day of apostles Philip and James, not an important festival. In England, some of its attributes were transferred to St. George's Day (23 April). The first harvest of Lughnassadh became Lammas, when the first loaf made from that year's grain was offered at church. This replaced the offering of the loaf at the local Pagan shrine, but as medieval churches were usually built on the site of the former

Fig. 5.1. The autumn quarter, centered on the rune Ken. Here, both the traditional beginning of the woodcutting season for winter fuel and the symbolic illumination of the beginning of the academic year emphasizes the meaning of the western quarter's rune of the flaming torch of light and knowledge. The autumnal equinox, the second harvest, is the beginning of the enclosure period of winter, symbolized by the university city enclosed by its protective walls. The sacred color of this western quarter is brown.

pagan shrines, there was little material difference in the Lammas observance between that of the Pagans and that of the Christians, either in location or content.

There are four possible solar years, too. The first is based on the solstices, and the second on the equinoxes. The Solsticial Solar Year can begin in December, at the winter solstice, have its middle in June at the summer solstice, and end again in December. This is the basis of the modern year. Alternatively, the year can begin at the summer solstice in June, have its midpoint in December, and end at the next June's solstice. The Anglo-Saxon year, which began at Yule/Christmas, was such a solsticial reckoning. If the equinoxes are taken as starting points, then the Equinoctial Solar Years can run from September to March and on to the next following September, or from March through September and on to the next March. The present British Financial Year is a degenerate version of this March equinoctial year, being a leftover of both the Julian Calendar and the medieval practice of starting the year on 25 March. This was abandoned gradually, being altered to 1 January, and so it has remained. The Republic of Venice changed to 1 January in 1522; Germany in 1544; Spain, Portugal, and the Roman Catholic Netherlands in 1556; Denmark, Prussia, and Sweden in 1559; France in 1564; Lorraine in 1579; the Protestant Netherlands in 1583; Scotland in 1600; Russia in 1725; Tuscany in 1751; and England in 1752. In the full annual cycle, the solar year and the vegetation year are integrated, creating the annual "eight-festivals" cycle. By this means, each season is divided by an equinox or solstice into two parts. Early autumn, for example, runs from Lammas to the autumnal equinox, while late autumn runs from the equinox until Samhain.

The fourfold division of the year is still recognized in British law. In England, there are four statutory Quarter Days, based on the solar calendar. Traditionally, they begin on 25 March, the Christian festival of the Annunciation of the Blessed Virgin Mary, commonly called Lady Day, and the beginning of the medieval British year; Midsummer Day, St. John the Baptist's Day, 24 June; 29 September, Michaelmas; and

Fig. 5.2. The wheel of the day—with day and night, morning and evening,
increase and decline—reflects the wheel of the year
which also cycles in the same way.

Christmas, 25 December. In Scotland, they are based on the old Celtic calendar. First comes Candlemas, 2 February; then Whitsuntide, 15 May; Lammas, 1 August; and finally, Martinmas, 11 November. The time periods defined by the English Quarter Days are unequal: between Christmas Day and Lady Day is a 90-day period (91 in a leap year). From Lady Day to Midsummer lasts 91 days; Midsummer to Michaelmas, 97 days; and Michaelmas to Christmas, 87 days. It is clear that with the English Quarter Days, the solar solsticial-equinoctial year has been modified seriously by the overlay of saints' days. The actual division is more even. From the vernal equinox to the summer solstice is 92 days and 20 hours; from the summer solstice to the autumnal equinox is 93 days and 15 hours; autumnal equinox to winter solstice is 89 days and 18 hours; and finally, from the winter solstice to the spring equinox is 89 days and 03/4 hours.

The problem of determining the exact dates for the agricultural year's quarter days has interested many people who have researched into the

Fig. 5.3. The circle of the year, with corresponding runes. Painting by Nigel Pennick, 1994.

skills and wisdom of the ancients. In his last book, *Archaic Tracks Round Cambridge* (1932, 27), the noted topographical researcher Alfred Watkins gave a spread of dates as significant. For the agricultural year, he gave:

First Quarter-day (Brid—St. Bridget—Candlemas), Feb. 1–4.

Second Quarter-day (Beltaine—May Day), May 1–6.

Third Quarter-day (Lugh or Lug—Lammas), Aug. 1–8.

Fourth Quarter-day (Samhain—Martinmas—Mayor chosen), Nov. 1–8.

And for the solar year:

First Quarter-day (Shortest day—Mid-Winter—Christmas), Dec. 23–25.

Second Quarter-day (Equal day and night—Lady Day), Mar. 21–25.

Third Quarter-day (Longest day—Midsummer—St. John's), June 21–24.

Fourth Quarter-day (Equal day and night—Michaelmas), Sept. 23–24.

Researchers into the astronomical alignments of stone circles and other megalithic structures, including Sir Norman Lockyer, Admiral Boyle Somerville, and Professor Alexander Thom have adduced strong evidence of alignment to sunrises and sunsets at these periods. Also, according to extant Druidic tradition, the Four Quarters of the May Year were determined by observing the days on which the declination of the sun, as viewed from an appropriate mark-place, was 16° 20' north or south of the equinoctial line. This happened four times in the yearly cycle, making the dates of the festivals in the modern calendar 4 February, 6 May, 8 August, and 8 November. The February date marks the end of winter and the beginning of spring; the May date marks the end of spring and the beginning of summer; the August date marks the end of summer and the beginning of autumn; and the November date marks the end of autumn and the beginning of winter. The days celebrated today are slightly different from this, being at the beginning of the respective months in the Gregorian Calendar. But they are close approximations to the original eightfold divisions, and fall within their allotted runic periods.

THE STATIONS OF THE MYSTIC YEAR

The complete harvest cycle relates the time of year and day to the various parts of the eternal cycle of life in a coherent way. Each of its significant events is known as a *Station* of the year, most of which correspond to the eight festivals of the Northern Tradition. Mystically, the whole cycle is present in the dramatic or physical enactment of the Mysteries of John Barleycorn. The daily cycle fits in exactly with the runic cycle, with the following correspondences.

STATION	TIME OF DAY	FESTIVAL	RUNE	SYMBOLIC EVENTS
First	16:30	—	As/ Rad	Death/Rebirth—parent plant brings forth the seed and then dies.
Second	18:00	Equinox	Ken	Calling/Summoning— ripening of fruit and harvest.
Third	21:00	Samhain	Hagal	Awakening—letting-go; the seed falls to earth.
Fourth	00:00	Yule	Jera	Enlightenment—rebirth of the light in the darkness; the spark of life burns on.
Fifth	06:00	Equinox	Beorc	Reconciliation—apparently dead, the seed comes to life again.
Sixth	09:00	Beltane	Lagu	Mystical Union—plant in full growth in harmony with the environment.
Seventh	12:00	Midsummer	Dag	Sanctification—flower opens and is fertilized.
Eighth	15:00	Lammas	Thorn	Completion—the circle turns.

THE LUNAR CYCLES AND THE MONTHS

Like the combined solsticial and harvest years, the Stations of the Year represent an eightfold division. Our more familiar months, and the zodiacal sign rulers of the year are both twelvefold. As everyday users of the Gregorian Calendar, we tend to think that months are defined by nothing more complex than the calendar months themselves—January, February, and so on. But these are not the only sort of months, being arbitrary divisions, relics of attempts by Alexandrian sages two thousand years ago to correlate as best they could the irreconcilable cycles of sun and moon. There are three important time periods in the calendar that correspond to the runic cycles, yet have no common measure. These are the week, the lunar month, and the solar year. There can be no accurate correspondence between the week and the lunar month, as the lunar month's duration is a day and a half longer than the days of the four weeks. Four weeks last 28 whole days, while a lunar month is 29 days, 12 hours, 44 minutes, and 2.87 seconds long.

The difficulty of defining precisely this lunar cycle was alleviated in the past by reckoning the lunar months in twos as a 59-day cycle. This is referred to symbolically in the Scottish *Ballad of Thomas the Rhymer,* where the eponymous historical bard met the Queen of Elfland:

> *From every lock of her horse's mane*
> *Hung fifty silver bells and nine.*

In northern Europe, Anglo-Saxon and Norse tradition understood two different sorts of month. One was the common-law month of four 7-day weeks, making 28 days. Astronomically, this was conveniently close to the sidereal month of the lunar cycle, which when compared with the fixed stars, lasts 27 days, 7 hours, 43 minutes, and 11.42 seconds. The second kind of month is the *moon,* the synodal month of approximately 29½ days between similar lunar phases. Before 1926, English law defined the legal month as the lunar month. Before the adoption of

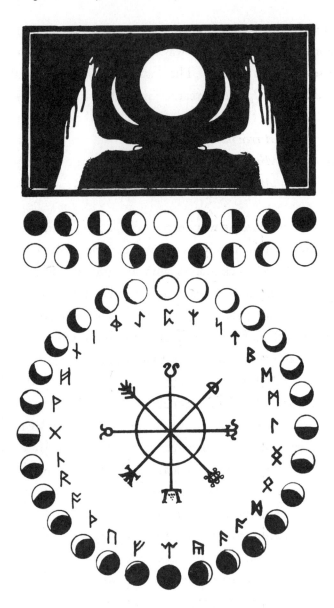

Fig. 5.4. Lunar Mysteries. Top: The upraised right hand signifies the first quarter of the Moon; the left signifies the last quarter, while both hands encircle the Full Moon. Middle: The mystic *nine phases* of the Moon and its *daemonium*. Lower: The wheel of the lunar cycle, with phases corresponding with the runes of the Anglo-Saxon Futhark. At the center, the eightfold wheel of the year shows its correspondences to this runic cycle.

the Julian Calendar in northern Europe, a year composed of thirteen 28-day months was used. In Norway, a month was counted as 28 days until the seventeenth century. The traditional German riddle of the *Year Tree* alludes to this lunar year:

> *A tree has thirteen boughs*
> *And each has four nests*
> *And in each nest, seven young ones.*

A calendar of thirteen 28-day months is a reckoning based on 52 weeks of 7 days apiece, immediately recognizable as the system used today. When we use the 52-week system now, we run the weeks onward so that if 1 January in the first year was Thursday, 1 January in the succeeding year will be Friday (assuming that the first year is not a leap year, when it will be Saturday). According to runelore, this 28-day cycle is reckoned by the early Anglo-Saxon rune row, which consists of 28 runes. This is dealt with in detail in Chapter 6. When the hitherto uninhabited island of Iceland was colonized from Norway around the year 870, the settlers used the calendar of 52 seven-day weeks as well as the old Norwegian year. The latter year consisted of twelve months, each of 30 nights, plus five intercalary days, the same system used in the ancient Egyptian calendar. Each of the months, and each year, of the thirteen 28-day months, began on Thursday, the most sacred day in Northern Tradition observance. However, this made the year a day short, and an extra, unnumbered day had to be added.

The present months are derived directly from the modified Roman calendar, with the same historic names. This sytem contains the remnants of an even earlier calendar, as betrayed by the real meaning of the months of September ("seventh"), October ("eighth"), November ("ninth"), and December ("tenth")—now the ninth, tenth, eleventh, and twelfth months. In the times when the runes were in common use, however, the Anglo-Saxon calendar began with the winter solstice, the fourth Station of the Year, which was known as *Geola* (Yule). The first month proper was called *Æftera Geola* (Later Yule). This contained *Modranecht* (Mothers' Night), which seems to have been the night of 25 December. *Æftera Geola* is roughly equivalent to the modern January. Next came *Solmonath* (Sun Month), equivalent to February. The festival of lights, of the returning sun, now known as Candlemas or Imbolc, precedes Solmonath. *Hrethmonath* (Hertha's Month) is equivalent to March, while *Eosturmonath* (Eostre's Month) paralleled April. Fertile May was called *Thrimilci* (Thrice Milk [Month]), while June was defined as *Ærra Litha* (Before Litha, the Summer Solstice). Similarly, July was called *Æftera Litha,* whose meaning is obvious. Next came *Weodmonath* (Weed Month), equivalent to August; here, however, *weed* refers not to unwanted plants, its modern meaning, but to luxuriant vegetation growth in general. September, the next month, was *Haligmonath* (the Holy Month); October was known as *Winterfilleth* (Winter-full); while November, as in the Celtic calendar, was the month when most farm animals were slaughtered. The Anglo-Saxons called it *Blotmonath* (Sacrifice Month). Finally in the year comes December, *Ærra Geola* (Earlier Yule), which completes the annual cycle of the Anglo-Saxon year. The calendrical system of the Anglo-Saxons has recently been explored by P. D. Brown in *Thirteen Moons* (2022), which is an illuminating study of the pre-Christian lunar year in England and Scandinavia.

Like Anglo-Saxon England, Iceland had a twelve-month year. However, it was not based on the winter solstice, and the months did not coincide with modern ones. In Iceland, the year began on Midsummer's Sunday, which fell between 22 and 28 July. Following this, the first month was *Heyannir* (Haytoil), July–August. Next came *Kornskurðamánuðr* (Corn-shearing Month), otherwise known as *Tvímánuðr* (Twain-month), which overlaps the Roman months of August and September. September–October was *Haustmánuðr* (Harvest Month), followed by *Gormánuðr* (Slaughter Month—October–November). November–December was *Frermánuðr* (Frost Month). The celebration of Yuletide is recalled in the name of the sixth month, *Hrútmánuðr* or *Mörsugr* (Ram-month or Fat-sucker), December–January, *Þorri* (Thorra's Month) came next, overlapping January–February. *Gói*, the eighth month, is equivalent to February–March, while the quaintly named *Einmánuðr* (Single Month) is March–April. The tenth month has two names: *Gaukmánuðr* (Cuckoo-month), and the more agriculturally based *Sáðtíð* (Sowing-tide). Next, for May–June, came *Eggtíð* (Eggtide), and the final month was *Sólmánuðr* or *Selmánuðr* (Sun-month or Dairy-month), June–July, bringing us back to Midsummer's Sunday once more.

Today, modern followers of Ásatrú use their own names for the months. Although different groups tend to use slightly different names, the most widely used system begins with January as *Snowmoon. Horning* is the name for February; *Lenting* is March. April is called after the (goddess?) *Ostara*, while *Merrymoon* is the Merry Month of May. *Fallow* is June; *Haymoon*, July; and *Harvest* occupies August. *Shedding* is September; *Hunting*, October. *Fogmoon* is November, and the final month is *Wolfmoon*. According to East Anglian esoteric lore, the soul of the Earth at any place is considered beneficial only in January, March, May, July, August, and October. "Bad Soul" months are February, April, June, September, November, and December. It is especially bad in December. This soul can be conceived as a spirit, or an impersonal power, or the magically active essence of the Earth. However we interpret these qualities today, our forebears certainly lived according to the lore of the months.

THE ETERNAL FIRST:
THE RUNES OF THE HALF-MONTHS

Because each rune relates to an hour of the day cycle, it also relates to one-twenty-fourth part of the solar year cycle, a period of just under 15¼ days. This is the runic *half-month* or *fortnight*. The old definition of the fortnight was actually fifteen days; bracketing fourteen nights is a survival of the twenty-four-fold division of the solar year. Each of the twenty-four runes of the Elder Futhark rules the half-months in sequence through the year. The beginning date of the runic time cycle of the year is 29 June. This comes from the summer solstice standing at the exact center of the rune Dag. The greatest power and influence of the rune comes at the central point of the half-month. The first rune of the Elder Futhark is Feoh, and the half-month ruled by this rune runs from 29 June until 14 July. From then until 29 July is ruled by Ur, followed by Thorn from 29 July until 13 August. Lammas falls in the half-month of Thorn. From 13 to 29 August is the half-month of the god-rune, As. Rad runs from 29 August until 13 September, when Ken takes over. It is in the half-month of Ken that the autumnal equinox falls.

From 28 September until 13 October is ruled by the rune Gyfu. From this point, the Wyn half-month heralds the beginning of winter on 14 October—Winter's Day, marked on the ancient runestocks with a Tree of Life rune-hoard sigil. In Pagan Norway, this was the festival of Winter Nights (*vetrnætr*), welcoming the coming winter. On 28 October, the day known as Fyribod (Forebode), Hagal begins. The Mother Rune rules over the Samhain period until 13 November. Then, until 28 November comes Nyd, followed by Is from 28 November until 13 December, the first cold period of the winter. The half-month covering Yuletide, including the winter solstice, from Little Yule, 13 December, until the 28th, is ruled by Jera. This is followed by the half-month of Eoh, which ends on 13 January, Tiugunde Day. This is an important mark-day in the traditional calendar, being the day of Wassailing, a score of days after Yule. Here was the festival of Midwinter's Sacrifice (*midvintersblót*), marking the middle of the winter season, heralding peace and a good harvest in the year to come. From 13 to 28 January, Peorth rules, and after Peorth, Elhaz until 12 February. The half-month of Elhaz contains Imbolc, and the runestock sigil marking Imbolc is a version of the Elhaz rune. From then until 27 February, Sigel rules, then Tyr until 14 March. The vernal equinox, festival of Eostre, comes under the Mother Goddess rune Beorc, which gives way on 30 March to Eh. On 14 April, Man takes over from Eh. The beginning of Man half-month marks the Norse festival of Victory Sacrifice (*Sigrblót*), for victory in all future undertakings. This day marks the commencement of the summer half of the year. Man, in turn, gives way to Lagu on 29 April. Lagu is the rune ruling Beltane, and yields to Ing on 14 May. Ing rules until 29 May, Oak Apple Day, when Odal takes over. The half-month of Odal ceases on 14 June, when the final rune, Dag, comes into season, culminating at the summer solstice and ending on 29 June.

THE RUNES AND
THE ROMAN CALENDAR

The old Roman calendar, upon which later calendars are in part based, has three dividing-points in each month. These are believed to have been derived from an earlier lunar calendar, perhaps Etruscan in origin. But whatever the origin of this calendar, each month begins on the Kalends (the first); then, after a few days comes the Nones; and later, around the middle of the month, the Ides. In January, February, April, June, August, September, November, and December, the Nones are on the 5th of the month, and the Ides on the 13th. In March, May, July, and October the Nones are on the 7th of the month, and the Ides are on the 15th. In both the Church calendar and the runic calendars, several of these mark-days in the Roman calendar are key points. In January, the Ides (13th) is St. Hilary's Day in the Church calendar, Tiugunde Day in the country calendar, and the beginning of the runic half-month of Peorth. In November, the Ides marks St. Brice's Day and the beginning of the runic half-month of Nyd. The Ides of December marks St. Lucia's Day, Little Yule, the beginning of the half-month of Jera. The runic periods of the year, corresponding and significant holy days in the traditional country calendar, are as follows. Only a few of the beginnings of runic half-months were not marked by holy or notable days in the later country calendar.

RUNE	DATES	SIGNIFICANT DAYS	RUNESTOCK EMBLEM
Feoh	29 June	Ss. Peter/Eurgain/Trunio	key, flower
	7 July	Nones of July	
	10 July	Knut, the Reaper	
Ur	14 July	Ss. Cynllo/Elyw/Garmon	rake, stave
	15 July	St. Cewydd; Ides of July	
	26 July	Sleipnir	
Thorn	29 July	Ss. Bleiddan/Lupus/Olaf; Thor	axe
	1 August	St. Almedha; Kalends of August, Lammas	
	5 August	St. Ceitho; Nones of August	
As	13 August	St. Cuby; Ides of August	dog and goat
	15 August	St. Mary; the Great Mother Goddess	
	25 August	the Discovery of the Runes	
Rad	29 August	Beheading of John the Baptist	
	5 September	Nones of September	
Ken	13 September	St. Cyprian; Ides of September	
	23 September	St. Tegla; Autumnal Equinox	balance
Gyfu	28 September	Vigil of Michaelmas	
	29 September	Michaelmas; Heimdall	
	7 October	St. Keina; Nones of October	
Wyn	13 October	Edward the Confessor	fir tree
	14 October	Ss. Brothen/Tudur; Winter Nights	
	15 October	Ides of October	
Hagal	28 October	Ss. Simon/Jude; Fyribod	treble cross, sledge
	1 November	Kalends of November, Samhain	binding knot
	5 November	Nones of November, Bonfire Night	

RUNE	DATES	SIGNIFICANT DAYS	RUNESTOCK EMBLEM
	11 November	Ss. Edern/Elaeth; Martinmas	goose neck, axe
Nyd	13 November	Ss. Brice/Britius/Gredifael; Ides of November	
	23 November	Ss. Dienolen/Clement; Wayland	
Is	28 November	not marked	
	5 December	Ss. Cowrdaf/Stinan; Nones of December	
Jera	13 December	Ss. Lucia/Ffinan/Gwynan; Little Yule, Ides of December	
	17 December	Saturnalia, first day	
	21 December	Winter Solstice, Yule	barrel, spear head
Eoh	28 December	Bairns' Day	
	1 January	Kalends of January New Year's Day	sun
	3 January	Sometimes called the Kalends in medieval weather lore	
	5 January	Nones of January	
	7 January	St. Distaff; Frigg	
Peorth	13 January	Ss. Hilary/Kentigern; Tiugunde Day, Ides of January, *Midvintersblót*	reversed horn, wild boar
	20 January	Ss. Fabian/Sebastian	axe for cutting firewood
Elhaz	28 January	not marked	
	1 February	Kalends of February, Brigantia	elhaz-like sigil
	2 February	the Wives' Feast Day	
	5 February	Nones of February	
Sigel	12 February	not marked	
	13 February	Ides of February	

RUNE	DATES	SIGNIFICANT DAYS	RUNESTOCK EMBLEM
Sigel	14 February	St. Valentine; Vali	
	15 February	Ss. Oswy/Sigfrid; Faunus, Siegfried	
Tyr	27 February	not marked	
	3 March	St. Winnal; Aegir	
	7 March	Nones of March	
Beorc	14 March	St. Cynog	broomstick/torc
	15 March	Ides of March	
	19 March	Minerva, Freyja	
	23 March	Vernal Equinox	
Eh	30 March	not marked	
	1 April	Kalends of April, All Fools' Day; Loki	
	5 April	St. Derfel Gadarn; Nones of April	
	13 April	Ides of April	
Man	14 April	St. Caradog; *Sigrblót*	fir tree
	16 April	Ss. Padarn/Magnus	pickaxe, commence fieldwork
	23 April	St. George	
Lagu	29 April	St. Sannan	
	1 May	St. Asaph; Kalends of May, Beltane	May Tree
	7 May	Nones of May	
Ing	14 May	Second of the six best days for sowing	millstone
	15 May	St. Carannog; Ides of May	
	18 May	Erik, King	
Odal	29 May	St. Erbyn; Tyr; Oak Apple Day	
	7 June	Nones of June	

RUNE	DATES	SIGNIFICANT DAYS	RUNESTOCK EMBLEM
Dag	14 June	Ss. Dogmael/Vitus; Vidar	
	15 June	Ss. Curig/Julitta; Ides of June	
	21 June	Summer Solstice	

Most saints' days in the Christian Church are clustered at the beginning of each month, between the Kalends and the Ides. Few saints' days are or were celebrated at the very end of the month, after the 25th. The only major exception is December, where there is a cluster around Christmas. This Christmas cluster is a continuation of the sacred days of the Roman Saturnalia and the northern Pagan festivals of Yuletide. Elsewhere in the year, the saints' days have also taken over the festivals of the elder faith. Often, the "saints" are not named after people who really existed, but after divine principles, such as St. Lucia, who symbolizes the holy light at the beginning of the Yuletide period, and St. Dogmael, who signifies the rising light of the midsummer period. Where they are canonizations of real people, their attributes are assimilated to the appropriate time of year and the earlier divinities worshiped then. For example, the Norwegian saint Olaf was slain with an axe at the Battle of Stiklastad in 1030. Subsequently, his images, set up in churches, always portrayed him with an axe, and he assimilated the attributes of Thor. Pagans worshiped his image as that of Thor when their worship was prohibited. St. Olaf's Day, 29 July, is the beginning of the runic half-month of Thorn, sacred to Thor. If a full moon falls on St. Olaf's Day, then a severe winter is indicated. Several shrines of St. Olaf existed in England, including an important one in Southwark, London; another in the City of London; and one giving a name to the village of St. Olaves in Suffolk. It is probable that they were erected on the sites of former sacred places of the Thunder God.

St. Dogmael (otherwise worshiped as St. Dygwel or St. Dogwell)

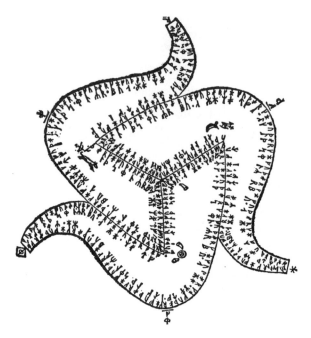

Fig. 5.5. Medieval calendar from Scandinavia, using runes
to indicate calendrical sequences.

never existed as a person. His day was celebrated in Celtic Britain at the beginning of the runic half-month of Dag. This saint's name appears to be a canonization by the Church of the Anglo-Saxon day mark *Dægmæl,* the rising sun at 7:30 a.m., real time. In heralding the beginning of the midsummer half-month of Dag, St. Dogmael reflects another light-saint, Lucia, whose Little Yule of 13 December heralds the midwinter half-month of Jera.

RUNESTOCKS, OR CLOG ALMANACS

In the days before the invention of printing, calendars, and perpetual almanacs were carved on wooden staves. In his book *Restitution of Decayed Intelligence in Antiquities,* the first edition of which was published at Antwerp in 1605, Richard Verstegan wrote of the Saxons' calendar lore:

They used to engrave upon certain squared sticks about a foot in length, or shorter or longer as they pleased, the courses of the Moones of the whole yeare whereby they could alwayes certainly tell when the new Moons, full Moons, and changes should háppen, as also their festival daies; and such a carved stick they called an *Al-mon-aght,* that is to say, *Al-mon heed,* to wit, the regard or observation [heed] of all the moones; and here hence is derived the name of *Almanac.* (Verstegan 1628, 58)

Fig. 5.6. This image from Olaus Magnus, *Historia de Gentibus Septentrionalibus* (A Description of the Northern Peoples) published in 1555, depicts runestave alamancs.

The making and use of these staves continued from Saxon times until the nineteenth century in an unbroken tradition. The knowledge required for making calendar staves, like the staves themselves, was handed down in families and never entered the realm of printed instruction. Calendar staves or runestocks (Swedish *runstav*) are of two main types: those made from four-sided staves, square in cross-section; and those carved on two-sided, flat staves. Four-sided staves were divided usually according to the solstices and equinoxes, while the flat ones covered the winter and summer halves of the year. As well as the equinox-solstice "seasons," the four sides of the square-section runestocks relate to the four quarters of the heavens and the land. Less commonly, in addition to the square-section and flat staves, there were also "books" of flat staves, seven in number, tied with a leather thong. Thirteen of the fourteen sides were inscribed with information about a specific week of the year. Sometimes these are known as "wend-runes," because the runes were written back and forth; this description also applied to spirals bearing runes written from right to left. Unlike the square or flat staves, which carried a whole year's information, these last two kinds of almanac were used as calendars for seasons, or three-month periods.

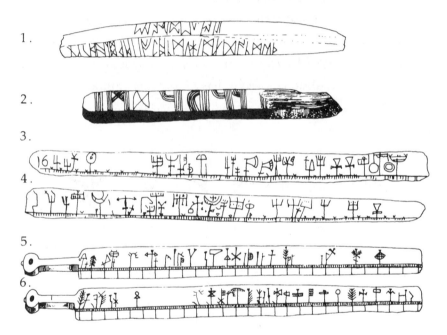

Fig. 5.7. Runic and calendrical staves: 1. Yew wand, Westeremden, Frisia; 2. Yew stave, Britsum, Frisia; 3 & 4. Primestave, Stavanger, Norway (1644); 5 & 6. Clog almanac, England (seventeenth century).

Various kinds of calendar staves have their own traditional names. In England, most of them were known as clog almanacs, or just clogs, derived from an old word for a worked piece of wood, still used today to describe a wooden shoe. In Norway, calendar staves were known as *primstav* (primestaves), *messedagstav* (*messedag*-staves; *messedag* meaning "mass day"), or *rimstav* (rimstocks, from the Old Norse word *rím*, "calendar"). The simplest are *messedag*-staves, which record only the basic days, with festive days marked by corresponding symbols. Primestaves provide the means for calculating lunar cycles in relation to solar cycles, in addition to recording the days of the week. The Swedish runestocks have the first seven characters of sixteen-character Younger Futhark rune row: Fé, Úr, Thurs, Óss, Reið, Kaun, and Hagall. These runes do not represent specific days of the week, however, but a seven-day repeating cycle. If in one year 1 January falls on a Monday, then that date will be a Tuesday the next year (or on a Wednesday if the first year is a leap year), and so on. Some runestocks use the late runic row known as the *Dotted Runes* to mark the seven day-letters, carved along the edge. Saami tradition, however, has a set of quasi-runic characters to signify each day of the week (Fig. 5.8).

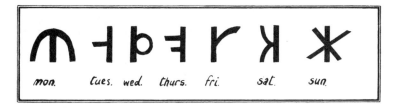

Fig. 5.8. The quasi-runic traditional Saami sigils for
the days of the week.

In addition to the seven-day cycle, Swedish runestocks used runes for the nineteen numbers needed to denote the Golden Number of the lunar/solar cycle. But because this rune row had been reduced to sixteen letters, three additional ones, compound bind-runes, were developed. These are Árlaug (17), Tvimadur (18) and Belgthor (19). Like the Elder Futhark, this runic row had a specific order. But its order when used in relation to the Metonic cycle numbers (see Chapter 6) was slightly different from the usual sequence. The characters are: Fé, 1; Úr, 2; Thurs, 3; Óss, 4; Reið, 5; Kaun, 6; Hagall, 7; Nauð, 8; Ís, 9; Ár, 10; Sól, 11; Týr, 12; Bjarkan 13;

Laugr, 14; Madur, 15; Ýr, 16; Árlaug, 17; Tvimadur, 18; and Belgthor, 19. Recent research has also revealed a direct connection between a very late surviving Swedish version of a traditional rune poem, attested as late as 1600, and the wooden runestock calendars or almanacs.*

Surviving examples of traditional stave almanacs bear a profusion of ideographic symbols and archaic north European numerical notation (see Figs. 5.7 and 5.9). Many runestocks have a system of numerical characters known as Stave Numbers, a continuation of the old notation of northern Europe. Naturally, there are several versions of Stave Numbers, but they all possess common features. Almost all of them parallel the Roman system of numbers, but most of them are composed of an upright stem onto which various strokes are cut. Several variants are shown in Fig. 5.9. In Stave Numbers, the number ten is usually marked by a cross-stroke. But because of the nineteen-year periodicity of the solar-lunar cycle, and the use of Stave Numbers exclusively for this purpose in later days, the final runestock stave number is 19. However, the conventional runestock notation is the symbol for 20, the *score,* the number of completion and return. (The twentieth Elder Futhark rune is Man, representing the microcosm and "the measure of all things.")

In addition, detailed studies by the cryptographer Alf Monge have revealed that there was also a cryptic runic calendar notation in use in medieval Scandinavia and other places reached by Viking Age voyagers. He found that the runemasters used a form of notation that enabled them to pinpoint any specific day and year by means of the Golden Number and other calendric symbols, encoded in runes. Finally, a Northern Tradition system of notation was sometimes used for denoting the year (in the present Common Era calendar). This is based upon Roman numerals, yet unless one is given the key to it, it may be mistaken for a monogram or personal mark. The system is shown in

---

*For a translation of the poem and an exploration of its background, see the essay by Michael Moynihan, "The Early Modern Swedish Rune Poem," in the recent anthology *The Rune Poems: A Reawakened Tradition* (Brown and Moynihan 2022), 49–63.

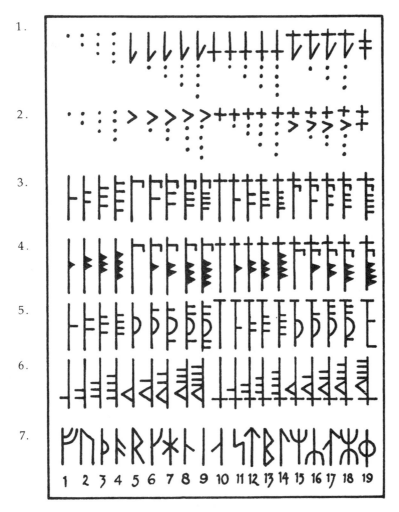

Fig. 5.9. Runestock numerical notation. Lines from top to bottom:
1 & 2. England, sixteenth century; 3. Germany, 1480; 4. Austrian Tirol, 1526;
5. Sweden, seventeeth century; 6. Pfanten, Allgau, seventeenth century;
7. Sweden, 1755.

Fig. 5.10, and readers will be able to work out the system for themselves. These forms of esoteric notation continued in use long after the advent of Arabic numerals. Arabic numerals never appeared on runestocks except as year dates.

Runic calendars may start at any convenient point. Every day is the

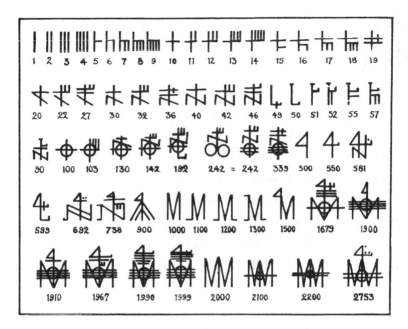

Fig. 5.10. Monogrammic year notation. See text for details.

beginning of another year, and throughout history, different cultures and political systems have seen different days as New Year's Day. The most familiar of these is our own New Year's Day, 1 January, which is derived directly from the midwinter solstice. This has been the beginning of the annual reckoning since Viking times. In Scotland, the festival of Hogmanay, celebrating the solar deity Ogmios or Hogmagog, still overshadows Christmas. Before about 1960, when the modern commercialized Christmas of the consumer society began to emerge, Christmas Day was an ordinary working day for most Scots people. Medieval Christian reckoning set the year's first day at 25 March, the Annunciation of the Blessed Virgin Mary. Danish rimstocks often began on Old Winter's Day, 14 October. Marked by a fir tree engraved on the stave, Winter's Day was reckoned to be the beginning of the winter part of the year. The Celtic year was reckoned from Samhain, beginning at sunset on 31 October.

Naturally, the year can be divided in various ways, as mentioned above: by solar phenomena, the agricultural year, the seasons, lunations, and into fixed months and days. The later runestocks, fashioned out of a four-sided, square cross-section stick, aptly divide the year into four. But this division is not usually by season or month, but by the four solar quarters. Taking the equinoxes as the baseline of equal day and night length, the winter half of the year is the period when the days are shorter than the nights. On the contrary, its complementary opposite, or *daemonium,* the summer half, is the period when days are longer than nights. Midway between the equinoxes are the winter solstice, the shortest day (and the longest night) and the summer solstice, the longest day (with the shortest night). They form the intermediate markers on the runestocks. The first side of the runestock begins at the commencement of the growing light, the first quarter of the year from the midwinter solstice to the spring equinox. The second side of the almanac is the period of lengthening days after the equinox, culminating in the longest day. These first two sides comprise the lengthening-day pair, symmetrical around the equinox point. The third side is the period of declining day-length from the summer solstice to the autumnal equinox; and the fourth marks the dwindling day-length when nights are longer than days, as far as winter solstice. Like the first two sides of the stave, these two are symmetrical around the equinox-point. The relationship between increasing day-length and decreasing night, and vice-versa, is expressed in the Ing rune, where the crossing-points mark the equinoxes and the wide points the solstices.

UNLUCKY (OR "EGYPTIAN") DAYS

Runestocks usually provided useful information of various kinds as well as the basic calendar data. They marked the auspicious day for collecting herbs, the beginning of the runic cycle, St. Peter's Day, 29 June; for cutting wood, the beginning of the fishing season, planting and harvesting. They also listed other, more esoteric days. For example, a Swedish runestock dated 1710 in the possession of the Royal Society of Antiquaries of

Scotland had a series of marks denoting the "black days." These were the days sometimes known as *Dies Ægyptiaci,* Egyptian days, inauspicious days inherited from the Alexandrian calendar markers, and traditionally considered unlucky. On some of these days, it was considered to be unlucky to commence any undertaking, and on others, only certain doings were permissible. In their original form, Egyptian Days had a triadic nature, each part of which might be auspicious or inauspicious. These days had widespread recognition, for qualities of each of them were transferred to the corresponding saint of the church. They are found in old Scottish Abbey calendars, and several ancient Continental European calendars. The 1710 runestock has 1, 2, 4, and 29 January; 11, 17, 18, and 29 February; 1, 4, 14, and 16 March; 10, 17, and 18 April; 7 May; 9 July; 10 and 18 September; 6 October; 6 and 10 November; and 11 and 18 December. Their sigil is I=. Later additions to the *Dies Ægyptiaci* were made at some time, and the full list of days recognized as unlucky now includes some of the above, to which must be added 10, 15, and 17 January; 8, 10, 26, and 27 February; 17 and 20 March; 7, 8, 16, 20, and 21 April; 3, 6, 15, and 20 May; 4, 8, 10, and 22 June; 15 and 21 July; 1, 19, 20, 29, and 30 August; 2, 4, 6, 7, 21, and 23 September; 4, 16 and 24 October; 5, 15, 29, and 30 November; and 6, 7, 9, 15, 22, and 28 December.

MODERN CALENDARS AND
THE RUNIC CYCLES

Although we are compelled to use the present-day calendar in our everyday doings, we must always be conscious of the fact that it is not perfectly fitted to natural cycles. Because of the complex relationships of solar, lunar, and planetary cycles, all calendars are working approximations of the way that things really are. The present Gregorian calendar is used by most nations of the world except Islamic ones. Little is known of early calendars in northern Europe. When they were superseded by the Julian Calendar, those parts that could not be discarded were retained and inserted within the new framework. So the newer calendar incorporated the older sacred feast days and days of importance within the agricultural year. Because knowledge of time cycles and calendars was the preserve of specialists, little has survived from antiquity. The best preserved and most ancient non-Roman calendar in the Northern Tradition is the Coligny Calendar from near Bourg-en-Bresse, Aine, France, which is dated at around 50 BCE. It is the remains of an enormous bronze plaque that measured about 1 meter by 1.5 meters (3 ft. 3 in. by 4 ft. 10 in.). On it were engraved, in the ancient Gaulish language but in Roman characters, a sequence of sixty-two consecutive lunar months and two intercalary months. It was a lunar-solar calendar that reconciled the two cycles. The Coligny Calendar records a twelve-month, but lunar, cycle that covers a period of five years. The entire cycle is composed of sixty-two months: sixty ordinary and two intercalary months. One intercalary month starts the cycle, and the other is in the middle. The month called *Samon* (probably Samhain) starts the first half of the year, while *Giamon* begins the second half. Six of the months had 30 days, and the other six had 29 days. The 30-day months have the description *MAT* inscribed with them, while the 29-day periods have *ANM*. It is likely that *MAT* means "good," as in the Welsh *mad*, and that *ANM* means *an mat*, "not good." The Gaulish months were: Samonios (30 days long), Dumannios (29), Rivros (30), Anagantios (29), Ogronios (30), Cutios (29), Giamonios (29), Simivisonnios (30), Equos (29), Elembivios (29), Edrinios (30), and Cantlos (29). Both intercalary months were *MAT*, consisting of 30 days. According to Northern Tradition custom, it reckons in nights, and is divided into fortnights. The first part of the month is numbered from 1 to 15, while the second half is numbered up to 15 for *MAT* and 14 for *ANM* months. These represented the light and dark halves of the lunar cycle. Each month was composed of two sections, between which was engraved the word *ATENOUX*, which means "the returning night" or "renewal."

It is probable that this or very similar calendars were in use in Celtic Britain before the Roman Conquest. The Ogham year, for example, with thirteen months related to Ogham letters and their corresponding trees, survived in Irish bardic tradition until the eighteenth century, and is in use today by modern British Pagans. There are a few other fragmentary remains, too. But it is the old Roman calendar that has been used in most of Europe ever since it was set up by Julius Caesar in the year 45 BCE. Because by that year the calendar of Rome had become hopelessly inaccurate, Julius Caesar ordered a revision, which was carried out by Marcus Flavius and Sosigenes of Alexandria. When calculations were complete, the new calendar was instituted in what became known as the "Year of Confusion" (46 BCE). Then, two extra months were inserted into the year to bring the calendar back into line with the heavenly cycles. But because of a misinterpretation of one of Sosigenes's rules, the calendar soon needed further revision. This took place in 8 BCE, when the month of August was named to commemorate the ruling emperor. Despite this, the calendar is still known as the Julian, and not the Augustan calendar.

In all traditions, calendars have been promulgated by religious leaders, actually or nominally astronomer-priests. When the Roman Catholic Church took over from National Paganism as the state religion of the Roman Empire, the popes, high priests of the new religion, assumed the roles and titles of their Pagan forebears. Even today, the pope is called the *pontiff,* a continuation of the Pagan title *Pontifex Maximus.* So it was that a pope was responsible for the recalibration of the calendar that is still in use today. The Julian calendar was slightly inaccurate in reconciling year length with day numbering. Every fourth (leap) year was too long by 11 minutes 10.3 seconds, and there was no provision for rectifying the error. Over the years, the calendar became increasingly out of synchronization with the natural cycles, but it was left until 1582 before anything was done about it. The calendar ought to have been revised centuries earlier. When the Julian calendar was set up, the vernal equinox had fallen correctly on 21 March, but by 1582 it was occurring on 11 March. Then, finally, in 1582, Pope Gregory XIII ordered a revision. The recalculations were made by Clavius, a Jesuit monk, and an astrologer, Aloysius Lilius, who added new rules concerning leap years at the centuries' turn. They created the Gregorian

Calendar, otherwise called New Style (NS), which is still current. Having been superseded, the Julian Calendar was then called Old Style (OS). To bring in the new calendar, Gregory XIII decreed that 4 October 1582 was to be followed by 15 October, bringing day numbering back into line with the actual solar year.

Of course, having been ordained by the reigning Roman Catholic pope, the new calendar was adopted at once in Roman Catholic countries. But countries ruled by Protestant or Orthodox monarchs did not accept the change, and so various countries used different calendars for many years. Italy, France, Portugal, and Spain converted to New Style (NS) in 1582; Prussia, the German Roman Catholic states, the Netherlands, Flanders, and Switzerland on 1 January 1583. Poland changed over in 1586; Hungary in 1587. Then there was a gap of 113 years to 1700, before the Protestant states of Germany converted to New Style. The government of Sweden decided to change over gradually by the omission of eleven leap year days, from 1700 to 1740. When Germany, Sweden, and England adopted the Gregorian Calendar, the changeover saw the abandonment of the Julian-based (Old Style) runestocks and the general use of printed almanacs in their place.

In 1752, Britain and the rest of the British Empire went Gregorian. Here 2 September was followed by 14 September. Japan adopted the Gregorian Calendar in 1872, though internally, year-reckoning still goes by the year of the Emperor's reign. China converted on the abolition of the monarchy in 1912. Bulgaria changed from Old Style on the day after 31 March 1916 (OS), which became 14 April (NS). Most of Russia, except territories now belonging to Finland or Poland, changed on the day after 31 January 1918 (OS), which became 14 February 1918 (NS). Serbia and Romania changed next, when 18 January 1919 (OS) was followed by 1 February (NS). Greece changed in 1924, when 9 March (OS) was followed by 23 March (NS). In Turkey, which had used the Islamic Calendar alongside the Julian, 18 December 1925 (OS) was followed by 1 January 1926 (NS), and the last country to change, Egypt, followed 17 September 1928 (OS) with 1 October (NS). Some

Orthodox churches still use Old Style, but most of the various Greek Orthodox and the Romanian churches use the so-called New Calendar, which observes New Style dates for the fixed feasts, such as Christmas, but Old Style for the moveable feasts like Easter. To add to the confusion, the Orthodox Year begins on 1 September. Proposals for a new, radical revision are said to have been suggested by the Vatican in the 1960s. It is believed that this new calendar was to have dispensed with Friday 13ths and other supposed anomalies. But it was thought that, as in the sixteenth century, many countries would refuse to change, creating confusion. It seems that the Gregorian Calendar is set to be the world calendar for many centuries to come.

When the calendar was altered by the Church, many people objected to the change. Some people objected to "losing" ten or eleven days, but the main objections were from country people who depended upon observing the old country calendar for their livelihood. The Julian Calendar had been in use for many centuries and was by then the customary marker of the times for planting and harvesting. This calendar accommodated the older Pagan festivals with the observances of the Church. When the Gregorian Calendar was imposed, many people continued to observe the festivals according to the Old Style or Julian Calendar. Today, some people continue to observe the old festivals on the corresponding day of the Julian Calendar, but expressed in terms of the Gregorian.

If we need to calculate the runic period during which a historic event occurred, we may need to convert it from the Julian Old Style Calendar (OS) to the Gregorian New Style Calendar (NS). There are a few rules that need to be applied to the calculation. To convert dates after 1700 from Julian to Gregorian, then, adjustments must be made. For example, to convert dates in the period from 29 February 1700 (OS) until 28 February 1800 (OS), 11 days must be added to make the date into a New Style one. From 29 February 1800 (OS) until 28 February 1900 (OS), 12 days must be added, and after 29 February 1900, 13 days must be added. Of course, leap year days must also be taken into account. In the Julian Calendar, all years that are divisible by four are leap years. But in the New Style calendar, the first year of a century is only a leap year if it is divisible by 400. Thus, 1700, 1800, and 1900 are leap years in the Julian Calendar, but not in the Gregorian. The years 1600 and 2000 are leap years in both systems. Runic cycles can be best calculated for Old Style by determining the date of the summer solstice and calculating accordingly.

RUNIC NAMES AND THE TIME CYCLES

Using the runes in personal names is a way of enhancing that powerful personal quality known in the Northern Tradition as *megin* (might, power). The Anglo-Saxon king Aethelstan is a classic example of such a runic name that shows the magical principle. His name is composed of the Northumbrian runes Aethel (Odal) and Stan, meaning "stone of possession"—a very regal name befitting the strongman image that Aethelstan possessed. Runic names are composed of two parts, each of them being the name of a rune that can relate to a specific part of the time cycles. When used in this way, the first part of the name is the rune of the half-month in which the subject is born or decides to assume a new runic name. The other half is the rune corresponding with the hour of birth or name-taking. In this way, the name becomes a mnemonic for the time, expressing the special qualities appropriate to that period. Such names are a means of invoking the powers encapsulated in the runes into one's personal life. For example, the name Kenneth would be appropriate for a boy born at 11 p.m. on 21 September. The name is formed from the runes Ken and Ethel (Odal). Ken rules the year-period from 13 September until 28 September, while Odal is the hour-rune from 10:30 to 11:30 p.m. A girl born at 4:45 p.m. on 16 May could be named Ingrid. This name is formed from the combination of the runic periods of Ing and Rad (which has an alternative form of Rid). Ing rules the half-month from 14 May to 29 May, while Rad rules the hour between 4:30 and 5:30 p.m.* Someone born at

---

*All times are Local Apparent Time.

Fig. 5.11. The winter quarter, centered on the rune Jera.
This is the culmination of the cold, dark, part of the runic cycle,
when ice crystals in the air make haloes around the luminaries.
In this quarter, even in darkness, is the potential of rebirth, symbolized by
the winter sigil containing the potential of the seeds of spring growth.
The sacred color of this northern quarter is black.

8:27 p.m. on 27 October could be called Darwin, and so on. The meanings of these names can be interpreted as "the possession of knowledge" (Kenneth), "unlimited motion" (Ingrid), and "joy of day" (Darwin). Using this system, it is possible to create appropriate new runic names that may have never been used before.

The Elder Futhark has a number of alternative names that have been given to each rune. They can be used in the formulation of runic names. The usual variants are listed below: the standard form of the rune as used in this book is followed by the most commonly favored alternative forms. The first name given under "alternative forms" for the Elder Futhark is that recommended by runemaster Thorolf Wardle as "names for use today" in his booklet *The Runenames* (1984).

STANDARD FORM	ALTERNATIVE FORMS
Feoh	Feo, Fe, Fa, Fee, Feu, Feh, Fehu, Faihu, Frey.
Ur	Ur, Uur, Uraz, Uruz, Urus.
Thorn	Thurs, Dorn, Thor, Thurisaz, Thuris, Thiuth, Thyth.
As	Asa, Ansuz, Ansus, Aza, Ass, Æsc.
Rad	Rit, Rid, Radh, Reid, Reda, Rait, Rat, Raido, Raidha.
Ken	Kaan, Cen, Kenaz, Kusma, Kaun, Chaon.
Gyfu	Gibo, Gebo, Giba, Gibor, Gipt, Gewa.
Wyn	Wunna, Win, Winne, Winja, Wunjo, Wunnaz, Vend, Huun.
Hagal	Hagal, Hagalaz, Hægl, Hagel, Haal, Hagl.
Nyd	Naut, Need, Nid, Not, Noicz, Naudhiz, Nauthiz, Naudhr, Naudh.
Is	Iss, Isa, Eis, Iiz.
Jera	Yar, Jara, Jar, Jer, Ger, Gaar, Ar.
Eoh	Eo, Eihwaz, Eihwas, Eyz, Ihwar.
Peorth	Purt, Perthro, Pertra, Pairthra.
Elhaz	Akiz, Eolh, Eolx, Elux, Ezec, Algiz, Algis.

STANDARD FORM	ALTERNATIVE FORMS
Sigel	Sig, Sol, Sun, Sigi, Sigil, Sugil, Saugil, Sowulo.
Tyr	Tiu, Teiwaz, Tiews, Ti, Tir, Tyz.
Beorc	Birk, Berkana, Bercna, Brica, Bar, Bjarkan, Bairkan, Borg.
Ehwaz	Eku, Eh, Eoh, Ehwo, Aihws.
Man	Maan, Mannaz, Manna, Mann, Madur, Madhr.
Lagu	Lagu, Laf, Laukiz, Laguz, Lagus, Lago, Laugur, Laaz, Logr.
Ing	Ing, Ingwaz, Inguz, Enguz, Iggws, Ine, Yngvi.
Odal	Odal, Ethel, Aethel, Odil, Odhal, Othala, Othila, Utal.
Dag	Dag, Dagaz, Dags, Dagr, Dreg, Dar, Daaz, Tag.

The Anglo-Saxon and Northumbrian runes that are added to the 24-rune row of the Elder Futhark have only a few alternatives. These cannot be related directly to the basic time cycles, but are given here as they relate to the longer ones.

Ac	Acea, Acorn, Ar.
Os	Oss.
Yr	Yra, Ira, Ir.
Ior	Jura.
Ear	Era.
Cweorth	Cwerthro, Cweorp.
Calc	Aur.
Stan	Stane.
Gar	Gungnir.

6

THE RUNES, THE PLANETS, AND THEIR CYCLES

Earth I pray, and heaven above, heaven's might and halls on high.

ANCIENT ANGLO-SAXON CHARM

Astrologers have determined that when certain planets have certain relationships with the world and one another, then those influences are recognizable and relatively constant. In modern astrology, the astrological planets are the main celestial bodies that could be observed in the days before the telescope was invented. But they are not strictly planets in the modern sense, for they include the Sun and the Moon. They do not include the Earth, from which observations are made, and upon which these bodies cast their influences. The traditional astrological planets, then, are the Sun, the Moon, Mercury, Venus, Mars, Jupiter, and Saturn. Uranus, Neptune, and Pluto were discovered only when the telescope was put to use, as were the planet-sized satellites of the major planets.

The definition of a planet in astrology is different from that of astronomy. Astronomically, those bodies in the solar system that are in direct orbit around the Sun are known as planets. They are Mercury,

Venus, Earth, Mars, Jupiter, Saturn, Uranus, Neptune, and Pluto. Mercury's orbit is nearest to the Sun, and Pluto's takes it the farthest away. Of course, they vary greatly in size, from the largest, Jupiter, 142,984 km in diameter, to Pluto, which is about 2,200 km in diameter. As in all things, definitions color our perceptions of "reality." Although they are not classified as planets (because their orbits are around larger bodies, not the Sun), some satellites are larger than some of the planets. At least five of the satellites of the large planets are bigger than the planets Mercury and Pluto. These are Callisto and Ganymede, orbiting Jupiter; Titan, a satellite of Saturn; and Triton, which orbits Neptune. Titan, the largest satellite, approaches the size of Mars (5,150 km diameter for Titan, against 6,794 km for Mars), Europa and Io, other moons of Jupiter, are larger than Pluto, as is the Earth's Moon. Several other major planets' moons are planetary in size: Dione, Iapetus, Rhea, and Tethys of Saturn (1,120, 1,460, 1,530, and 1,050 km in diameter, respectively); Ariel, Oberon, Titania, and Umbriel of Uranus (1,160, 1,550, 1,610 and 1,190 km diameter, respectively). In addition, but not classified as planets in astrology, are some considerable "asteroids," better classified as minor planets. These include Ceres, almost half the size of Pluto, 1,003 km in diameter; Pallas, 608 km; Vesta, 538 km; Hygeia, 450 km across; and many other, smaller bodies. These orbit the sun in the area between Mars and Jupiter. Because the major planets are attended by up to twenty-three satellites (Saturn), these planets should not be seen as single objects, rather as planetary complexes containing assemblages of moons, rings and small orbiting asteroids whose various cyclic influences must produce varying gravitational and energetic effects. This is certainly true for Jupiter, Saturn, and Uranus. The dimensions of the bodies in the solar system are listed in Appendix 8.

THE SUN—SÓL

In traditional astrology, the Sun is called a planet because astrological conventions were settled when geocentric beliefs were predominant. Of course, we know now that it is the central point of the solar system, around which the planets, including Earth, orbit. It is the largest body in the solar system, and, being the fountain of energy, is the most influential. According to its position in relation to a place on Earth (the time of day), or in relation to the constellations (the time of year), the Sun affects the conscious element: the human ego, the real self. It affects the person's creative, self-expressive part. Ruled by the goddess Sól, the Sun has dominant, proud, faithful, and generous qualities. She is the power behind the twenty-four-fold cycle of the Runic Day, empowering each runic hour in turn. The Sun has many aspects, from the blazing power of the midsummer zenith to the depleted power close to the horizon at the winter solstice. As the blazing midsummer Sun, it is the Greek Helios or the goddesses Sól and Phoebe. The midday-midsummer sun is symbolized by the demigod Dag, the radiant, beautiful son of Nótt, the goddess of night. As the midwinter Sun, it is the darker, old form of Apollo, and the divinity that is celebrated at Sol Invictus—the festival of the Undefeated Sun, now assimilated as Christmas, birthday of the solar-related deities Osiris, Dionysos, Mithras, Balder, and Jesus. The Sun also manifests in a different way when it crosses the horizon, as the rising and setting sun. In the Northern Tradition, the rising sun is personified as the god Dellingr, the Dawn. He is the northern equivalent of Horus-of-the-two-horizons, who encompasses the rising and setting sun. From this Horus comes Herakles, better known as Hercules, and from him the post-medieval theatrical entity Harlequin is derived. In many sacred traditions, the Sun is seen as male, being ruled variously by the divinities known as Ra, Ahuramazda, Apollo, Helios, Balder, Ogmios, and Saint Elias.

THE MOON—MÁNI

The Moon is not strictly a planet, either, as it is the Earth's satellite. However, in real terms it is larger than the "planet" Pluto, and approaching the size of the planet Mercury, and its proximity to Earth renders it gravitationally the most influential celestial body. Like the other planets, the Moon generates no light of its own. It is literally the mirror of the Sun, reflecting its light. According to Agrippa, this makes the Moon's color "fair." Esoterically, the Moon represents the intuitive subconscious part of people—the withdrawn, solitary, and receptive. But, with the phases of its 29-day cycle, the Moon is changeable, affecting the impressionable and changeable parts of people. On the physical level, the Moon affects the involuntary elements within the physical body. Also, it is associated with illness. "One who is seized with terror, fright and madness during the night is being visited by the goddess of the Moon," wrote Hippocrates (cited in Jones and Jones 1977). The word *lunatic* comes from the Latin *luna,* "moon," and in English, we have a term like *moonstruck,* which originally meant "unable to think or act normally, due to the influence of the Moon." The Moon is the most anciently recognized measurer of time, a marker of the divine power of measure and number.

The four phases of the Moon are a visible expression of the threefold/ fourfold structure of life. Starting invisible in darkness, the Moon manifests as the crescent, grows to the First Quarter "Half-Moon," then to fullness. From Full Moon, it wanes to Last Quarter, then back to darkness. In contexts where the Moon is perceived as a female deity, the threefold phenomenon are manifested as Artemis, Selene, and Hecate in Greek Paganism; or as Diana, Luna, and Proserpina in ancient Rome. In modern Wicca it is the threefold goddess of Virgin (First Quarter), Mother (Full Moon), and Old Woman (Last Quarter). In the Northern tradition, the three phases can be seen as Hjuki (waxing), Máni (full), and Bil (waning), with the first two male gods and the third a goddess. On a more esoteric level, the Moon possesses nine phases, which relate magically to the nine non-invertible runes of the Elder Futhark. Also, when a Full Moon falls on a Monday, then the motherly lunar powers are at their most potent. Any Full Moon, however, is suitable for many lunar-linked activities. For example, a traditional rhyme from East Anglia recommends invoking the luck-generating qualities of the Moon at her fullness:

Pray to the Moon when she is round,
Luck with you will then abound,
What you seek for shall be found,
On the sea or solid ground.

MERCURY—ODIN

Mercury is a rapidly moving planet, the nearest to the Sun. Its motion gave its name to the word "mercurial." Traditionally, it is said to be "glittering" in color. In the Northern Tradition, it is ruled by Odin, god of wisdom, denoting the use of the intellect and memory in all its forms, from speaking to writing and pictorial communication. He has a changeable disposition but has the ability to synthesize; to bring seemingly separate things together coherently to form a union.

VENUS—FRIGG

Venus in the Northern Tradition is equated with Frigg, consort of Odin. At different points of its cycle, Venus is both the "Morning" and "Evening Star"—white in the morning, reddish in the evening, respectively. Influentially, Venus is connected with the spiritual side of a person manifested in the physical. She affects the emotions and affections, and rules peace and harmony, love and beauty, in a creative way. Traditionally, Venus signifies receptive, feminine sexuality and the almost irresistible magnetic attraction of the female sex for the male. Venus rules the compromises necessary for obtaining the things we need.

MARS—TYR

Mars is red and fiery, ruled by Tyr, the northern warrior skygod. He signifies the primal impulse of energy; endurance; thoughtful, justified aggressive action; courageous, daring power, but under full control. He controls the physical side of things, which can means either constructive or destructive power. Traditionally, Mars signifies active, masculine sexuality, ruling the element of fire, and the life-sustaining blood. Tyr's bane or *daemonium* is the Fenris-Wolf; in stellar terms, the star Antares.

JUPITER—THOR

Physically, Jupiter is the largest planet in the solar system, appearing "citron in color, near to paleness and clear" according to Agrippa. In the Northern Tradition, Jupiter is equated with Thor, signifying physical well-being, controlled optimism, energetic growth, and material success. He also rules the more profound aspects of the human being's mental life, in speculative, exploratory thought, and an enthusiastic response to the challenges of life. In northern legend, Thor leads expeditions into uncharted territory such as Utgard (*útgarðr*).

SATURN—LOKI

Saturn's color is blue, leaden and shining. Connected with the shadowy Anglo-Saxon god Sætere, or Loki, the bisexual trickster fire-god, Saturn represents the more restrictive and negative aspects of the human personality. He brings austerity, emotional coldness, a detached caution, excessive self-limitation, despondency, and perhaps fear of life itself. Saturn also rules depressiveness, apprehension, and terror. In an organizational sense, Saturn-Loki rules over the delaying entanglements of bureaucracy, exercising arbitrary control over life. At worst, he rules over disgrace, calamity, disaster, and complete ruin.

URANUS—URD

Like most of the solar system's large bodies and all of its smaller ones, this planet was unknown in ancient times. It was discovered in March 1781 by the astronomer William Herschel. It was first named *Georgium Sidus* (George's Star) after the reigning king of Britain, George III.

Outside Britain it was called Herschel by other astronomers. Finally, it was officially called Uranus, as astrologers had been using the name Ouranos for some time to describe the then-hypothetical eighth "planet." In color, it is greenish. It is associated with the Northern Tradition Nornic deity Urd, being ascribed the power of disruptive change or reformation, which produces enlightenment on a higher plane, but criminality and mindless violence on a lower level.

NEPTUNE—AEGIR

This was discovered in 1846 by Johann Galle. Neptune's qualities are connected with the Northern Tradition sea-god Aegir (Ægir). Its color is pale green. It is seen as a dissolving influence, producing confusion and delusion. But it is also a link with the sea of the unconscious, and is associated with spirit contact. Impracticality, uncertainty, vacillation, anxiety, and even guilt have been associated with Neptune, who, as Aegir, is as changeable as the level of the sea.

PLUTO AND CHARON—VILI AND VÉ

Discovered in 1930, Pluto and its satellite or co-planet Charon, discovered 1978, can be thought of as parallels of the Northern gods Vili and Vé, the second and third brothers of Odin. After Pluto's discovery, astrologers transferred the attributes of "negative Mars" to it. These are a disturbing influence, erratically eruptive, but with the ultimate effect of eliminating the old and regenerating the new. In its lower form, Pluto influences reprobate, perverted criminality. In its higher form, it is evolutionary, influencing the creative and regenerative urges. However, its influence must be negligible, and it may not even be a planet in the accepted sense. It is quite possible that Pluto and Charon are escaped satellites of Neptune, for their orbit actually crosses that of the latter planet, and comes closer to the Sun. Another indication of the "lost satellites of Neptune"–status of Pluto and Charon is that Charon is known to be almost half the size of Pluto, a unique dimension ratio for known planetary systems. At some time in the future, Pluto and Charon are likely to collide with, or be recaptured by, Neptune. It is probable that the asteroids, of which Ceres is over 1,000 km across, and several of which are over 500 km in diameter, which are much closer to Earth, have more influence upon the Earth than Pluto and Charon.

PLANET "X"

This designation is something of an "in joke," because it signifies both the "x" factor of the unknown in algebra and also the roman numeral X, which is ten, for the tenth planet. It is hypothesized that Planet X produces certain motions noted in the orbits of Neptune and Pluto/Charon that can only be accounted for as the influence of an outer planet. No name has been agreed for this hypothetical planet, but if we carry the "x" analogy further, it could be named after the goddess Gefn, patroness of the rune Gyfu, which is written "X." This would go some way toward the realignment of the major planets' gender balance, which has suffered at the assumptions of male astronomers. Everything in the universe is balanced, and this applies to the gender attributes of the planets, too.

THE NINE WORLDS

Like modern astronomy, northern cosmological mythology tells of the existence of Nine Worlds. But these "worlds" are not intended to be taken literally, as representing the so-called planets of the solar system from Mercury to Pluto. These "worlds" are cosmic principles rather than physical bodies, each encapsulating its own unique set of elements. There are various alternative ways of visualizing the arrangement of the Nine Worlds. But whichever way we look at them, the Earth is the middle plane of this cosmology, with four worlds "above" and four worlds "below" in some way. This is why the Earth is called

Midgard (Miðgarðr)—Middle Earth (a name used by J. R. R. Tolkien in his fantasy trilogy *The Lord of the Rings*). The Eddic Poem *Völuspá* recounts the *völva* (seeress) saying: "Nine worlds I knew, the nine in the tree" (st. 2, trans. Bellows). These Nine Worlds are: Ásgarðr (Asgard, the realm of the Æsir), Vanaheimr (Vanir Home), Múspellsheimr (the fiery realm of Múspell), Miðgarðr (Midgard, the middle realm), Jötunheimr (Home of the Giants), Niflheimr (Home of Mist), Svartálfaheimr (Home of the Black Elves), Ljósálfheimr (Home of the Light Elves), and Helheim (Home of Hel, goddess of the underworld). Only the abodes of the divinities of the Æsir and of people are given the name "gard" (from Norse *garðr*, "enclosure, yard"). Dwarves, giants, and denizens of the Demonic Empire dwell in a "heim" (*heimr*)—home. In her book *Leaves of Yggdrasil* (1990, 157–60), the noted modern *völva* Freya Aswynn has equated the Nine Worlds with the nine non-invertible runes of the Elder Futhark. They are: Asgard—Gyfu; Muspellheim—Dag; Vanaheim—Ing; Midgard—Jera; Jötunheim—Is; Niflheim—Nyd; Svartálfaheim—Eoh; Ljósálfheim—Sigel; Helheim—Hagal.

PLANETARY LIFE PERIODS

According to tradition, the astrological planets rule over certain periods of a person's life. Máni (Moon), rules from birth until four years of age (4 years); Odin (Mercury) from 4 to 14 (10 years); Frigg (Venus), from 14 to 22 (8 years); Sól (the Sun) from 22 to 41 (19 years); Tyr (Mars) from 41 to 56 (15 years); Thor (Jupiter) from 56 to 68 (12 years); and Loki (Saturn) from 68 to 98 (30 years).

THE DAYS OF THE WEEK

The days of the week in modern English are named after the gods and goddesses of the Elder Earth who rule them. They are direct parallels of the Roman divinities of the week, being equated with the qualities of the Sun, the Moon, and five major planets. On their corresponding days, the planetary powers are considered to be at their most influential, and so corresponding activities are more likely to be successful then.

Sunday is dedicated to the sun, envisioned as the goddess Sól (or Phoebe in the East Anglian tradition).

Monday is the sacred day of the Moon goddess, who goes by many names. (In the Norse tradition specifically, however, Máni is the male brother of Sól.)

Tuesday is the day of Tiwaz, Tiw, Tuisco, or Tyr, defender and god of justice.

Wednesday is the day of Woden or Odin, an aspect of the Allfather, god of wisdom, energy, enlightenment, and battle, equivalent to Hermes-Mercury.

Thursday is the day dedicated to Thunor or Thor, the god of thunder, who parallels Zeus-Jupiter of the southern European pantheon. Thursday is the most holy day in the Northern Tradition. It is the week's sacred day equivalent to the Friday of the Muslims, the Saturday Sabbath of the Jews, and the Sunday of the Christian religion.

Friday is the day dedicated to the goddess Frigg or Freyja, Venus in the southern European pantheon. It has always been considered unwise to take the risk of making a journey or beginning new things on a Friday, especially if it bears the date 13th, which in August, September, October, November, and December coincides with the commencement of a new runic period. But rather than being invariably bad in itself, more often Friday is seen as dangerously unpredictable, as in this old East Anglian adage:

Friday's the day will have its trick,
The fairest or foulest day of the week.

Saturday is named after the obscure Anglo-Saxon deity Sætere or Seater, believed to be equivalent to the god Saturn. More powerfully, Saturday is the day of the trickster-god Loki, and also associated with the Norns, the Three Fates. Its Old Norse name was *Laugardagr,* "pool day," which was traditionally "wash-day."

WEEKDAY POLARITIES

The engendering of the days of the week can be determined from the gender of the ruling divinities. As mentioned above, in the Northern Tradition, the Sun is feminine. The Moon, too, is usually feminine, although it is also sometimes considered male, as with the Norse Máni. Of course, any absolute engendering of something is only a generalization, for all of us have within us attributes and elements associated with our opposite gender. So it is with the planets and their corresponding days, where a certain maleness may be found in the female ones, and vice versa. The Northern Tradition is one of dynamic balance between the genders, and the days of the week are so divided. Sunday, Monday, and Friday are generally ruled by feminine divinities, while Tuesday, Wednesday, and Thursday are under male deities. Saturday is ruled by the changeable deity, Loki, who is bisexual. The division of seven is thus 3–1–3, with the odd one out representing both and nothing at the same time.

NORTHERN TRADITION ASTRONOMY

When we examine the history and origins of Northern Tradition astronomy, we find that it has a dual origin. Of course, it includes the techniques and traditions of Mediterranean calendar-making and astronomical definition; but also it contains an indigenous element that becomes appropriate only as one approaches Earth's polar regions.

As early as 330 BCE, the Greek astronomer Pytheas visited Norway to take observations of the midnight sun. He is reported to have visited wise men in the district of Nidaros, the present Trondheim, to gain information about astronomy and calendars. This early scientific interchange is one recorded instance of what may have been a relatively common practice in Pagan times. Legend tells that the Hyperborean Abaris (perhaps a druid or *vates* from Britain) visited Pythagoras to exchange knowledge. Pytheas's visit to the North is recorded by Cosmos Indicopleustes in *Christian Topography* (bk. II), and in Geminos's *Introduction to the Phenomena* (chap. 6). Geminus quotes Pytheas: "the barbarians showed us where the Sun goes to sleep; for around these places it happens that the night becomes very short, 2 hours for some, 3 for others, so that, a little while after setting, the Sun rises straight-away" (Evans and Berggren 2006, 162).

This sophisticated astronomical knowledge was transmitted by word of mouth, generation after generation, and added to by accurate observations made by farmers and seafarers. One and a half thousand years later, the information was written down. In the twelfth-century Icelandic text *Oddatala* (Oddi's Tally), we have a surviving record of the accurate pre-Christian observations and calculations of the great Northern Tradition astronomer, Oddi Helgason, known as "Star Oddi." This remarkable scientist, a devotee of Thor, was no nobleman, but a farm laborer who lived and worked on Thord's farmstead at Muli in the north of Iceland, at the beginning of the tenth century. At the appropriate times of the year, Oddi Helgason's job was to look after Thord's fishery on Flatey island, and at night, he observed the stars. Not only did he observe them, but he made accurate observations, which he recorded. His accurate calculations were used later by Churchmen when they attempted to correlate the Icelandic-Norwegian calendar with their own Alexandrian one.

The direct observation and record of natural celestial phenomena by Oddi Helgason, within the framework of traditional Northern astronomy, was more accurate than the Christian astronomical knowledge of his era. This can be seen from his most important surviving work, which concerns the height of the sun at midday. At Flatey, the different between the height of the sun at midday on the two solstices is very marked. At midwinter, it stands at 0° 35' above the open horizon, but at midsummer, it stands 47° 20' above the horizon. Oddi Helgason expressed this difference not in degrees, which were not in use in Iceland then, but in natural measure—solar diameters. Helgason established the total increase of the sun as 182 radii, based upon each of the 26 weeks between the solstices, an increase or decrease of 1 radius larger or smaller than the preceding week. The *Oddatala* records:

> The sun's path increases to the sight by ½ a sun wheel in the first week after the [winter] solstice; in the second week, one wheel; in the third week 1½; in the fourth, 2 wheels; in the fifth, 2½; in the sixth, 3; in the seventh, 3½; in the eighth, 4; in the ninth, 4½; in the tenth, 5; in the eleventh, 5½; in the twelfth, 6; in the thirteenth, 6½; in the fourteenth, likewise 6½. In these two weeks, the sun's course increases the most, because here is the midpoint between the solstices [i.e., the vernal equinox] . . . In the fifteenth week, the sun's course is increased by 6 wheels; in the sixteenth, by 5½; in the seventeenth, 5; in the eighteenth, 4½; in the nineteenth, 4; in the twentieth, 3½; in the twenty-first, 3; in the twenty-second, 2½; in the twenty-third, 2; in the twenty-fourth, 1½; in the twenty-fifth, 1; in the twenty-sixth, half a wheel. There, it has reached the Summer Solstice, and by the same amounts as it was counted during its increase, the sun's course now decreases. (Reuter 1985, 11–12)

This is another of the numerical sequences or progressions, like the "St. Peter's Game" (see below), that underlie runic cryptography and the magical element of the time cycles.

CYCLES OF SUN AND MOON

The nineteen-year cycle is a vital reconciler of solar and lunar cycles. Nineteen is the smallest number of years that is a multiple of a complete lunation period (the synodic month). There are almost 235 synodic months in 19 Julian years, a period known as the Metonic Cycle or the Minor Cycle. This is called after the Pagan ancient Greek astronomer

Meton, who noted in the year 432 BCE that, after a period of nineteen solar years, the phases of the moon fell on the same day of the same month to within about two hours. Only after 310 Julian years does the moon take a step backward, that is, does the computed full moon fall one day earlier than it "should." In the Northern Tradition, this 310-year cycle, requiring the recalibration of the Metonic Cycle, is named after a mythological Swedish king, Aun. He was reputed to have lived for over three hundred years, and during his lifetime the moon took a day's journey backward. The dates of full moons showing their position in the nineteen-year cycle were inscribed in golden characters on the astronomical monuments of Athens, and so the numbers used today are known as the *Golden Number*.

An instance of the cycle's importance to country folk can be understood from an anecdote recounted by the seventeenth-century Swedish antiquary Olaus Rudbeck. In 1669, Rudbeck met a man at the Disting fair at Uppsala. Disting was originally the *thing* or legal meeting sacred to the female deities, the *Dísir*. Disting was a major festival for Pagan Sweden and held for centuries afterward. Rudbeck's acquaintance had a runestock that he had inherited, uncalibrated, from his great-grandfather. Along with other indications, the runestock showed when the Disting Full Moon fell in January each year. In 1669, the Full Moon fell on St. Paul's Day (25 January) rather than on Disting (26 January), indicating the end of the Aun cycle. Because of this, he told Rudbeck, he was able to use the runestock again as a calendar.*

Nowadays, the Golden Number is used mainly by the Church for calculating the "correct" date for Easter. This is done by using the *Epact,* which is the age of the calendar moon, diminished by one day, on 1 January. But in its calculations, the Church uses a "Hypothetical Moon" as opposed to the real observable lunar phases. This has no connection with the runic cycles, based as they are upon the actual

---

*For more on the position of Disting among the old Norse Pagan festivals of the lunar calendar, see P. D. Brown's research in *Thirteen Moons* (2022), 12–21 and 32–42.

observable celestial phenomena, and not a calculated system. Here in England, the tables used by the Church were enshrined into law by an eighteenth-century Act of Parliament (24 Geo. II, cap. 23), so the legal Full Moon does not take place when that which orbits our planet shines with her full light upon us!

This ecclesiastical use is clearly secondary and derivative, several steps removed from its main function of recording the solar/lunar cycles. In the Northern Tradition, the mystery of the nineteenth rune refers to the Golden Number of this cycle. It shows the position of the year in the Metonic Cycle. It also refers to the nineteen Nodal Returns in the eclipse cycle. The sequence of eclipses of the sun and moon are related to a cycle, the Nodal or Saras Period of 18.61 years. But the Metonic cycle of nineteen years is not the same as this eclipse cycle. Eclipses occur when the Sun, Moon, and Earth are in syzygy—alignment in the same phase perpendicular to the ecliptic. Solar eclipses take place at New Moon, and lunar eclipses at the time of Full Moon. The Moon's orbit is at an angle around 5.15° to the ecliptic. When its orbit intersects the ecliptic, its *nodes,* then and only then can the Moon be in line with the Earth and Sun, when eclipses occur. For an eclipse of the Sun to occur, the Moon must be at or near one of its nodes (the Dragon's Head and the Dragon's Tail), and in conjunction with the Sun. The nodes of the Moon's orbit only coincide with the Sun twice a year. The apparent motion of the Sun in the ecliptic makes the Moon complete a revolution in respect to its nodes in 27.2 days (a Draconic or Nodical Month), when its return to another conjunction with the Sun is 29.5 days long (a Synodic Month). The upshot of these cycles is that they coincide every 6,585 days (to within 11 hours of one another). If the Sun and Moon are in conjunction with one of the lunar nodes, the time taken to the return to the same node is 346.6 days. A period of 242 Draconic Months, 223 complete lunations, and 19 returns of the Sun to the same orbital node of the Moon, all come together. This is the Saros Cycle, which lasts for 18 years, 10 days, 7 hours, and 42 minutes. It is the rule for predicting eclipses. In the Northern Tradition, solar and lunar eclipses have a poetically symbolic interpretation. Here, they are associated with the wolves, Sköll and Hati, whose names mean *mockery* and *hatred*. These malevolent wolves had the task of overtaking the luminaries and devouring them, so that the world would be enveloped once again in primeval darkness. The Eddic poem *Grímnismál* (st. 39) puts this more poetically, incidentally also referring to the gendered qualities of the Moon (male) and Sun (female) in the Northern Tradition:

> *[Sköll] is the wolf that to Ironwood*
> *Follows the glittering god,*
> *And the son of Hrothvitnir, Hati, awaits*
> *The burning bride of heaven.* (trans. Bellows)

At specific times, these wolves overtake the solar and lunar goddesses and attempt to swallow them. But the time is not yet right for them to be obliterated, and, aided by the gods, they are repulsed, and the luminaries reappear in their former glory.

Fig. 6.1. In the Northern Tradition, the demonic wolf is emblematical of the eclipses of the Sun and Moon, and also the fall of Odin, through whose agency we have the Runes.

The numbers connected with these cycles can be found in symbolic form in various traditions. For example, the Norse board game Hnefatafl—which was played in Scandinavia, England, and Scotland before it was superseded by chess—used a board divided into a grid of 19 by 19 points. Like other board games from Europe and Asia, Hnefatafl clearly had a cosmological origin in the Metonic Cycle, where the playing pieces could be taken to represent the apparent motions of the planets amid the fixed stars.

THE ANCIENT EGYPTIAN CALENDAR AND THE GOLDEN NUMBER CYCLE

The Ancient Egyptian Calendar, sometimes known as the Alexandrian Calendar, was the basis for the Julian Calendar, used on runestocks in Northern Europe. The Julian Calendar was the baseline to which the Golden Number for lunar calculations was added. The Egyptian year consisted of 365 days, beginning on the first of Thoth, equivalent to 19 July. It was divided into three seasons, each of four months. Each month comprised 30 days, and 5 epagomenal (intercalary) days were inserted at the end of the twelfth month to keep the calendar in line with the solar year. The twelve months were called Thoth, Paophi, Hathyr, Choiak, Tybi, Mecheir, Phamenoth, Pharmouthi, Pachon, Pauni, Epeiph, and Mesore. This was the standard civil calendar, which differed in significant ways from the funerary calendar and the sacred ritual calendar. In the Egyptian calendar was the Sadu Cycle of thirty years. The ordinary Egyptian calendar was a shambles, however, because although it had three seasons—Akhe, "Inundation"; Proye, "Winter"; and Shomu, "Summer"—there was no attempt to keep it in line with the solar year. Because of this, it drifted so that after 120 years the calendar was a whole month in front of the astronomical year. Although a Ramesside papyrus (ca. 1600 BCE) laments "Winter is come in Summer, the months are reversed, the hours in confusion" (Gardiner 1961, 64), nothing was done about this disgraceful state of affairs.

The Egyptian farmers predicted the annual flooding of the Nile, upon which they depended, by observing the stars, especially the heliacal rising of Sirius, and the calendar remained only for formal, ceremonial, use. Only after Alexander's Greek conquest was something done. In 237 BCE, the *Decree of Canopus* by King Ptolemy III Euergetes began to use a leap year day to keep the calendar where it was. Finally, the Roman Emperor Augustus legally imposed the Julian Calendar, which ironically had been calculated by Egyptian astro-mathematicians, upon Egypt. The Egyptians, however, continued to use the old calendar for another four centuries.

In the year 323 CE, calendar-makers at the Egyptian city of Alexandria, then one of the world's greatest scientific, astronomical, and mathematical centers, started the Golden Number sequence, which is still continued today. Because the lunar month is approximately 29 days 12 hours, it was decided that alternate periods of 29 and 30 days should be used to calculate lunar cycles in the calendar. These are the *menses cavi* and *menses pleni,* short and full months. In the year 1076 AUC (the Roman calendar), the year 323 CE of the present reckoning, the Alexandrian sages observed that the New Moon nearest to the vernal equinox fell on the 27th of the Egyptian month of Phamanoth, equivalent to 23 March, the Golden Number 1. From then on, alternating periods of 29 and 30 days of the Moon were inserted into the calendar: 29 days after 27th Phamanoth was Pharmuthi 26th, equivalent to 21 April; 30 days after that, Phamacon 26th, equivalent to 21 May, and so on through the year, the Golden Number was set against the appropriate dates.

So the first year of this Golden Number system began at the vernal equinox, 323 CE. The Julian equivalents for Year 1 were thus: 23 March, 21 April, 21 May, 19 June, 19 July, 17 August, 16 September, 15 October, 14 November, and 13 December. But as 324 had the Golden Number of 2, the number 2 was put next to 12 January. After that, 2 was put against 10 February, 12 March, 10 April, 10 May, 8 June, 8 July, 6 August, 5 September, 4 October, 3 November, and 2 December. From there into 325, another 30 days were added and the number 3 placed against 1 January. By adding on 29 and 30 days alternately, the whole calendar could be calculated, so that every day of the year had a coded number between 1 and 19 against it, the number of the Metonic Cycle of Sun and Moon. The sequence works out in such a way that every following number is created by adding 8 to the preceding one, and every preceding number by adding 11 to the following one. The numerical sequence of the Golden Numbers is thus as follows: 1, 9, 17, 6, 14, 3, 11, 19, 8, 16, 5, 13, 2, 10, 18, 7, 15, 4, 13, and so on.

Two years after the formulation of this numerical sequence, the Christian Church fathers met in council at Nicaea. Apart from the usual bitter doctrinal arguments that characterized such meetings, they went there to discuss the vexed question of the calculation of when Easter should be celebrated, which meant—in practice—the reconciliation of the lunar with the solar cycles. There, they decided to adopt the system of Golden Numbers, which had been worked out satisfactorily by the Alexandrian sages two years earlier. Of course, natural cycles are unfortunately not quite as precise as that, not being composed of round figures for human convenience. So, further corrections were necessary, by the insertion of embolismal months. These were inserted in the sequence 5, 8, 11, 13, 16, and 19, when an extra full month of 30 days was added to bring the cycle of the moon back into calibration with the calendar months. This numerical sequence is the second block of six numbers in the complete 19-year row of Golden Numbers, dividing them 6–6–7. In years with the Golden Number 2, an extra short month of only 29 days was added. In the old Swedish runestocks, the longer-term adjustment was remembered by the cryptic rhyme, "The Moon steps 12 and 20 during Aun," during which period the numbers 12 and 20 were used instead of 11 and 19. Further adjustments have had to be made in the long term, too, as slight discrepancies, negligible in the short term, have accumulated. However, the Alexandrian system was found to be quite satisfactory, and was incorporated into the northern runestocks as a sequence of runic characters, with specific relationships with the runic time cycles.

The mystic key to the late runes is the sequence that the Metonic Cycle imposes. When the runes are taken in their straightforward numbering, with Feoh as 1, and so on, then they are numbered in sequence from 1 to 19. But there is another number sequence inherent in the nineteen-year cycle, that is the actual order of numbers according to the 8 and 11 rule. When the runes are placed against this order, an encoded, mystic sequence, is formed: 1, Fé; 9, Úr; 17, Thurs; 6, Óss; 14, Reið; 3, Kaun; 11, Hagall; 19, Nauð; 8, Ís; 16, Ár; 5, Sól; 13, Týr; 2, Bjarkan; 10, Laugr; 18, Madur; 7, Ýr; 15, Árlaug; 4, Tvimadur; and 13, Belgthor. This sequence was used in the Middle Ages by runic cryptographers. The central block of the 19-year sequence contains the years in which embolismal months are inserted in order to keep the solar and lunar calendars in harmony. These are the runes numbered 11, 19, 8, 16, 5, and 13; equivalent to Sól, Belgthor, Nauð, Ýr, Reið, and Bjarkan.

There are also several other calendric cycles derived from Graeco-Roman usage that have some relation to the runic time cycles. They are the *Roman Indication,* which is a period of fifteen years, begun in about the year 300 CE. Another interesting cycle is the so-called *Solar Cycle,* also known as the Major Cycle. This is a period of 28 years, in any given year of which the days of the week recur on the same days of the month. To obtain a better concurrence between these periods, more accuracy is achieved by combining the cycles. For example, three Saros Periods, making 54 years and 31 days, give a better correlation than the single 18.61 cycle. An almost perfect correlation is attainable with 48 Saros Periods, 893.28 years.

THE LUNAR SELES

The Lunar Seles or Mansions are related to the runes through the shorter Anglo-Saxon rune row. As mentioned above, this system is a development of the Elder Futhark by one order-change and the addition of newer runes. Traditionally, the lunar mansions form a "lunar zodiac" of 28 divisions, each of which marks generally the apparent distance traveled by the Moon in one Earth day. The ecliptic is usually divided equally into 28 divisions of 12° 51'. This has been recognized for many millennia. At Stonehenge, for example, the 56 Aubrey Holes that surround the main megalithic structure are clearly related numerically to the 28 lunar mansions. The early European version of this system is poorly recorded, but there are well-defined comparable systems known from Arabian, Hindu, and Chinese astrology. There, the mansions are known as Manzils, Nakshatras, and Sieu, respectively. The former system was probably derived from the Greco-Egyptian systems of Alexandria, and so, as with many esoteric systems, shares a common origin with European usage. Each of the 28 lunar seles is believed to signify an influence and is numbered consecutively with a rune from the 28-rune row, beginning with Feoh and ending with Ear, leaving out the terrestrial "Midgard Serpent"–rune, Ior. It is possible to use the lunar seles with the traditional astrological planets, when the nature of the sele is seen to be modified in accordance with the quality of the planet present in it. In terms of runic astrology, the corresponding runes of the lunar seles and the planets can be compared and appropriate prognoses reached.

Actually, the lunar seles are each designated segments of the heavenly circle, but they are marked by specific stars. Early systems of lunar mansions began with the star Alcyone (η Tauri) in the Northern constellation or asterism known as The Boars' Throng. From antiquity, contrary to the geocentric doctrine, it was taught that this star was the nowl at the center of the universe, around which all the stars revolved. To the Babylonian Magi, it was known as Temmenu (Foundation Stone), while the early Arab astronomers called it Al Wasat (Central One). Both the Arabic and Hindu systems of lunar mansions begin here. The Arabic Mansion beginning at Alcyone is named Al Thurayya (Many Small Ones), while the Hindu equivalent is called Krittika (General of the Heavenly Army). In runic astrology, it takes the name and quality of the corresponding rune. The beginning points of each of the 28 lunar seles are marked mainly by the following stars and asterisms. In many cases, the meanings of their corresponding runes are most appropriate.

RUNE	NORTHERN TRADITION STAR NAME EQUIVALENT	CLASSICAL NAME	ASTRONOMICAL DESIGNATION
1 Feoh	Boars' Throng	Alcyone	(η Tauri)
2 Ur	The Follower	Aldebaran	(α Tauri)
3 Thorn	The Shield	–	(λ Orionis)
4 Os	The Brand	Alhena	(γ Geminorum)
5 Rad	Thiazi's Eyes	Castor & Pollux	(α & β Geminorum)
6 Ken	The Bee Skep	Praesaepe	(44M Cancri)
7 Gyfu	The Giver	–	(α Leonis)
8 Wyn	The Lord	Regulus	(β Leonis)
9 Hagal	The Girdle	Zosma	(δ Leonis)
10 Nyd	The Coming Judge	Denebola	(β Leonis)
11 Is	The Beautiful One	Zavijava	(β Virginis)
12 Jera	The Wheatsheaf	Spica	(α Virginis)
13 Eoh	The Stave	–	(ι & κ Virginis)
14 Peorth	North & South Scales	–	(α & β Librae)
15 Elhaz	The Byrnie	Graffias & Isidis	(α & β Scorpii)
16 Sigel	Fenris-Wolf	Antares	(α Scorpii)
17 Tyr	The Sword	Lesath	(λ Scorpii)
18 Beorc	Birka	Pelagus	(ζ Sagittarii)
19 Eh	Sleipnir	–	(π Sagittarii)
20 Man	The Slain and Restored Goats	Giedi & Dabih	(α & β Capricornii)
21 Lagu	The Stream	–	(ξ & μ Aquarii)
22 Ing	The Lucky Star	Sadalsuud	(β Aquarii)
23 Odal	The Royal Lucky Star	Sadalmelik	(α, etc. Aquarii)
24 Dag	The Doornail	Scheat	(β Pegasi)
25 Ac	The Acorn	Alpheratz	(α Andromedae)
	The Carrier	& Algenib	(γ Pegasi)
26 Æsc	The Key	Mirach	(β Andromedae)
27 Yr	The Bow	Sharatan	(β Arietis)
28 Ear	The Last Ones	–	(γ & δ Arietis)

There are also 28 Lunar Stations, which are marked by specific stars.

ST. PETER AND PETOSIRIS

The mystic numerical sequence known in Finland as *Pietarin leikki* and Sweden as *Sankt Peders Lek* (Saint Peter's Game), is related to the lunar cycle of the 30-day full month. It is also related in an arcane way to the design of labyrinths, and Saami traditional cosmology, where it is found carved on staves and rock faces. This sequence is described in a strange Christianized folktale about St. Peter and 30 other people on a ship during a terrible storm that threatened to sink the overloaded vessel. St. Peter decided that to avoid the ship going down with all hands, 15 people must be thrown overboard. But to make it fair, he added, everyone should stand in line, and then every ninth person would be thrown overboard. As there were 15 Jews and 15 Christians on board, St. Peter arranged them in such a sequence that all of the Jews should be thrown into the sea to drown, while all of the Christians remained aboard to survive. Clearly, this story is just a mythical explanation of the sequence's origin as an anti-Semitic sick joke. However, the existence of such a sequence without a purpose would make even the story meaningless. The sequence, which is recorded on calendars from Scandinavia as late as 1755, has the traditional notation of XXXXIIIIIXXIXXXIXIIXXIXIXIIXXI. The method of counting is to take the ninth one away, then to count again from there another nine, taking that one away. The sequence diminishes as shown below. An asterisk denotes the removed character.

```
X X X X I I I I I X X I X X X I X I I X X I X I X I I X X I
X X X X I I I I * X X I X X X I X * I X X I X I X I * X X I
X X X X I * I I * X X I X X X I X * I X X I X I X I * X X I
X X X X I * I I * X X I X X X * X * I X X I X I X * * X X I
X X X X I * * I * X X I X X X * X * * X X I X I X * * X X *
X X X X I * * I * X X * X X X * X * * X X I X * X * * X X *
X X X X I * * * * X X * X X X * X * * X X * X * X * * X X *
X X X X * * * * * X X * X X X * X * * X X * X * X * * X X *
```

Fig. 6.2. The spring quarter, centered on the Goddess Rune, Beorc, brings the rejuvenation of the Sun, and the ascendancy of the light over the darkness. This is the quarter of regeneration and partnership.
The sacred color of this eastern quarter is red.

Finally, in eight circuits of the line, the designated 15 are removed. The numbers involved in this sequence are 30, the number of items; 9, the number counted off; and 8, the number of times the line is counted to remove the 15 designated ones. The sequence of removal is as follows: X X X X 14 4 7 12 1 X X 10 X X X 5 X 28 X X 15 13 11 X 6 3 X X 9. This makes the sequence of removed figures numbers 9, 18, 27, 6, 16, 26, 7, 19, 30, 12, 24, 8, 23, 5, and 22. Transferred to the Northumbrian Futhork, the numbers removed in sequence correspond with the runes Hagal, Beorc, Yr, Ken, Sigel, As, Gyfu, Ehwaz, Cweorth, Jera, Dag, Wyn, Odal, Rad, and Ing.

The "game's" connection with St. Peter gives it an obvious relationship to the calendar. St. Peter's Day, 29 June, is the first day of a new runic year cycle, beginning with the rune Feoh, signifying literally cattle, but symbolically wealth, abundance, and power. According to Christian mythology, St. Peter is the keeper of the keys of the doors of Heaven and Hell, an appropriate figure for a beginning-time. St. Peter is associated with entrances and passage, which was manifested often in religious art. The ancient holy well of St. Peter at Peterchurch, Herefordshire, whose waters were reputed to have the power to cure rheumatism, once had a dramatic sculpted head of the saint, out of whose mouth the waters flowed. This image of the face at the beginning of some place or time can be seen in the imagery of the maw of Hell and in the two faces of Janus, the Roman divinity of January.

Another part of this complex mythological imagery calls St. Peter "the Rock," from the Greek etymology of his name. According to tradition, Peter was the rock on whom the Church was founded. Accordingly, the chief church of the West, in the Vatican at Rome, was dedicated to St. Peter. It was founded over the supposed tomb of Peter, in a pagan cemetery dedicated to the goddess Cybele. But the name Peter may not refer to the disciple of Jesus anyway. It may refer to the ancient Egyptian astrologer-priest Petosiris who is ascribed with writing important astrological texts for a King Nechepso, and which are generally believed to be of the Ptolomaic period, around the second century BCE. Petosiris's material is said to have had a major influence on the school of astronomy and astrology at Alexandria in the following century. This was exactly the time and place of the calendar reforms whose effects are felt to this day, and which can be found—as the "Egyptian Days" and other markers—on runestocks.

In the north, however, it is clear that the name St. Peter is in the main a substitution for a Pagan deity of beginnings, numerical sequences, and astronomical markers. The connection between the cosmic world pillars (rocks) and the St. Peter's Game sequence is clearly intended to be illustrated in the old engraving of the Saami cosmic holy mountain, reproduced here. These twin peaks are solar markers, like the original twin Heelstones, which, it has recently been discovered, stood in front of Stonehenge to "bracket" the rising sun. They echo the twin obelisks that stood either side of the entrance of many temples in ancient Egypt. But, as explained in Chapter 4, the Greek etymology of St. Peter is also connected with the name of the geomantic markers known as perrons. The solar nature of perrons is clear, both as gnomons to cast the sun's shadow and thus denote the passing of time, and also in their symbolism of a shaft surmounted by an orb, often gilded in former times. Equally, perrons can be used to mark the passage of the moon and even of the stars. One of the attributes of St. Peter is that of marking the passage of time. In Christian mythology, St. Peter is supposed to hold the keys to Heaven, but also those to Hell, which would make him an external guardian of the underworld. An old English spell shows the magical connection in folk tradition. When someone was dying, it was customary to try to speed their end by performing certain actions with a key and reciting:

> *Open lock*
> *End strife*
> *Come death*
> *And pass, life.*

In Celtic mythology, the underworld guardian figure is Gwynn ap Nudd, "Light, son of Darkness," the master of the faerie kingdom, whose sacred mountain in England is Glastonbury Tor. Gwynn is thought of as being master of and unifier of the polar opposites; his servants wearing livery that was red on one side and blue on the other. These colors symbolize fire and ice, the formative active and static forces of the universe, manifested in the year cycle as summer and winter. In parallel with this, the conventional iconography of St. Peter shows him holding two keys, one of gold and the other of silver, the keys to Heaven and Hell. Esoterically, these keys represent the Sun and the Moon. The obvious interpretation of these mythical attributes is that the key to Heaven is the information about the cycles of the visible heavens above, and the key to the underworld is knowledge of the motions of the Sun, Moon, and the planets when they are invisible, beneath the earth. It is therefore appropriate that the Christian archetype of St. Peter should have been chosen to take over the role of year guardian and reconciler of the solar and lunar cycles.

RUNIC CYCLES IN THE GREAT YEAR

During a period of 25,920 years, the point of the vernal equinox has a retrograde motion through the constellations. This is caused by the nutation of the Earth's rotation, rather like the secondary rotary motion described by the axis of a spinning toy top. This phenomenon is known as the Precession of the Equinoxes. The period of one rotation is known as the Precessional Year, the Platonic Year (*Annus Platonicus*), or Great Year. Customarily, the 25,920-year period is divided into twelve equal time zones, sometimes known as *Platonic Months,* each corresponding to an arc of the zodiac. Customarily, each period through which the vernal point regresses is named after a corresponding sign of the zodiac, impressing some important aspects of its qualities upon the events of the age. In runic astrology, a similar division is made to the year, corresponding not to the signs of the zodiac, however, but to the runic half-months of the year. Dividing the Great Year of 25,920 years by 24, this makes each runic half-month of the Great Year equal to 1,080 years in length. During this period, the vernal point regresses by 15°. The number 1,080 is important, for traditionally it is the number of breaths that an adult person takes in one hour. In the Northern Tradition, it is associated with the divine intelligence and with the prophetic powers of the Norns. The moon's radius is 1,080 miles, ten times the esoteric lunar number 108, and one-tenth of the Indo-European mystic number 10,800. There are 10,800 stanzas in the *Rig Veda,* and, according to the Greek pre-Socratic philosopher Heraclitus, civilization is destroyed by fire every 10,800 years—ten runic half-months of the Great Year.

Fig. 6.3. Runic wheel showing the relationship between the zodiac, the seasons, the eight festivals of the year, and significant solar directions.

According to many astrological sources, it is believed that the vernal point is still retrograding through Pisces, making the present time part of the astrological Age of Pisces. But the greatest difficulty with the Great Year is in determining the beginning-point for the runic cycle within it. This can be seen by the disagreement in various astrologers' calculations made for the dawning of the Age of Aquarius. Because there are no agreed fiducials, this makes determination of beginning- and ending-points a very vexed proposition. The beginning of the Age of Pisces has been put, among other dates, at 255 BCE, 158 BCE, 125 BCE, 97 BCE, 46 BCE, 1 CE, and around the year 1000. To find your own preferred start of the Aquarian Age, add 2,160 years to any of the dates above. The runic time periods relate to the astrological ages of the Great Year in the same way that the conventional signs of the zodiac relate to the runic half-months. The 12 signs of the zodiac in the year all overlap the 24 runic half-months of the year with periods corresponding as follows:

ZODIAC SIGN	YEAR DATES	RUNES	RUNE COMPLETELY WITHIN SIGN
Cancer	21 Jun–20 Jul	Dag/Feoh/Ur	Feoh 29 Jun–14 Jul
Leo	21 Jul–21 Aug	Ur/Thorn/As	Thorn 29 Jul–13 Aug
Virgo	22 Aug–22 Sep	As/Rad/Ken	Rad 29 Aug–13 Sep
Libra	23 Sep–22 Oct	Ken/Gyfu/Wyn	Gyfu 28 Sep–13 Oct
Scorpio	23 Oct–22 Nov	Wyn/Hagal/Nyd	Haga! 28 Oct–13 Nov
Sagittarius	23 Nov–20 Dec	Nyd/Is/Jera	Is 28 Nov–13 Dec
Capricorn	21 Dec–19 Jan	Jera/Eoh/Peorth	Eoh 28 Dec–13 Jan
Aquarius	20 Jan–18 Feb	Peorth/Elhaz/Sigel	Elhaz 28 Jan–12 Feb
Pisces	19 Feb–20 Mar	Sigel/Tyr/Beorc	Tyr 27 Feb–14 Mar
Aries	21 Mar–20 Apr	Beorc/Ehwaz/Man	Ehwaz 30 Mar–14 Apr
Taurus	21 Apr–20 May	Man/Lagu/Ing	Lagu 29 Apr–14 May
Gemini	21 May–20 Jun	Ing/Odal/Dag	Odal 29 May–14 Jun

Similarly, the astrological ages relate to the Great Year, and the runic half-months have the same relationship to the ages as they do to the zodiac in the solar year of 365 days. But of course, the "running order" is reversed because of the retrograde motion of the vernal point. Although the precise starting point of the Age of Aquarius is uncertain, the runic Great Year half-month Sigel, 1,080 years in length, overlaps the end of

Pisces and the beginning of Aquarius. This makes the present era, at the end of the Age of Pisces or the beginning of the Age of Aquarius, solidly in the runic age of Sigel, a solar age. The use of power, derived ultimately from the sun, and nuclear energy, in imitation of stellar mechanisms, may be manifestations of this age. The destructive element of the rune Sigel, which can sweep away everything in its path, has been very apparent in the increasingly devastating wars of the last two centuries. Symbolically, both the Nazi and Japanese forces of World War II used solar symbols in their vicious attempts at world domination. The Nazi party used the swastika, traditionally a solar symbol, and the SS used the Sigel rune, while the Japanese had the rising sun as their emblem. But on the other side, the Age of Sigel is not all destruction. As a rune of individuation, the Age of Sigel also represents the evolution of the individual, and spiritual growth.

7

THE RUNES IN THE CIRCLING HEAVENS

The stars' motions, the whirling meadow, is supported by the hub; "post and stars" go together in the Old Norse idiom.

OTTO SIEGFRIED REUTER

NORTHERN TRADITION ASTRONOMY AND ASTROLOGY

The Northern Tradition does not see in the seemingly random scatter of the stars at night the same constellations as those described in modern astronomy and astrology. Although they bear no resemblance to the objects or animals described, the constellations and their names familiar to modern astrologers and astronomers are derived mainly from Babylonian and Egyptian sources, with Greek and Arab additions and modifications. In runic work, however, it is more appropriate to use the traditional names from northern Europe, which have been handed down by word of mouth over the centuries. Of course, the Northern Tradition constellations are strictly of the northern sky and relate to the myths and beliefs of northern religion. As the astronomy

refers to latitudes of 50 degrees and northward, most of these traditionally named stars, asterisms, and constellations are in the winter half of
the sky. The farther one goes northward, the light evenings and short
nights of summer make the stars of the summer half less and less necessary for navigation and orientation. Over the centuries since they were
in general use, a few of the old names were lost as the Arab names took
over. But most of them are still known, and the others have been recon-
stituted by documentary research, folkloric studies, and by the application of advanced esoteric techniques.

As its name implies, the Northern Tradition is grounded in the
experience of people living in the northern lands of Europe, and, according to those beliefs, the north pole of the heavens is the most sacred
part of the sky. The invisible hub of the stellar vault, around which the
other stars appear to rotate, has been known by many poetic kennings,
such as "up north," the "center of the Moon's Hall," "Odin's spear" (the
Northumbrian rune Gar), and as the apex of the World Pillar, Irminsul.
Over the millennia, owing to the precession of the equinoxes, this point
has been marked by a succession of stars. In neolithic times, α Draconis
was the Pole Star, and around the beginning of the present Common
Era calendar it was approaching the star that became known in Viking
times as *leiðarstjarna,* the Lodestar (32 Camelopardalis, also known as
4339 Camelopardalis). The north pole of the heavens approached this
star until around the year 800 CE it was at its closest. But, owing to
the precession of the equinoxes, the present Polaris α Urs Minoris), the
Nail or Nowl (Navel) attained its present status as Pole Star around
the year 1400. In Anglo-Saxon England, the Lodestar was also known
by the rune name of *Tir,* and would have been a sacred star of the god
Tiw (Tyr).

The star known as the Nowl, the present polar marker, is one of
the *Fifteen Stars* of traditional medieval astronomy, prominent stars and
asterisms used in orientation, navigation, and astrology. Their attributes
are described in detail below. Close to the Nowl are the constellations
of Woden's (or Odin's) Wagon and Our Lady's Wagon. These are iden-

tical with the constellations known as Ursa Major and Ursa Minor. The name of the latter Wagon constellation, which contains the Nowl star, describes the vehicle of Frigg, the Great Mother Goddess, the Queen of the Heavens whose spindle is the north celestial pole. In the Northern Tradition, the modern constellation of Orion is not seen as a single entity, being composed of the Plough star (Rigel, β Orionis) and Frigg's Distaff. This latter constellation is composed of the three stars known now by their Arabic names of Alnitak, Anilam, and Mintaka, and collectively as the Belt of Orion. The latter constellation is the circumferential spinning counterpart of the Nowl, Frigg's Spindle. The three stars can be seen as representative of the Three Norns, expressers of our Wyrd.

The Boars' Throng is the asterism otherwise known as the Pleiades, or the Seven Stars. The name comes from the Norse *svínfylking* ("swine array"), a wedge-shaped battle formation of warriors. In Viking times, these fearless warriors of Odin fought as the vanguard of the army, breaking through the enemy to let in their comrades, who were following behind. The boar is one of the most hallowed animals in the Northern Tradition, being sacred to the sky-god. Consequently, the Boars' Throng marks the beginning of the Northern Tradition stellar year, and the first Sele of the Moon (Lunar Mansion) is denoted by the main star, once believed to be the center of the universe, Alcyone (η Tauri). This asterism of the Fifteen Stars is close to the constellation of the Lesser Wolf's Jaws, which include the classical six-star constellation of the Hyades and the Follower (Aldebaran, α Tauri). The Lesser Wolf's Jaws lies directly on the ecliptic, intercepting the sun's path, so this constellation is considered to be violent and troublesome, associated with storms. The Lesser Wolf's Jaws face the stellar array named the Battle of the Gods, which contains the classical constellation of Auriga. This constellation includes the goats of Thor's chariot, and also Heidrun, the little she-goat of Odin, the Northern Tradition name of the first magnitude star Capella (α Aurigae).

The Greater Wolf's Jaws is a large stellar array that includes the classical constellation of Andromeda; part of the Milky Way; and the semicircle of stars through Pegasus to Cygnus, including Deneb Adige (α Cygni). The open jaws face the pole of the sky, the destructive wolf's jaws threatening the Cosmic Axis, Yggdrasil. Thiazi's Eyes (Castor and Pollux, α and β Geminorum) represent the eyes of the giant Thiazi, slain by the gods and thrown into the sky as a memorial. Aurvandill's Toe (Corona Borealis, more precisely the main star, Alphecca, α Coronae borealis) mythologically represents the toe of the giant Aurvandill, which was cast into the sky by Thor.

The constellations of the Northern Tradition are markers of the seasons, and have direct connections with the customary seasonal rites and their associated myths. For example, at the end of autumn, the Torch Bearer heralds the approach of Loki's Brand onto the Bridge of the Gods, where the Battle of the Gods is taking place. At midwinter midnight, Loki's Brand stands at the southern end of Irmin Street (Milky Way), with the Greater Wolf's Jaws and Aurvandill's Toe opposite each other as vernal and autumnal constellations. In navigation, the rising-points of notable stars and constellations like Frigg's Distaff (due east) were used as markers until the advent of the magnetic compass, which arrived in Europe from China around 1150. The legendary names of the stars relate the qualities of time, direction, and space to cosmic myth, a holistic universal view that is much at odds with modern materialism, yet which is a truer model of the image of human beings. When in conjunction with the planets, they are believed to indicate certain specific qualities of the time that will be manifested then.

The stars and asterisms commonly known as the *Fifteen Stars* are important traditionally because they are ascribed with certain qualities and influences. These stars above all others were held to exert known powers and were the basis of much talismanic work by the magi of the medieval period. In making talismans, in addition to the prevailing powers of the astrological planets, the influence of relevant members of the Fifteen Stars were taken into account. In astrology, too, the Fifteen Stars are credited with certain powers. Customarily, these powers have usually been explained in terms of planetary or godly qualities. Because of this, the Fifteen Stars can be used in classical astrology in exactly the same way as the better-known planets. Like the planets, they have certain esoteric yet rational correspondences that can be used in many other ways, too. These very important Fifteen Stars, with their Northern Tradition names and equivalents, are as follows.

It is appropriate to begin the circle with the Boars' Throng, otherwise known as the Pleiades, since this asterism has customarily been taken as the first lunar sele. It is also known as the *Seven Stars,* after which many public houses in England and Wales are named. As the Boars' Throng, it is visualized as a representation of a *svínfylking* squad, a northern martial-arts warrior band. It is ascribed the astrological nature of Máni and Tyr, bringing turbulent ambition, traditionally being malevolent in effect. If rising, the Boars' Throng is said to bring afflictions to the face, especially the eyes and general sickness or wounds. But also, as befitting its warrior name, it brings military advantage. Culminating, the asterism is said to bring destruction, ruin, and disgrace; with Sól (the Sun) it brings illness of the throat and face, sometimes power with infirmity, as with the planetary Tyr (Mars). With Máni (the Moon), similar problems are indicated, and with the planetary Odin (Mercury), losses through litigation, business failure, and bankruptcy. With the planetary Frigg (Venus), strong passions and licentiousness are indicated. In conjunction with the planetary Tyr, the Boars' Throng brings accidents, especially in connection with fire. With the planetary Thor (Jupiter), the Boars' Throng indicates hypocrisy, deceit, and fraudulent business concerns with possible imprisonment. With the planetary Loki (Saturn), there may be chronic sickness, and with the planetary Urd (Uranus), disharmony, many troubles, and unexpected losses. With Aegir, strength and gain, but with many mishaps, perhaps a secret, corrupt, and/or dishonorable profession. The Boars' Throng is associated with quartz, quicksilver, and the herb Fennel (*Foeniculum vulgare*). Its magical qualities include the raising of the wind and the revelation of hidden things. Its corresponding runes are Tyr and Ken.

The Day Star (Arcturus, α Boötes) is a golden-yellow star of the first magnitude. It is believed to be of the nature of the planetary Tyr and Thor, a quality that brings self-reliance, prosperity, riches, and fame, and justice through power. If rising, the Day Star is said to bring good fortune, which may be attended by many problems brought on as the result of personal misjudgment. Culminating, it indicates a profitable business and a good personal reputation, and if with Sól, Máni, or the planetary Thor, adequate wealth and honor. With Sól, the Day Star indicates success in business, accurate judgment, and a harmonious home. But if with Tyr, respiratory problems may occur. The Day Star with Odin may make the subject popular and hard-working, well-off but extravagant. It may also bring with it strong religious urges, high office in a company or business, regular promotion, and good health. With Frigg, the Day Star is said to bring popularity and much friendship, as with Tyr, which denotes the subject to be popular with many friends. It also indicates considerable gain but offset by equal extravagance. Thor may bring benefit through legal matters, or gain through business with foreign countries, but this may be tinged with hypocrisy. With Loki, it can bring honesty, but this is overshadowed by materialism, resulting in selfishness, even miserliness. Difficulties early in married life are indicated, but it is generally favorable for children. With Urd, the signs are good for middlemen, especially those associated with antiques or collectables. Here, it indicates an official position in a club, society, or organization. It is also favorable for marriage and children. With Aegir, it signifies good business abilities aided by considerable ingenuity. However, this may be balanced by loss in middle age and subsequent dependence upon a marriage partner. Magically, the Day Star is allied with the stone Jasper, the metal Gold, the herb Ribwort (Plantain, *Plantago lanceolata*), and the runes Thorn and Dag. It is associated with the curing of fevers.

The star known as Fenris-Wolf (Antares, α Scorpii) is a first magnitude binary, emerald green and red in color. In ancient Persian astronomy, it was one of the Royal Stars. In Europe, it is ascribed the nature

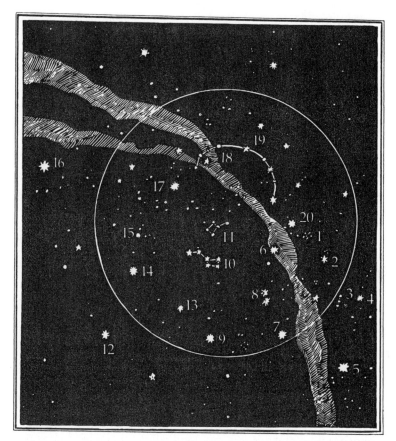

Fig. 7.1. The Northern Stars and Asterisms: 1. The Boars' Throng;
2. The Follower; 3. Frigg's Distaff; 4. The Plough Star; 5. Loki's Brand;
6. Heidrun; 7. Torch Bearer; 8. Thiazi's Eyes; 9. The Lord; 10. Woden's Wagon;
11. The Lady's Wagon; 12. The Wheatsheaf; 13. The Coming Judge;
14. Day Star; 15. Aurvandill's Toe; 16. Fenris-Wolf; 17. South Star;
18. The Biter; 19. The Doornail; 20. Torch Bearer.

of the planetary Tyr and Thor, with a martial and generally malefic nature. Fenris-Wolf brings headstrong obstinacy to destructiveness and malevolence, tending to destruction by obstinacy. If rising, Fenris-Wolf indicates riches and honor gained through violence, but whatever benefits may be gained, they will be evanescent. If culminating, the star indicates good fortune. With Sól, Fenris-Wolf can bring insincerity manifested as religious and political dishonesty, which may bring riches and honor that end disastrously. Also indicated are violence either suffered or committed, a fear of treachery, lack of trust, and general casualties of the subject's life. With Máni, popularity, broad-mindedness, and an interest in philosophical matters are possible, also changeability of opinions and activity in local affairs. With Odin, the Fenris-Wolf can bring suspicion, wrongful accusations, unpopularity, corruption, and a danger of sickness. With Frigg, it indicates insincerity, dishonesty, and selfishness, all of which are unfavorable for the subject's health or personal gain. With Tyr, the Fenris-Wolf can produce life-destroying habits and addictions, and foment quarrelsomeness, but is favorable for gain. With Thor, it signifies religious fanaticism and hypocrisy exacerbated by inherited wealth. With the planetary Loki, it may produce unmitigated materialism, leading to loss through argumentativeness and litigation, leading to chronic failure, making many enemies and producing sickness. With Urd, it indicates all kinds of heartless extremism, iconoclasm, lawlessness, and destructively revolutionary tendencies. With Aegir, Fenris-Wolf can produce a shrewd, cunning, perhaps thieving, untruthful, person who nevertheless gains much through hard work. Equally, it may produce some form of mental unbalance, leading perhaps to the fanatical support of a pernicious religious cult and thus to final downfall. The star Fenris-Wolf corresponds to the stones Amethyst and Sardonyx, the rune Tyr, the metal Iron, and the lethally poisonous herb Meadow Saffron (Autumn Crocus, *Colchicum autumnale*).

The Follower (Aldebaran, α Tauri), is a pale, rose-colored star of the first magnitude. It is located in the Northern Tradition constellation of the Lesser Wolf's Jaws, positioned almost directly in opposition with the wolf star, Fenris-Wolf (Antares). It is ascribed a comparable nature to Tyr, the voluntarily disabled conqueror of the Fenris-Wolf, but it also has some aspects attributable to the planetary Odin and Thor. It brings intelligence, eloquence, integrity, popularity, good fortune, courage, and honor, but with aspects of ferocity and a gaining of power and wealth through others. If culminating, it indicates honor and preferment in an appropriate career, good favors and fortune. If rising, and in conjunction with Máni, it is considered to be beneficial, but if it is in conjunction with both the ruler of the Ascendant and Máni, it denotes a possible danger of violent death, especially if the ruler of the Ascendant is a masculine planet.

With Sól, it indicates great energy and doggedness, bringing material honors, which might prove transient. There is possibly a danger of litigation, bankruptcy, and general financial loss. With Sól and Tyr there is indicated a possible liability to contagious diseases, while with Máni, business will be good, with plentiful credit, but with the danger of sudden collapse. Here, it is good for domestic or religious matters. But if Tyr or Loki is with Fenris-Wolf, then the traditional interpretation is that death by hanging or stabbing is indicated. With Sól or Máni culminating or rising, it indicates honor and power gained through violence with great struggle and losses, while with the planetary Odin, it points to prominence through public communications, material gain, and learned company. With the planetary Frigg, it infers potential honor through creative arts, accompanied by good health and happy personal relationships. With the planetary Tyr, it is said to bring success in military matters. This, however, is accompanied by great dangers, the native being susceptible to illness and accidental or violent death. The planetary Thor indicates honor in sacred matters and possibly the attainment of high rank in the military. With the planetary Loki (Saturn), it denotes possible mental affliction, bringing sarcasm or vitriolic eloquence and also legal ability. This may result in material success, but with losses through mercurial associates. With Urd, it appears that the native will be nature-loving, and may enjoy scientific, domestic, and political success, and public honors. He or she might also have esoteric interests that may lead to disfavor. In connection with the planetary Aegir, scientific, artistic, or mediumistic abilities are indicated. There may be loss through fire or electrical malfunctions, gain through metals, machines, or technical instrumentation, especially if planetary Tyr is in a strong position. This conjunction is unfavorable for children, and a danger of accidents is indicated. The Follower has the corresponding stone of Diamond, the rune Feoh, and its herb is the Christmas Rose (Black Hellebore, *Helleborus niger*).

Heidrun (Capella, α Aurigae) is a first magnitude white star in the Battle of the Gods constellation. Capella literally means the Little Nanny-Goat, which, in the Northern Tradition is Odin's goat Heidrun. It has the influences of the planetary Odin and Tyr, bringing honor, wealth, and eminence in public matters. It infers that the subject might have an almost obsessive inquisitiveness and a love of novelties. If culminating, the Nanny Goat indicates military advancement, especially through high-tech weaponry, with accompanying destructiveness, a general waste and squandering of resources, bringing further serious troubles in its wake. With Sól, it may bring changeability, quick and careless talk resulting in misunderstanding, but also military honors and wealth. With Máni, there is the danger of indiscretion, sarcasm, quarrelsomeness, disharmony, and a risk of accident. With the planetary Odin, the Goat, there may be the danger of libel actions and many quarrels, but with the potential of success after many problems. Frigg and the Goat indicate possible literary abilities applied with little material gain. With Tyr, the subject should be gifted intellectually, but may squander the ability on trivial pastimes. With Thor, libel or slander is indicated through overenthusiasm, also serious conflict with relatives. With Loki, Heidrun indicates that the subject could be addicted to luxury, with many bad habits leading to loss of wealth and bad health at the end of life. Urd riding Heidrun can bring eccentricity and obsession leading to dependence on others. With Aegir, it is said to bring unfulfilled ambition, courageous but ill-considered projects, much travel, and illness in mid-life. Heidrun's corresponding stone is the Sapphire, its rune Wyn, and its herb Mint *(Mentha spp.)*.

The Goat's Tail (Deneb Algedi, δ Capricorni) is a small star in the classical constellation of Capricorn, being of the nature of the planetary Thor and Loki. It brings polar opposites: beneficence and malevolence, happiness and sorrow, gain and loss, life and death. If culminating, it might bring notable fame, authority, and wealth as a result of personal talents. With Sól, loss is indicated, a fall from high places, loss of money and property. With Máni, success only through dedicated hard work, but even this will be lost eventually, perhaps through the theft of one's original ideas by others who market them better. The Goat's Tail and Odin produces suspicious melancholia and poverty, perhaps of a solitary, academic nature, while with Frigg an unfulfilled ambition is indicated. With Tyr, there is a likelihood of the subject being an adherent to unpopular causes, but perhaps ending in success. With Thor, like Frigg, there may be disappointment through unfulfilled desires, and loss through litigation and religious matters, with a danger of imprisonment. With Loki, it can bring a subject who is strongly opinionated and unpopular. With Urd, the effects of past actions may cause the subject to lead a strange life with many bizzare and unusual problems. With Aegir, there is the danger that the subject may fall under someone else's influence. They may also be superstitious or recklessly speculative, making many enemies. This star corresponds with the runes Jera and Eoh, the herbs Marjoram (*Origanum vulgare*) and Mandrake (*Mandragora officinarum*), and the stone Chalcedony.

Loki's Brand (Sirius, α Canis Majoris) is the brightest star in the sky, a brilliant white and yellow binary star. It takes of the nature of the planetary Tyr, Thor, and Loki, bringing honor, power, fame, and guardianship. Culminating, it brings high office with renown and material wealth, while with Sól and Máni, it indicates business success. With Odin, Loki's Brand also signifies business success, but attended by unnecessary worries and possibly disablement through accident. With Frigg, it can bring gain by inheritance giving a luxurious and extravagant lifestyle. With Tyr, it may bring courage and work in connection with metals, while with Thor, business success is indicated once more, along with assistance from relatives and travel. With Loki, the Brand indicates success, this time as the result of steady perseverance, domestic harmony, with wealth from inheritance and gifts. With Urd, gain and influence may be terminated by sudden death, while with Aegir, Loki's Brand denotes illumination in intuitive matters, including good organizational ability, bringing success in a chosen career and a natural death. Beryl is the corresponding stone to Loki's Brand, while Mugwort (*Artemisia vulgaris*, one of the oldest known medicinal plants) is its herb, and the runes corresponding are Elhaz and Dag.

The Lord (Regulus, α Leonis) is a triple star composed of one blue and two whites, which is ascribed the nature of the planetary Tyr and Thor and assigned to Heimdall. Rising, it indicates great wealth, fame, and honor mitigated by illnesses and other problems. Culminating, it signifies good fortune and honors, while with Sól, the Lord star denotes power and authority which does not last. With Máni, esoteric interests and influential friends are indicated, with threats from enemies. With the planetary Odin, it signifies an honorable and just subject whose generosity may be abused. With Frigg, there is the possibility of many disappointments and problems through love affairs, while with Tyr, fame and honor may accrue through strength of character. With Thor, the star denotes fame and success within an organization. With Loki, it may bring good health, a happy home life, and gain through speculation. With Urd, it can produce an energetic, spontaneous subject with selfish traits; while with Aegir, it may signify control over others, but in a generally benevolent manner. The Lord's stone is Granite; its rune is Man; and its herb, like that of Loki's Brand, is also Mugwort.

The Nowl (Polaris, α Ursa Minoris) is a yellow and white double star. Because of the precession of the equinoxes, it is still approaching the celestial north pole. It will reach its nearest point in the year 2095 CE, when it will be 26' 30" from it. Then it will recede, and other stars will take over its nature. In the year 4500 CE, μ Cephei will be the boreal polar marker. The Nowl is of the nature of Frigg and Loki, causing a lot of trouble and illness. Naturally, the corresponding stone of the Nowl is the Magnetic Lodestone, and its plant is the poisonous herb Lesser Periwinkle (*Vinca minor*). Its corresponding runes are Tyr, Yr, and Gar.

Aurvandill's Toe (Alphecca, α Coronae Borealis) is a second magnitude star of the nature of the planetary Odin and Frigg, bringing honor and recognition with poetic and artistic ability. With Sól, Aurvandill's Toe indicates a brilliant, inventive mind, subject to adverse but harmless publicity. With Máni it could bring public honor, but also much suffering through litigation, conspiracies, and personal squabbles. But eventually, they should be overcome. With the planetary Odin, the physical things in life are likely to be thought to be secondary to the things of the mind. This may bring loss through the action of more active rivals. With the planetary Frigg, Aurvandill's Toe is thought to be very favorable for love affairs, artistic and musical abilities, also favorable for friendships in general. With Tyr, the Toe can bring a keen mind, expressed as an ability in writing. But this may bring with it material gain. With Thor, honor, artistic ability and material gain are indicated. With Loki, the subject may have strong but well-controlled passions. But this quality may be accompanied by poor health. This conjunction may produce an economical but poor subject with few children, disappointed in love. With Urd, it indicates selfishness and possible mental problems, but also psychic powers. There may also be losses through litigation and inconstant friends. The planetary Aegir is thought to bring aggressiveness, abrupt attitudes, disharmony, and many changes during the life of a subject. Rosemary (*Rosemarinus officinalis*) is the herb associated with Aurvandill's Toe, while its stone is Topaz, and its corresponding rune Wyn.

The Raven (Algorab, δ Corvi) is a double star of third magnitude, one pale yellow and the other purple, said to have the nature of the planetary Tyr and Loki combined. It is reputed to bring a destructive, malevolent nature, which is associated with dishonesty, underhanded business practices, and general scavenging. Whichever planets it is associated with, the Raven is likely to bring out their more disadvantageous qualities. The Raven's corresponding stone is Jet, and its herb Henbane (*Hyoscyamus niger*).

The South Star (Vega or Wega, α Lyrae) is a sapphire-colored star known in medieval times as *Vultur Cadens,* the Falling Vulture. It is of the nature of the planetary Odin and Frigg, bringing hopefulness, idealism, and beneficence, but also sobriety and pretentiousness. Traditionally, the South Star is used for geomantic orientation and as a navigational aid. With Sól, natives are reserved, hypercritical, and unpopular, when it may bring transient fame. With Máni, the South Star indicates possible fraud, bringing public disgrace, litigation over libellousness, but some gain through financial dealings. The South Star and Odin signify suspiciousness, withdrawal, and business losses, perhaps through dishonest practices. With Frigg, it indicates that the subject may be miserly and unloving, while with Tyr, it denotes unfashionable opinions, especially in scientific matters, but held with tenacious courage. The South Star and Thor indicate legal losses and risk of imprisonment. With Loki, it may define self-opinionated, powerful passions, bringing vicious arguments with superiors or authority. With Urd, it again indicates powerful passions, considerable gains balanced by equal losses, bringing many enemies and numerous disappointments. With Aegir, the South Star signifies fearfulness and liability to accidents, but a long life and natural death. The South Star's stone is Chrysolite, its rune is Is, and its corresponding herb is the Common Fumitory (*Fumaria officinalis*).

The Torch (Algol, β Persei) is a white binary star that carries with it a very bad reputation. It is ascribed the combined natures of the planetary Thor and Loki, being associated indisputably with misfortune and violence, bringing a dogged and turbulent nature. According to Arabic tradition, this is *Ra's al-Ghul,* the Ghoul's Head (or Demon's Head), the most malefic star in the heavens. In classical Greek tradition, it is the head of the petrifying demonic Titan, the Gorgon, Medusa. When culminating, the Torch is supposed to indicate personal disaster. If in conjunction with Sól, Máni, or Thor, however, it is believed to bring victory over others in conflicts. Its malevolent reputation states that when the Torch is with Sól or Máni, violent death or life-threatening illness may be feared, perhaps connected with the head, face, or respiratory system; when with the planetary Tyr, tradition states that the subject is likely to be a murderer who will come to a violent end. Whichever planets it is associated with, the Torch indicates the expression of their worst and least favorable qualities. It corresponds with the stone Diamond and the herb Christmas Rose (Black Hellebore, *Helleborus niger*).

The Torch Bearer (Procyon, α Canis Minoris) is a yellow-white and yellow double star that is of the nature of Máni and the planetary Thor, bringing sudden activity, violent exertion, anger, carelessness, and pride. When rising, the Torch Bearer is said to bring craftiness, lust, dissipation, waste, and loss in trade. With Sól, there should be assistance from friends, many gifts, and rich inheritance. With Máni, it can bring restless mobility, changeability, disagreements with colleagues, schisms, and even divorce. With Odin, troubles with the opposite sex are indicated, offset by good health and material gain. Frigg and the Torch Bearer indicate favorable dealing with influential people, resulting in personal gain. With Tyr, it can bring violence, cruelty, scandal, and ruin, while with the planetary Thor, there should be much movement, and assistance from friends. Loki's influence gives ability in judgment, domestic harmony, and good health. With Urd, there may be a philosophical attitude to life, an enquiring mind attached to no school, dogma, or sect, bringing many friends from all walks of life. With the planetary Aegir, the subject should be sensitive and lucky, perhaps a successful intuitive gambler. Its stone is Achates, its rune Nyd, and its corresponding herb is Pennyroyal (*Mentha pulegium*).

The Wheatsheaf (Spica, α Virginis) is a white binary star sometimes known as Arista, with the nature of the planetary Odin, Frigg, and Thor. A star of orientation, many ancient Egyptian and Greek temples were aligned upon it, including the prime temple of the Mother Goddess in the Mediterranean region, the great Temple of Diana at Ephesus, one of the classical Seven Wonders of the World. It brings material possessions, success, fame, and peaceful disposition, but also barrenness, injustice, and unscrupulousness. When rising or culminating, the Wheatsheaf indicates unlimited good fortune, happiness, wealth, and undeserved fame or advancement. With Sól, it signifies immense wealth and favorable affairs in all matters, while with Máni, personal advancement may be through the application of innovation. With the planetary Odin, the Wheatsheaf can bring tidiness, meticulousness, and ingenuity, and perhaps profitable investments. With Frigg, friendship with people of the opposite sex, and with Tyr, popularity, but with some lack of judgment are signified. With Thor, it can bring social popularity and wealth. Loki's influence may indicate suspicion and cautiousness, but with a basically benevolent intention. With Urd, it is basically fortunate, denoting gain through marriage, and the planetary Aegir may produce comfortable surroundings, with some extravagance. But a long life is not indicated. The Wheatsheaf's corresponding stone is Emerald, while its rune is Peorth, and its herb is Sage (*Salvia officinalis*).

In addition to the customary Fifteen Stars, there are some other important stars recognized in the Northern Tradition as being in possession of special or notable characteristics: Thiazi's Eyes, the Plough Star, and the Biter.

The Northern Tradition constellation known as Thiazi's Eyes are composed of the two stars known by their Greek names of Castor and Pollux (α and β Geminorum). In East Anglia, the stars are also known as the Eyes of Wandil, a demon of darkness cast up into the sky by the powers of light. Castor is a bright and pale-white binary star. It is considered to be the northern or left of the two eyes of Thiazi, of the nature of the planetary Odin. It is said to bring a keen intellect, distinction in law or publishing and many travels. However, honor and fame are often followed with losses, disgrace, and terrible problems. If rising, eye problems are indicated. With Sól, valuable esoteric work is indicated, but attended by many dangers, including injuries to the face and blindness. With Máni, a lack of confidence is likely. Again, blindness and eye injuries are indicated. With the planetary Odin, great psychic abilities are possible, but little personal gain will accrue from them. With Frigg, a strange, unorthodox life may be the result, with many successes countered by equal disasters. With Tyr, it is possible that a malevolent nature will lead to a wasted life, while with Thor, esoteric and philosophical interests may lead to a loss through litigation, with the additional danger of criminal proceedings. With Loki, timidity and an untrustful nature is indicated, coupled with considerable intellectual ability, which is hampered by communication problems, but which may lead to gain through persistence. With Aegir, a desire to please everyone may lead to pleasing no one.

Pollux is a tawny star, of the nature of the planetary Tyr, with an audacious brave and spirited nature. Traditionally, it is considered to be the southern or right of the two eyes of Thiazi. When rising, it is associated with bad eyes and blindness, wounds, sickness, and imprisonment. When culminating, it indicates honor and advancement, but with a danger of downfall. With Sól, it may bring esoteric interests, but also many ailments or various violences leading to dire consequences. With Máni, it again indicates danger from conflict, violence, and ocular injury or disease. With Odin, it can bring a troubled mind or place the subject in an unpopular profession, leading to losses both through family conflict and unrelated enemies. With Frigg, there is a likelihood of strong, uncontrollable, passions, while violence threatens with Tyr. With Thor, losses through litigation are indicated, with possible imprisonment, while with the planetary Loki, bad temper and bitterness are signified, with danger from occupations connected with horses or other large animals. With Urd, psychic ability is indicated, along with personal vanity, and, perhaps, government employment. With Aegir, much change is indicated, with the possibility that the native may have an ability in speaking foreign languages and perhaps also employment connected with exploration or research. The corresponding rune of Thiazi's Eyes is Ehwaz, and its herb is Ragwort (*Senecio jacobaea*).

The Plough Star (Rigel, β Orionis) is a bluish-white binary of the character of the planetary Thor and Loki, bringing benevolence, renown, and happiness through inventiveness. When rising, the Plough Star indicates good fortune and lasting honors. Culminating, it denotes great military or religious preferment, coupled with irritability and anger. With Sól, boldness and courageousness is indicated, but recklessness will bring many enemies. The Plough Star and Máni may bring

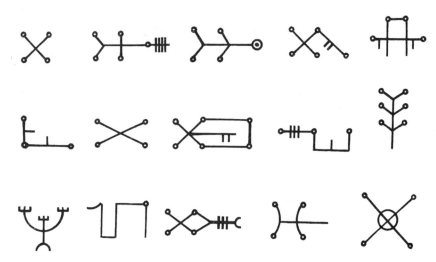

Fig. 7.2. Sigils of the Fifteen Stars. Top line (left to right):
The Follower (Aldebaran); The Torch (Algol); The Raven (Algorab);
Aurvandill's Toe (Alphecca); Fenris-Wolf (Antares). Second line:
Day Star (Arcturus); Heidrun (Capella); The Goat's Tail (Deneb Algedi);
Boars' Throng (Pleiades); The Nowl (Polaris). Third line: Torch Bearer
(Procyon); The Lord (Regulus); Loki's Brand (Sirius);
The Wheatsheaf (Spica); and the South Star (Wega).

worries and disappointments, producing a general malaise, but with the planetary Odin, success in the scientific field of endeavor is indicated. With Frigg, it is said to bring honors in mid-life, with a good marriage for females. With Tyr, military or mechanical obsession is indicated, while with the planetary Thor, benefits may accrue from foreign business. With Loki, the indications are generally good, bringing benefits from the elderly, the clergy, and members of the legal profession. With Urd, explorations of all kinds are indicated, while with Aegir, learned occupations are favored.

The Biter (Deneb Adige, α Cygni) is a brilliant white star in the constellation of the Greater Wolf's Jaws, with the nature of Odin and Frigg. It is associated with an inventive, ingenious intellect, quick to learn and advantageous. The star's runic correspondence is Elhaz and its herb the Sedge *(Carex elongata).*

RUNIC CYCLES AND BIORHYTHMS

Within our lives, although we may think of things as being constant, we are in fact under the influence of many invisible rhythms. Far from being stable, everything in our lives is in constant flux. But these eternal changes are by no means chaotic or unstructured. They exist in the form of cyclic processes, which can therefore be analyzed and understood. The most basic and recognizable of these cycles is within all of us. It is a human bodily time cycle: the diurnal, 24-hour rhythm, related directly to the Earth's rotation. In general, human body temperature has a high point in the middle of the day, and a low point correspondingly in the middle of the night. It has been noted, however, that people known as "larks," who tend to be introverted and are active early in the morning, have a high point before noon. Conversely, "night owls," who tend to be extroverts, have their temperature high in the evening. These cycles, if disrupted by long-distance travel, can take up to a week to become re-established in the new time zone. There is a genuine difference between the body's reaction during the night and day. Pregnant women have twice as much likelihood of going into natural labor at midnight than at midday. In experiments, scientists gave rats a large dose of X-rays (just to see what would happen). Those dosed by night perished, while those given the same dose by day survived. Similar results were obtained by overdosing rats with amphetamines. In runic terms, these differences are between Dag (midday: bright light, activity) and Jera (midnight: completion).

The cycle of the moon is also of importance. In a study of half a million births, undertaken in New York in 1959, W. and A. Menaker showed that mothers were more likely to give birth when the moon was waxing rather than waning. The Sooty Tern on Ascension Island has a 9.7-month breeding cycle determined by every tenth full moon. Excessive bleeding during operations was also correlated with lunar cycles by Dr. Edson Andrews in Florida in 1966. He found that the instance of postoperative hemorrhage was clustered around full moons. Related in some way to these basic cycles of day and lunar months are biorhythms. These are bodily functional cycles that were probably recognized in ancient times, but which have been studied scientifically only since the end of the nineteenth century. Then, the Viennese doctor Hermann Swoboda noticed from his daily records that there appeared to be cyclic patterns in the illnesses of patients he was monitoring. On further study, he discovered a significant pattern of 23- and 28-day cycles. The 28-day cycle, of course, is apparent in women as the menstrual cycle, but Dr. Swoboda and, independently, Dr. Wilhelm Fliess of Berlin, discovered that the same cycle is also present in men. Both medical practitioners came to the conclusion that the shortest cycle lasted 23 days, during which physical energy, alertness, and resistance to illness fluctuated. The 28-day cycle seemed to govern hormonal oscillations, weight loss and gain, and emotional "ups and downs." These two cycles became known as the *Physical Cycle* (23 days) and the *Emotional Cycle* (28 days). The third biorhythmic cycle was discovered (or rediscovered) by Dr. Alfred Teltcher at Innsbruck. This is an *Intellectual Cycle,* whose period is 33 days in length.

Interestingly, the three cycles coincide almost exactly with three of the major runic rows of the Elder Futhark family. Each day of the 23-day cycle can be assigned to the first twenty-three runes of the Elder Futhark, which can then be taken in correspondence with the corresponding runes of the other two cycles. Similarly, the 28-day and 33-day cycles can be measured by runes, assigning a rune of the Anglo-Saxon Futhork to the first cycle, and runes of the Northumbrian system to the second.

Studies of these three biorhythmic cycles have shown that they begin at birth. High points come first in each cycle. The physical cycle is at a peak on the sixth day, then falls to a critical, "crossover" point at 11½ days, then falls to its nadir around 17 days, returning to the critical "crossover" point, as at birth, on day 23. Likewise, the emotional cycle rises to a high after 7 days, drops back to criticality at 14 days, is at a low at 21, and returns to its beginning "crossover" point after 28. This 28-day emotional cycle may be related to the days of the week, so that the days of the week upon which one was born will recur within subsequent cycles. Someone born on a Tuesday will have highs and lows, and critical periods on Tuesdays, and so on. When seen in biorhythmic terms, the traditional rhyme that describes the qualities affecting the lives of babies born on different days of the week ("Monday's child is fair of face, Tuesday's child is full of grace," etc.) takes on a new relevance.

The 33-day cycle operates similarly, having first a high point around day 8, then a "crossover" on day 16, a low at 25 and back to critical at 33. Because the cycles are of different duration, they go out of synchronization at the beginning, birth, and only after a period of about 58 years do they reach a nodal point once more. Interestingly, this is close to the 59-year cycle of eclipses of sun and moon.

In each of the cycles, the major points that affect us significantly are the highs, lows and "crossovers." These major points bring us to specific states of activity, low or high. For the 23-day physical cycle, high days bring energy, alertness, and stamina. Critical days, when the cycle is changing rapidly from one state to the other, are unpredictable times, when there is a danger of misjudgment. Low days bring slow reactions, tiredness, and poor sleep patterns. The 28-day cycle of the emotions works similarly. On high days, one is enthusiastic, expressive, even elated, and able to deal with emotional problems. On critical days, the "crossover" may show itself in irritability and poor judgment. Low days are depressive, melancholy, or reflective, with emotional problems seemingly insoluble. The intellectual cycle's high days bring mental alertness, creativity, and ability to solve problems. At the "crossover," judgment is impaired and unpredictable, preventing quick decisions. Low points bring mental tiredness, slow thought, lack of insight, and writers' "blocks." This is the time of "stupid mistakes." But things are not as simple as that. Because these cycles are of different lengths, peaks or troughs will coincide sometimes, interacting with one another to produce combined effects. Low or critical points of all three cycles close together may have a profound effect. When runes are applied to the cycles, other insights can be gained. Studies on biorhythms have also shown statistical correlations between low points and illness. In 1973, a study of 200 hospital deaths by Dr. Harold Willis at Missouri Southern State College, showed that 56 percent of these occurred on the patient's critical day. Of heart attack deaths, 63 percent were on critical days. Only 20 percent of days are critical, making these results statistically significant. These cycles differ from other cycles in one fundamental way; while impersonal cycles are calculated externally to one's age, biorhythms are part of an individual human's life.

CYCLES AND PERIODIC EVENTS

The Ages of the World

An awareness of time cycles permeates traditional lore. There are several versions of adages that tell of the lifespans of various living organisms in terms of a number and its square, cube, fourth power, and so forth. One goes:

> *Three wattles are the life of a hound, 9 years.*
> *Three hounds are the life of a steed, 27 years.*
> *Three steeds are the life of a man, 81 years.*
> *Three men are the life of an eagle, 243 years.*
> *Three eagles are the life of a yew tree, 729 years.*

The life of a yew tree is the completion of one age, and there are seven ages in this phase of the world until its doom, Ragnarök, the end of a greater cycle of 5,103 years. In fact, all of these times supposedly lived by the different organisms are symbolic and not an average. It is interesting, however, to compare the Northern Tradition life of a man at 81 years (3 × 3 × 3 × 3) to the biblical span given at threescore years and ten (2 × 5 × 7). Of course, as the universe is eternal and ever regenerating, this 5,103-cycle is but a miniscule part of greater terrestial and cosmic cycles. Another version of this traditional calculation still exists, in a damaged form, at Westminster Abbey in London. There, in the Sacrarium, the Cosmati Pavement was made as an alchemical image of

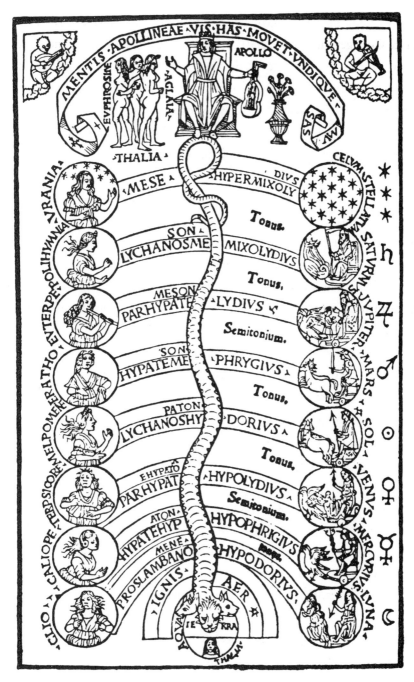

Fig. 7.3. Italian woodcut of 1496 showing the harmonic correspondences of the planetary cycles with the elements. Note the triadic motifs in the three-headed serpent and the three fates.

the microcosm by the mosaic artist Odoricus in 1268. Although now partly obliterated, it bore an inscription that explained the endurance of the world in the lifespans of hounds, steeds, stags, men, ravens, eagles, and sea serpents. According to this thirteenth-century version, the end of this phase of the world will come in the year 19,683 CE.

CUSTOMARY CYCLES

Some cycles are symbolic and commemorative, which, while taking their place in public life, are considered to have no esoteric meaning. The system of cycles known as *Jubilees* are derived from Jewish practice but are now applied to companies and royalty. Originally, a Jubilee took place every 25 years, and a centenary after 100 years. But, in Britain at least, this was altered by the Victorians when celebrating the long reign of Queen Victoria. She reigned from 1837 until 1901. She should have had only two Jubilees, a "Silver" one in 1862 and a "Golden" one in 1887. She died before the "Diamond" one was due, 75 years after her accession, in 1912. But in 1897, her "Diamond" Jubilee was celebrated, changing the tradition from 75 to 60 years. This truncated version is used generally today to celebrate royal and corporate anniversaries.

STRUCTURAL CYCLES

There have been several attempts to show that various things ranging from the weather to business and politics are subject to fixed cycles, from which certain inferences, some of them astrological, can be drawn. Among the most famous of these are Buchan's Periods. Buchan studied the weather and came up with dates that, he said, were significantly colder or warmer than the average for the time of year, regardless of the general weather prevailing at the time. Buchan determined that 7–10 February, 11–14 April, 9–14 May, 29 June, 4 July, 6–11 August, and 6–12 November are cold periods; while 12–15 July, 12–15 August, and 3–9 December are warm periods. The veracity of Buchan's observations has long been contested.

In his researches on longer, less verifiable cycles, Rodney Collin claimed to have found various recurrences that relate to multiples of synodic periods. They include a cycle of 41 months that is supposed to be reflected in prices, industrial production, and sales; a barometric-pressure cycle of 7½ years, which is reflected in tree rings and lake deposit layers; a nine-year cycle, supposedly connected with the main asteroid belt, which affects such diverse things as stock-market prices and suicides; and a 117-month cycle (9¾ years), observable in certain animals. The number of lynx trapped in Canada show a remarkable periodicity over a long time span. Statistics in the possession of the Hudson Bay Company from 1735 until the 1970s, when analyzed by Edward Dewey and O. Mandino, showed that they fell into a 9.6-year cycle of numbers. This cycle also applies to the red, colored, silver, and cross fox; the rabbit, muskrat, skunk, martin, mink, coyote, and timber wolf. When discovered, this cycle had been going on for over 230 years. On analysis of other animal numbers, it was found that the same cycle existed in salmon abundance in Canada and England; birds of prey, such as the owl and goshawk in North America; tree-ring widths in Arizona; barometric pressure at Paris; and ozone levels in the atmosphere at Paris and London. Major military engagements and British financial crises are also supposed to adhere to this cycle! Others have noted a 7.6-year cycle of barometric pressure at New York, 12 times the "creativity cycle" of poets, writers and musicians, which is said to be 7.6 months in duration.

In addition to this bewildering plethora of studied cycles, there is also the astronomically defined cycle of sunspots, with a duration of 11 years and 2 months. This cycle affects the electromagnetic environment of the Earth, and terrestrial weather patterns. William Herschel, discoverer of the planet Uranus, noted in 1801 that the weather appeared to be related to sunspot activity. The cycle itself was discovered and defined in 1843 by the Danish astronomer Heinrich Schwabe. However, it is not constant, as examination of old records has revealed periods when the cycle broke down. The best documented is the so-called Maunder Minimum, which lasted from 1645 until 1715. The German astronomer Gustav Sporer also discovered that there was an earlier period, from 1400 until 1510, when sunspot activity was minimal. But two sets of dates are insufficient basis on which to predict a cycle. In the earlier part of this century, the Russian researcher A. L. Chizhevsky studied data from 72 countries dating from 600 BCE until the twentieth century and demonstrated to his satisfaction that major military outbursts were related to the sunspot cycle. But as this idea was contrary to the doctrine of dialectical materialism, he was imprisoned by Stalin. Within the sunspot cycle is a 27-day cycle of recurrent magnetic storms, which occurs in the years approaching sunspot minima.

Longer cycles have been studied by various researchers. In addition to the 9.6-year battle cycle, Collin claimed yet another "war cycle" of 15 years (connected with Saturn and Mars-Loki and Tyr). Collin also claimed an 18-year cycle affecting building and land prices. Between the end of the American Civil War in 1865 and the U.S. entry into World War II in 1941, American stock-market cycles were so predictable that a 70 percent success rate would have been achieved by those who invested accordingly. This cycle came to an end with World War II, and did not re-establish itself, showing that cycles of this kind can be disrupted, and accordingly are caused by a combination of relatively stable factors. Where they have existed for long periods, they also belie the claims of politicians, whose apparent successes may be attributed to natural cycles rather than political acumen. Even longer cycles have been suggested, though the means of finding the evidence to define them are very obscure. For instance, weather in Europe is supposed to have a 36-year periodicity. There is also a cycle of "swings" between male and female imagery in clothing fashions, taking 84 years, and a "psychic cycle" of 165 years. To Collin's war cycle, Dewey and Mandino added a 142-year cycle of major wars, though the history of the twentieth century seems to have negated this one.

ESOTERIC TIME CYCLES

Various European esoteric traditions tell of other longer cycles that cause recurrences of process. German folklore preserves a knowledge of a cycle lasting 700 years. This tells of the rising from the Earth of a hidden *Great Treasure* every 700 years. This treasure is manifested by strange portents and lights on the Earth. Esoterically, it can be manifested as a Cauldron of Inspiration, otherwise appearing in its variant guise of the Holy Grail. Because of this, the cycle has come to be known as *Óðrærir* in the Northern Tradition.* The years of change of the 700-year cycle can be calculated as 1556 BCE, 856 BCE, 156 BCE, 544 CE, 1244, and 1944. Around these years of change, periods of great disruption and dissolution are supposed to occur.

According to one of the admittedly many calculations, the year 158 BCE is associated with the beginning of the astrological Age of Pisces. This is very close to 156 BCE, which is a significant year in the 700-year cycle. The next key year in the cycle, 544 CE, has been associated with the death of King Arthur. This marked the end of an era, the collapse of the ancient British regal tradition, and the triumph of the Anglo-Saxons in England. St. Benedict, founder of the great Christian monastic order, also died in that year, having created a new type of organization that was to make its mark on history. In 1244, the heretical Christian sect known as the Cathars were finally extirpated in a crusade, bringing another chapter of esoteric history to an end.

The last change in the 700-year cycle took place in 1944, the year that the Nazis' attempted conquest of Europe and the USSR reached its nemesis. In that year, the atomic bomb was proved feasible. Shortly afterward, nuclear fission was unleashed upon the world at Hiroshima and Nagasaki. The Great Treasure, which could have been of benefit to humanity, was manifested negatively in the disastrous culmination of

---

*In the Norse mythological tale of Odin's winning of the Poetic Mead, one of the three vessels he transports it in is called *Óðrærir,* a name that means "raiser of poetic ecstasy."

the worst war yet. In this cycle, the "Grail" has manifested as nuclear technology. According to this tradition, the next change for humanity will be in the year 2644. But, until then, the Space Age, born in 1942, had given humans a new form of consciousness, that of our planet as an object in space. The preliminaries to the moon landings in the late 1960s produced, for the first time, photographs of a beautiful blue and white sphere floating in the blackness of space, a stunning image of the real status of our planet.

DIUTURNAL CYCLES

The longest detectable cycles are the approximately 240-million-year sea level change cycles, which contain shorter and lower-order cycles of 30 million years. These periodic fluctuations relate to galactic conditions. They are a result of the motion of the solar system through the galaxy, and the effects of tidal forces and unimaginably long periodicity within the galaxy itself. These remote tidal forces affect the Oort cometary cloud, which reaches out several light years' distance from the Sun, which in turn is thought to influence vastly long climatic cycles on Earth. Giant comets, with diameters greater than about 100 km (60 miles) are believed to arrive in Earth-crossing orbits every 100,000 years or so, breaking up to form great masses of interplanetary debris, the Apollo asteroids. This debris encounters the Earth as major meteor streams. When objects of some size encounter the Earth, then a major cataclysm takes place. This can affect the Earth's climate for centuries. Large enough meteor streams can trigger off ice ages. There is historic and mythic evidence for extraterrestrial catastrophism. In earlier times, the approach of comets was viewed with trepidation. All over the world, they are associated with fire from heaven, earthquakes, and tidal waves. Comets were seen as portents of disaster, and folktales describing "the end of the world," including Ragnarök, contain all of the elements of meteoric strike. Historically, Gildas's late sixth-century account *The Ruin of Britain* tells of a cataclysm in which "fire heaped up and . . .

did not die down until it had burned almost the whole surface of the island" (Gildas 1978, 27). Some scientists have interpreted this as a reference to the effects of a comet fragment impacting the Earth and causing an explosion in the upper atmosphere (see Rigby, Symonds, and Ward-Thompson 2004).

In 1845, the comet Biela broke up without influencing the Earth. Dire prophecies of bombardment by meteoric debris were not fulfilled, and, since then, no Earth-threatening comet has come close. The spectacular meteor storms of 1872 and 1885 were the result of the Earth encountering the debris of this comet. But the "non-event" of Biela, and similar "failures" of the much-heralded comets Kahoutek and Halley in more recent years, have created a false sense of security. In the past century, after the Biela fiasco, the idea that the Earth's history was punctuated with catastrophes of extraterrestrial origin was discounted, and geological and organic evolution began to be explained by most scientists in terms of gradual, slow-acting, non-cyclical and non-discontinuous processes. But in 1908, a massive fireball exploded over the Siberian forest at Tunguska, proving that extraterrestrial bodies could collide with the Earth and cause enormous devastation. In 1968, some fear was generated by the press in Australia and parts of the United States that the Apollo asteroid, Icarus, was about to cross the Earth's orbit, and might collide with us. The Apollo asteroids were discovered in the 1930s, and by the 1970s, about 20 had been discovered. Now, it is thought that there may be 1,000 in the solar system. Icarus passed within half a million miles of Earth in 1968, a "near miss" by astronomical standards. In late March of 1989, an "asteroid," estimated to weigh 400 million tons, passed by the Earth by half a million miles. Experts calculated that, had it collided with our planet, it would have made a crater up to 30 miles across if it had hit the ground or, if it had fallen into the ocean, mile-high waves would have devastated coastlines. A "hit" at some time in the future is a mathematical probability.

It is possible that some of the longer-term cycles preserved in folk tradition may refer to the periodicity of planetary cataclysms, as occasioned by meteoric or asteroid impacts. According to recent calculations, it is possible that the Earth may undergo such a major encounter with such an interplanetary body about every 1,500 years, releasing the equivalent of 5,000 megatons of energy, equivalent to a nuclear world war. The legend of Ragnarök may have happened many times in the past, and may come again one day.

8

INTERPRETATION OF RUNIC CYCLES

Quarrel not rashly with Adversities not yet understood; and overlook not the Mercies often bound up in them. For we consider not sufficiently the good of Evils, nor fairly compute the Mercies of Providence in things afflictive at first hand.

SIR THOMAS BROWNE, *CHRISTIAN MORALS*

CHRONOMANTIC METHODS

In the previous chapters, I have given the basic principles and data for using the runic time cycles. Here, in the final chapter, I give some methods that may be used to work out the runic-astrological influences acting in more specific cases.

THE ZODIAC AS A TIME-MARKER

Although the zodiac is the basis of modern astrology, it does not coincide with the real extent of the constellations after which the divisions or "signs" are supposed to be named. Neither does it take the precession of the equinoxes into account, representing the position of the signs in times long gone. Because of these factors, the Sun is at present in each "zodiacal" constellation at different times in the year from those customarily ascribed to the sign. This means that the signs being used now have no direct relationship with the constellations. Just like the Church's unreal "official" phases of the Moon used in the calculation of Easter, the zodiacal signs are a hypothetical rather than an actual astronomy. But, despite this non-correspondence, they still denote something to do with the quality of the time that they represent. Instead of being descriptions of real constellations, the zodiacal signs are actually symbolic labels for describing certain periods of time. As near as can be calculated, given the irregular and indeterminate dimensions of the actual constellations, the signs are as follows. It can be seen that they are nothing like the zodiac signs used in modern astrology. Because they are not human constructs, like the zodiacal division, they do not begin and end at midnight, but at various times during the day. Compared with the signs used customarily in astrology, the constellations are:

CONSTELLATION	ACTUAL DATES	CUSTOMARY DATES
Pisces	21 Mar–18 Apr	19 Feb–20 Mar
Aries	18 Apr–10 May	21 Mar–20 Apr
Taurus	10 May–18 Jun	21 Apr–20 May
Gemini	18 Jun–21 Jul	21 May–20 Jun
Cancer	21 Jul–10 Aug	21 Jun–20 Jul
Leo	10 Aug–17 Sep	21 Jul–21 Aug
Virgo	17 Sep–3 Nov	22 Aug–22 Sep
Libra	3 Nov–16 Nov	23 Sep–22 Oct
Scorpio	16 Nov–13 Dec	23 Oct–22 Nov
Sagittarius	13 Dec–21 Jan	23 Nov–20 Dec
Capricorn	21 Jan–14 Feb	21 Dec–19 Jan
Aquarius	14 Feb–21 Mar	20 Jan–18 Feb

But neither the modern zodiac nor the runic divisions of the year are based directly upon the apparent position of the Sun in various constellations: they are an equal division of the year circle by 12 or 24. Both can be seen better in terms of a cosmic clock that marks the passage of a certain sequence of time-qualities that can only be fully expressed in symbolic terms. In addition, this twelvefold modern zodiac does not coincide directly with the twenty-four-fold runic circle, but there is another, complementary, parallel in Northern Tradition chronomancy. These were explained in Freya Aswynn's work, *Leaves of Yggdrasil* (1990, 157–60), in which she correlated the twelve palaces listed in the Norse scripture known as *Grímnismál* with the signs of the modern zodiac. These several periods correspond as follows:

PALACE	ZODIAC SIGN	DATES	RUNES	RUNE COMPLETELY WITHIN SIGN
Himinbjörg	Cancer	21 Jun–20 Jul	Dag/Feoh/Ur	Feoh 29 Jun–14 Jul
Breiðablik	Leo	21 Jul–21 Aug	Ur/Thorn/As	Thorn 29 Jul–13 Aug
Sökkvabekkr	Virgo	22 Aug–22 Sep	As/Rad/Ken	Rad 29 Aug–13 Sep
Glitnir	Libra	23 Sep–22 Oct	Ken/Gyfu/Wyn	Gyfu 28 Sep–13 Oct
Glaðsheimr	Scorpio	23 Oct–22 Nov	Wyn/Hagal/Nyd	Hagal 28 Oct–13 Nov
Ýdalir	Sagittarius	23 Nov–20 Dec	Nyd/Is/Jera	Is 28 Nov–13 Dec
Landviði	Capricorn	21 Dec–19 Jan	Jera/Eoh/Peorth	Eoh 28 Dec–13 Jan
Valaskjálf	Aquarius	20 Jan–18 Feb	Peorth/Elhaz/Sigel	Elhaz 28 Jan–12 Feb
Noatún	Pisces	19 Feb–20 Mar	Sigel/Tyr/Beorc	Tyr 27 Feb–14 Mar
Bilskírnir	Aries	21 Mar–20 Apr	Beorc/Eh/Man	Eh 30 Mar–14 Apr
Thrymheimr	Taurus	21 Apr–20 May	Man/Lagu/Ing	Lagu 29 Apr–14 May
Fólkvangr	Gemini	21 May–20 Jun	Ing/Odal/Dag	Odal 29 May–14 Jun

Because the conventional zodiac signs have little connection with the actual constellations that they purport to represent, the *Grímnismál* palace names can be used instead of the conventional zodiac signs in work referring to the Northern Tradition.

RUNIC HOROSCOPES

As with classically based astrology, it is possible to draw up a "runic horoscope"—a plan showing the positions of all the planets within the celestial sphere, but with reference to the corresponding runic circles of Earth and the heavens rather than the zodiacal divisions. Just as the common "Sun sign" of an individual is the sign of the zodiac in which the Sun appeared at the moment that the native was born, similarly, the runic sele is that part of the annual runic cycle in which the Sun stood during the person's birth. The precise times can be found in Appendix 2. In addition to the annual runic sele, the ruling-hour rune at a person's time of birth will determine certain qualities of the personality. The hour rune is the place on the diurnal runic cycle in which the Sun stands at any time of day or night.

Fig. 8.1. Runic astrological correspondences with Man the Microcosm.

These qualities are related to the ruling qualities of the runes themselves. There will also be secondary runic influences from the other runic cycles, such as the cycle of the day, the lunar cycle, and the influences of planets and the fixed stars. The horoscope is divided into 24 equal sectors or runic seles (houses or mansions), each of which extends for 15°. Each of these seles expresses the corresponding quality of the rune representing it. The circle commences with the first runic sele, Feoh, and the rest follow at 15° intervals around the circle. The fiducial for the commencement of the runic circle thus lies at 7° 30' after the midsummer solstice, within the zodiacal sign of Cancer. Although the starting-point of the celestial runic circle is with the commencement of the rune Feoh, which begins at 7½° to the west of the southern *ætting*. The starting point of the classical zodiac circle is at the point known as 0° Aries, the point of intersection of the Celestial Equator and the ecliptic. This is equivalent to the *ætting* of the vernal equinox, 0° Aries. In the runic circle, this is equivalent to the midpoint of the Goddess Rune, Beorc. As each rune extends for 15° of the circle, this can be written as 7°.

The complete angular correspondences of these seles have been given on page 79. As with a traditional zodiacal horoscope, the positions of the planets at any time can be found and transferred to a diagram of the 24 runic seles by consulting an ordinary nautical almanac. It must be noted that the tables in a nautical almanac are based on Greenwich Mean Time (GMT) and must be corrected to real time (LAT) for an accurate runic reading. The almanac gives the planetary positions in terms of the number of degrees, reckoning clockwise, from the Greenwich meridian, a figure known as the Greenwich Hour Angle (GHA). These can be entered directly on the runic circle.

Classical astrology has its origins in the Near East, which lies at latitudes far south of northern Europe. Because of this, it contains embedded within its system the subtropical astronomy of Babylon and Egypt. Like the 12-hour sundial, which gave so much trouble when imported into northern Europe by the Church, some astrological traditions are based on the more equitable summer and winter solar phenomena of the south. The concept of the Ascendant is one of these. But as in customary zodiacal astrology, the runic sele rising at the moment of birth on the eastern horizon can be taken as an indication of the external appearance of the subject. These are the qualities that will be immediately apparent to another person, both in outward appearance and behavior. It will govern relations with others. The way in which the personality is expressed through the will shows the influence of the ascendant rune.

DEFINITION OF SELES

It is possible to define the precise runic seles by various methods similar to the "house systems" of astrology (such as the Equal House, Campanus, Morinus, Regiomontanus, and Placidus methods). For example, the Equal House system divides up the ecliptic into 12 parts, centered upon the ecliptic pole. The other systems vary in different ways. The Campanus system divides the great circle overhead into equal parts, while the Morinus system divides equally the Celestial Equator from the ecliptic pole. The Regiomontanus system divides the Celestial Equator regularly, with lines centered on the north and south points of the horizon. But, as applied to the runic seles, some of these are much more appropriate than others for far northern latitudes. For example, the Placidus system is inappropriate for the higher latitudes, becoming more and more distorted, with a consequent unequal allocation of signs. The Placidus system removes all of the runic seles of Odal, Dag, Feoh, and Ur, and some of Ing and Thorn from horoscopes calculated around 70° N and northward! Clearly, this division is unsuited to Northern Tradition work.

At any given time, any planet or star will be in a certain position relative to the circle of the runes, which is fixed with regard to the eight directions. At that given moment, any planet or star above the horizon will appear to stand within one of these 24 runic divisions. As explained above, the Sun will be in the corresponding rune of the hour.

Planetary and stellar qualities are expressed through the runes. Put simply, the planetary qualities are as follows: Sól, self-expression; Odin, mentality; Frigg, harmony; Tyr, energy; Thor, expansion; Loki, limitation; Urd, change; Aegir, uncertainty, and Máni, response. If they are considered a "planet," the Pluto/Charon planetoids as Vili and Vé bring elimination. At any time when a planet or fixed star is in any runic sele or "house," the runes can be considered to express the corresponding aspects of the planetary qualities. Simply, Feoh expresses them richly; Ur, powerfully; Thorn, protectively; As, divinely; Rad, actively; Ken, enlighteningly; Gyfu, generously; Wyn, joyfully; Hagal, transformingly; Nyd, necessarily; Is, statically; Jera, completely; Eoh, defensively; Peorth, fatefully; Elhaz, attackingly; Sigel, brilliantly; Tyr, energetically; Beorc, purifyingly; Ehwaz, conjoiningly; Man, humanely; Lagu, flowingly; Ing, expansively; Odal, possessively; and Dag, changingly.

Each of the 24 Elder Futhark runes has a planetary deity ruling over it or connected with it in some subtle way. Sól rules over Sigel and Dag; Máni over Lagu. Odin rules As, Gyfu, and Odal. Wyn and Man are ruled by Odin jointly with Frigg, who also rules Feoh, Ken, Jera, Peorth, and Beorc. The rune Tyr is ruled by its namesake, as is Rad. Thor rules Thorn and Elhaz, while Loki rules Nyd and Is. Ur is under the rulership of Urd, as are Hagal and Eoh, and, finally, Aegir rules Ehwaz and Ing. As with the other correspondences, these particular affinities have their own effects. Of course, a full interpretation of a runic horoscope will involve every aspect of the qualities of both the "planets" and fixed stars and the runes. There is enormous potential for detailed readings with insightful results for those who develop an aptitude for the astrology of the runes.

THE MEANING OF THE PLANETS
IN THE RUNIC SELES

The position of any planet in any runic sele expresses a certain quality, which is composed of the planetary nature modified and expressed through the rune. These qualities are expressed in the individual's horoscope. Here, they are listed according to the runic seles, commencing with the first rune, Feoh.

Feoh

With the fire/earth rune Feoh, Sól (the Sun) manifests the unfettered creative power, which leads to great productivity and rich abundance. This can be expressed as the accumulation of wealth that is maintained. But there is the distinct possibility of selfishness, leading to discord over monetary matters. Also, if other planetary-runic combinations are less favorable, then this wealth, though obtained, may be squandered. With Ur, she expresses the primal creative power that underlies all things. It is a powerful time for getting things going, especially with regard to cooperative or collective matters, but perhaps not in the role of leader.

Máni (the Moon) in Feoh indicates domestic security achieved through appropriate management. However, it can also signify an over-dependence upon the mother, both in emotional and financial terms. When the planetary Odin (Mercury) is with Feoh, the subject's intellectual qualities may be used for the conscious or subconscious control of others. But also they may bring a brilliant memory and an exceptional grasp of financial matters. With the planetary Frigg (Venus), Feoh indicates a domestically orientated outlook, though this combination is not a good prognosis for lovers, for affairs may involve manipulativeness. The planetary Tyr (Mars) and Feoh can bring anger and forcefulness, which may be channeled into financially profitable business ventures. But this combination can also lead to frustration and self-injury.

The sele of Feoh with the planetary Thor (Jupiter) present indicates material well-being and monetary success, accompanied by kindness, generosity, and hospitality. The controlled strength of Thor perfectly controls the potential waywardness of the steer, bringing benefit to both. With the planetary Loki (Saturn), Feoh is unsettled. Wealth may be squandered or hoarded, while the individual's talents may remain hidden in isolation. Overspending and consequent debt are indicated by Loki's presence here. With this runic sele, the planetary Urd (Uranus), the planetary Aegir (Neptune) and Feoh indicate the possible psychic abilities in the native, which may be used for financial gain. However, there is a strong possibility of their misuse, which must be guarded against.

Ur

Sól and the earthly Ur runic sele indicate that there will be success in the collective field, achieved through great perseverance united with the creative will. This power must be controlled, however, if it is not to run away with itself. With Sól, the Ur rune will mitigate these egotistical elements and channel them for the common good. With the Moon, Ur may bring an emotional grounding expressed as a deep love of home-life. In females, the motherly instinct will be strong and fiercely protective. Ur with Odin brings a probing intellect of almost boundless power, which likes to get to the fundamentals of things, but which has the tendency to set up new systems based upon personal opinions. This combination is good for the founders of new intellectual disciplines, or cults. Frigg and Ur interact by producing domesticity, which may border on possessiveness, but which is tempered by cooperation. With Tyr, Ur brings power, which may be expressed as irascibility. However, if channeled correctly, it can be used for the common good, and may make the subject a leader in some field of endeavor. Thor's placement in the sele of Ur can bring abilities of organization, both in the home and in public life. However, there may be a tendency to exert too much authority when it is not needed. The planetary Loki may react with Ur to produce unhappiness in childhood or adolescence, creating stubbornness and self-righteousness in later life. Subjects may strive in vain to live up to impossible standards. With Urd, Ur stimulates the urge to individuality, the desire to make a powerful new start. This may be expressed in novel forms of behavior, fashion, or art, accompanied by a stubborn refusal to conform to those things considered to be the norms of society. Equally, it may result in revivalism of traditional ways of doing things. Finally, Aegir combines with Ur to bring a strong artistic temperament.

Thorn

With Thorn, the solar power indicates a defensive nature, but one with internal strength and integrity, not easily swayed. It is an indication for good, the creation and maintenance of correct order. Natives with Sól in Thorn might consider themselves "born to rule." Máni and Thorn may bring the tendency to dominate emotionally. Order in both the home and in personal relationships are demanded by those with Máni in the sele of Thorn. There is also the wish for admiration from others, which may be overdramatized when it does not go quite to the liking of the person concerned. Odin and Thorn bring intellectual self-confidence, which may be expressed by an almost irresistible forcefulness. The person influenced in this may well be an authority on some relevant subject or field of endeavor, becoming defensive of his or her position, however. Thorn/Frigg indicates excessive showiness, attempting to be the center of attraction. Subjects tend to be possessive lovers, ardently defending their loved ones. With Tyr, this runic sele characterizes the qualities necessary for someone to be a valiant military chief or a leader in some other public field of endeavor. This combination indicates that the subject will be strongly attracted by, and attractive to, the opposite sex. Thorn is Thor's rune, and so the qualities of Thor are expressed here with utmost strength and vigor. This combination brings an abundance of benign energy, with the power to organize things successfully. Supreme confidence is the major advantage of this combination. But, as always, there is the danger of overconfidence, such as the time when Thor tried to catch the Midgard Serpent and failed!

With Loki, Thorn indicates a lust for control, the aggressive aggrandizement of unbalanced power, fiercely defending personal interests. Here, religious bigotry, egotism, and fanatical discipline may be the outcome. With the planetary Urd, this runic sele expresses breakthroughs in the use of materials, or reinterpretations of traditional forms in new ways. However, it also indicates a stubborn nature, perhaps alienating loved ones and those who ought to be one's supporters. Aegir and

Thorn suggests an artistic temperament that defends the right of the artistic to unfettered creativity.

As

With As, the "god rune," symbol of primal power, the solar power is manifested as the divine force at work. Like Sól and Thorn, it brings correct order and stability within the life of the native. Overall, it is a beneficial combination, expressing the analytical qualities of the person, with the ability to see through the external image into the deeper reality of things. Máni in As brings a preoccupation with order, neatness, and cleanliness. Subjects need to be thought well of, even if they are "back-room" workers who are not in the public eye. The planetary Odin with As brings the divine power of the intellect to bear on any profession with which the subject may be connected. There is neither obsessiveness over minute detail, nor the ignoring of essentials, but a capability of appraising any question accurately. The Frigg/As combination can bring a critical, jealous, possessive nature in matters of love. However, stability and warm-heartedness are at the foundations of these seemingly unwelcome traits. Tyr with As brings strong practical ability, but this may be marred by a personality that seeks to dominate. The subject with Thor in the As sele may tend to overdo things, either in personal life or at work. This may lead to arrogance or an exaggerated belief in one's self-importance, feelings that one is indispensable, or just plain overwork. There may also be the feeling that one is on a "divine mission" in one's life. Loki in As brings conflict, with ill-defined aims deteriorating into self-blame or punishment from outside. As with Thor, self-imposed overwork may lead to a breakdown. Urd with As may produce a subject who works for a general change in the common perception of the world, perhaps toward a more spiritual direction. This may be accompanied by stubbornness or revolutionary action. He or she may work for ecological causes. With Aegir, As indicates talents that may be squandered in areas where no progress is possible. Perhaps one might advance spiritually, if not materially, under such circumstances.

Rad

Here, Rad is the radiant power of the sunwheel; the irresistible strength of motion produced by each component in its right place, working correctly in accord with the other parts. With the Sun, it can indicate the egotism of the hero or celebrity, the using of others as a vehicle for the manifestation of the will of the individual. But also, it can produce a harmonious life in tune with the cycles of the heavens and life. But when in combination with other, less benevolent, planetary-runic aspects, it can go out of synchronization, and cause severe problems that can only be overcome by strenuous efforts.

With the Moon, the mirror of the Sun, Rad indicates a secondary, somewhat retiring role in life. There can also be an almost obsessive preoccupation with orderliness or neatness, with everything in its place like the spokes of a wheel. With the planetary Odin, Rad indicates the intellectual tendency to put everything into some sort of order; thus, it is the combination that favors analysts, collectors, and taxonomists. More generally, it can be seen as favoring the scientific view of things, perhaps applied as technology. Frigg and Rad combine to produce an active, analytical turn of mind, which may well make the subject overcritical of her or his partner(s). Tyr/Rad is a powerful combination ruling over mechanical ability, perhaps manifested in precision work. This ability requires great concentration, and there is the possibility of things getting out of hand. Rad with the planetary Thor produces a confrontation between expansiveness and inward-looking, which may be expressed as an internal conflict. With Loki, Rad leads to an overstretching of the individual's capabilities. This may be manifested as overactivity, more specifically, attempts to take on too much work, or to achieve the impossible. Inevitably, this attitude must lead to disappointment. With Urd, Rad can bring radical innovation, but these new insights may lead to rejection as the wheel of fortune rotates. Finally, Aegir and Rad is not a good combination, bringing a general "bogging down" of processes, which may lead to dire economic straits.

Ken

Ken, the rune of illumination, transformation, and regeneration, enhances the powerful Sól. With this combination, the native can be an illuminated person, valuing learning and inner spirituality, but also recognizing the worth of pleasure. It indicates intellectual excellence, and the creative qualities of synthesis and impartial judgment necessary in a teacher. With the Moon in it, the sele of Ken indicates a rather weak will, with a tendency to take too much notice of others' counsel, whether useful or not. This combination can produce a rather retiring nature, but one that may mask inner illumination. However, there is always the danger of following false prophets. With the planetary Odin, this sele enhances the intellectual capacity of the subject. But this may lead to an overintellectual approach toward life and an analytical, even judgmental, attitude toward others' behavior. There is also a strong objection to all forms of excess. With Frigg, the torch-rune's sele may indicate uncertainty in relationships, and the futile search for the partner perfect in every way, who does not exist. Tyr's presence in Ken can bring an overcritical nature, a narrow outlook that overlooks the good aspects of people and things. Thor and Ken indicate that in later life the native may become a wise judge of people and things, illuminated by the lessons of personal experience. Ken with Loki is somewhat conflicting, bringing a discipline to chaotic things that are often on the verge of collapse. Ken and Urd may bring new insights or literally shed new light upon esoteric matters, while the planetary Aegir brings change, often for the worse.

Gyfu

With Sól, Gyfu enhances the native's innate talents, and allows for complete self-expression. The solar combination with this sele also indicates a character that seeks out the "gifts of the gods," producing an insatiable curiosity for both curious things and facts. Máni and Gyfu is somewhat passive. The native may well be susceptible to accepting ideas or creeds in which she or he does not really believe. Here, there is a tendency to be affected by others' input, but on the positive side, it brings sensitivity and tolerance. With Odin, Gyfu denotes a beneficial use of the intellect for the good of all, perhaps producing useful results that others may use. With Frigg, this runic sele indicates a generous, selfless use of talent, evinced by good personal relationships, companionship, and a happy marriage. With Tyr, Gyfu is in conflict, manifesting as loss or sacrifice. But with Thor, this runic sele brings balance and good judgment. Here, a person's talents are used wisely both for the individual and for others. This combination indicates a considered, diplomatic nature in the native. Loki and Gyfu bring power and high rank in society. But the talent one has may be used unscrupulously in business for personal gain to the detriment of both one's rivals and one's partners. Gyfu with Urd may bring new talents into the world, the creation of new art forms or means of communication, which benefit everyone. Finally, Aegir in Gyfu's sele may indicate a change in the relative importance of certain abilities for society at large.

Wyn

Wyn mitigates the egotistical tendencies present in Sól, producing that blend of qualities necessary for a happy life. It enables the native to establish the necessary relationships for harmonious living, balancing the need for pleasure with strong-willed determination to achieve. However, Wyn also restricts the creativity of Sól to those areas that will benefit the native, and not bring problems. In the sele of Joy, the Lady of the Night brings emotional well-being that can be used positively for the achievement of one's legitimate desires. This can bring strong reactions, however, and the danger of selfishness. Odin and Wyn can bring a shrewd mind with ability in the psychological side of human relationships. When used wisely, this can bring harmonious relationships with others, but when misused, can bring resentment and intolerance. The planetary Frigg can bring a preoccupation with the joy of sex. The subject may continually seek out relationships, which are pursued with great vigor. Professions connected with agriculture are indicated by this combination. Tyr in Wyn revels in conflict. Here, we find those who enjoy fighting. Subjects with Thor in Wyn may undertake major business deals and get involved in long-term conflicts with rivals, but with a positive outcome at the end of the proceedings. The final outcome is balance. Loki and Wyn may bring responsibilities with which the subject then finds he or she cannot cope. Urd in Wyn can indicate great changes, but those that tend to a better—rather than a worse—state of existence. Aegir with Wyn may be expressed in the reciprocity necessary for harmonious relationships between people.

Hagal

With Sól, Hagal can be seen as negating many of the solar qualities, channeling them away from the service of the native into less pleasant and more rigid ways. It tends to suppress self-expression, minimizing the personal, and elevating the impersonal nature of things. There may be a tendency for the native to be critical, skeptical, unforgiving, and even fatalistic. The Moon is not in a good place when in Hagal, for at the root of things, it magnifies desire. This can be expressed as selfishness, jealousy, and obsession. It may seek restitution or revenge for perceived wrongs, and a selfish adherence to past and outworn behavior patterns. With the planetary Odin, Hagal can appear in the form of a ruthlessly perceptive intellect, which strives secretly for an alteration in conditions. Positively, it is transformative of situations. It gets to the root of matters analytically, but negatively, it may be scheming revolutionary destruction. With Frigg, Hagal may bring fundamental problems with sexuality, in the shape of passionate and possessive relationships, and a refusal to "let go." Hagal tends to enhance Tyr, empowering the subject with tenaciousness. With Thor, the sele of Hagal, with its inexorable transformative nature, clashes with the principle of direct action manifested in Thor. This may appear as financial or legal problems, perhaps in the form of unwise and unsound business ventures. Loki interacts with Hagal to magnify principle (or imagined principle) above pragmatism, perhaps leading to catastrophic stubbornness. With Urd, Hagal accelerates primal processes, while with Aegir, it enhances secretive tendencies, but also the more archaic forms of human spirituality.

Nyd

Nyd's adage "Know thyself" is appropriate to the egocentric nature that emanates from the Sun. It tends to slow down the creative processes, making self-expression difficult, but increases intensity. But its positive side is in bringing a calm, practical optimism to life, expressed as truthfulness, loyalty, and independence. The Moon is not well placed in the sele of Nyd. The power of thwarting and being thwarted is very apparent here. Odin's presence in Nyd indicates a cold, analytical quality of the intellect, a willingness to look at things as they really are, and to stand up for freedom of expression. The planetary Frigg in Nyd is constrained by tradition and the imagined thoughts of others. This, however, need not lead to unhappiness if handled appropriately. In Nyd, Tyr is expressed in the subject's flowing with the tide of events rather than fighting against them. However, by being in tune with the spirit of the age, the native can achieve important things. Thor in Nyd can bring a channeling of effort toward a venture in which the subject has a passionate belief. The native may feel "driven" by some internal need to achieve some goal that he or she sees as fulfilling a divine cosmic plan. Loki's presence in this sele is expressed in adherence to matters of principle, even to the individual's detriment. Nyd and Urd can produce a questing spirit in the individual, a search for one's "roots" or for new means of overcoming difficulties. With Aegir, Nyd is expressed as the acceptance of previously rejected ideas into the mainstream of thought, such as the reality of time cycles as affecting human life, or the re-emergence of the runes.

Is

As a runic quality, Is is the antithesis to that present in Sól. As the static principle, it tends to suppress or even negate the solar qualities wherever it encounters them. It can create rebelliousness against establishment, attempting to replace unnatural ways with natural ones, but also it can lead to hypocrisy in religious matters. With the Moon, Is signifies spiritual purity, or at least, single-mindedness. This may even lead to fundamentalism and bigotry. With the planetary Odin, Is is suppressive of the analytical faculties, making the subject concerned with superficial images rather than the underlying reality at the core of the matter. This may lead to the subject being considered a seer or pundit; yet his or her ability will lie only in gauging the external appearance, not in understanding the essential being behind the facade.

With Frigg, Is influences attitudes toward sexual roles in a conventional manner. The subject will tend to be open about her or his feelings, and emotional relationships will be uncomplicated. The sele of Is with Tyr may tend to channel the outgoing, active, nature of the planet into external activities, while important internal matters are left static. Is with Thor enhances the inexorable qualities of orderliness inherent there. With Loki, Is can indicate the presence of strong beliefs. But these may cause others to criticize and be marred by the subject's intellectual arrogance. Urd and Is can bring a reevaluation of knowledge or beliefs, while with Aegir the runic sele can negate the flux of ideas and replace it with a misguided, unchanging fundamentalism.

Jera

This rune expresses the cyclic nature of the solar cycle. It will enhance those solar qualities that tend toward correct orderliness, while suppressing those that elevate the ego above the collective good. Thus, Jera is a regulator of the solar qualities. It indicates that those creative projects that the native undertakes will reach fruition. In Jera, the Mirror of the Sun can bring cautious idealism, tending toward right orderliness. But the other side of this quality can be manifested in materialistic terms or by bigotry of a religious nature. Odin in Jera expresses the lighter side of the intellect, perhaps a preoccupation with superficialities rather than the deeper elements of being. However, the perception of these superficialities is an accurate one, and can be used to advantage by the subject to balance more "serious" considerations. Jera combined with the planetary Frigg brings material abundance and harmonious relationships, even though those relationships may appear unconventional.

Tyr and Jera indicate the satisfactory completion of any projects that the subject may undertake. With Thor, this sele indicates good sense and balanced judgment leading to material prosperity. In times when they are fashionable, the subject may tend toward traditional values and mores. Jera and Loki enhances the status quo, even to the point of repression. With Urd, the sele of completion and balance indicates a continuity of those things that really matter in life through a period of upheaval. Aegir's combination with Jera can bring uncertainty, especially on the spiritual level.

Eoh

With Sól, Eoh indicates a defensive nature, one tending to resist all things inimical to the individual's well-being. This can bring a practical, reserved, cautious nature. As the thirteenth rune, Eoh is sometimes considered unlucky or unfortunate, bringing events that are manifested in a seemingly capricious way. The Moon in Eoh indicates caution and defensive inactivity. Any ambition may be directed toward selfish materialistic ends to the detriment of the spiritual side of things. With Odin, Eoh signifies a magical view of the world, which can denote the native's delight in speculative, fantastic schemes. As with the yew runestocks of old, Eoh with the plantetary Odin is manifested as mathematical record and research. With Frigg, Eoh, as the yoke joining the old and the new, the combination denotes marriage with a partner considerably younger than the subject. Eoh and Tyr come together to achieve material well-being and social standing, regardless of other seemingly unfavorable circumstances. Thor and the rune-sele combine to assert orderliness in one's life, perhaps taking the form of defending conservative, traditional values against perceived change. With Loki, Eoh's defensive magical powers are enhanced. Stolid and intolerant, the subject may suddenly throw over his or her way of life and become quite the opposite. Urd with the sele of Eoh may bring catastrophic change cloaked in the guise of tradition, while Aegir's combination manifests in uncertainty and vacillation.

Peorth

Peorth brings another form of capriciousness, that of the lively dance or the playing piece on the game board. This often shows itself as a "fateful" nature, more accurately seen as events operating in accordance with Orlog. With Sól, this can lead to a personality that counters such uncertainty with independence and idealism. Vigor and purposeful activity characterize the native of Peorth-Sól. Sometimes these serious qualities are concealed behind apparent frivolity. With Máni in Peorth, the signs are that the subject will tend toward individualism, pursuing personal gain and preferment to the detriment of others. There is a likelihood that spiritual matters will not be thought to be of any great importance. The planetary Odin in the sele of Peorth will have his mercurial aspects enhanced, as in a game of chance. The subject will flow with the everchanging tide of life, and benefit from it. There is a possibility that the individual may possess telepathic or clairvoyant abilities. Peorth and the planetary Frigg indicate that the native will try to make friends with everybody. But this may be done in a rather undemonstrative way, rather like the impassive face put on by a gambler through triumph and disaster. This combination may be expressed in secret love affairs and other sexual adventures.

Tyr in the sele of Peorth indicates an energetic and intelligent application of the individual to her or his chosen task in life. The playful element can bring forth new ideas or techniques, but sometimes the subject may apply them before they are appropriate, leading to disappointment. Thor with Peorth wipes out distinctions, bringing the hidden into the light, though it may only remain there for a short period before descending once more into obscurity. The Loki/Peorth conjunction can bring seemingly capricious, arbitrary behavior, sometimes channelled creatively into a career environment that demands those qualities. Urd's conjunction with Peorth plumbs the depths of the inner secret contained within the rune. This may break the previously set barriers of human knowledge, creating a new insight into our existence. Aegir's combination with this sele can be manifested as a seemingly unconnected string of chaotic events, which, nevertheless, are the logical outcome of the individual's Wyrd.

Elhaz

Elhaz stands for the aggressive/defensive power of the Elk, and with Sól, it brings "rugged individualism." This may be manifested in an egotistical manner as a dictatorial commander or a "one-man band" in the individual's chosen profession. In combination with other rune-planet correspondences, this may be expressed as resistance to fatigue, or a threatening stance toward others who are seen as threatening. The Moon in Elhaz counters repression, enhancing the freedom of the individual. This may be manifested as unconventional family relationships. With the planetary Odin, the Elk rune sele places the native in the defended position of complete objectivity; he or she can observe without becoming personally involved. To these subjects, the truth matters above all else: they are the living examples of the old Druidic motto: "The truth against the world."* The "Fortean" worldview, observing all things that many might find incomprehensible or disturbing, is the ideal of Odin/Elhaz subjects.

With Frigg, Elhaz brings some distance or reticence from others. Relationships may tend toward the impersonal, but subjects will have their own independent ideas on sexuality. Relationships may thus tend to be transitory. With Tyr, Elhaz may bring innovation, but this may bring the subject into conflict with the established order of things. The supremely powerful combination of Elhaz and Thor means that the subject need fear no one. The upshot of this is that the native will be

---

*"Gwir yn erbyn y byd," a motto of the Welsh antiquarian and bard Iolo Morganwg (Edward Williams, 1747–1826).

supremely tolerant of all others' lifestyles, so long as they live in general accordance with natural law. With Elhaz, Loki indicates orderliness almost to the point of obsession. Positively, Loki brings loyalty, but there is a negative aspect, too, which is an aggressive and insensitive nature. With Urd, Elhaz brings idealism, and a willingness to make the effort to penetrate to the essential core of things. Aegir and Elhaz denotes the necessity for the correct placement of things according to their natural qualities.

Sigel

Sigel is the solar rune *par excellence,* so with Sól, the solar qualities are double enhanced. In the runic year cycle, its direction is that of the summer solstice sunrise. In this sele, the solar power is at its greatest potential strength. Correspondingly, creativity is enhanced by the Sun in Sigel. But this is countered by an enormously powerful ego, which may lead to exaggerated claims or opinions in the native. With the lunar luminary, Sigel engenders vulnerability, and a reflective nature. Subjects with this combination may be especially susceptible to external influences, but will always attempt to exert their independence and reach their self-set goals. Odin's combination with Sigel brings clarity and illumination; the eclectic absorption of disparate influences and their synthesis into new insights and new ways of doing things. Intuition is the strong point here. Frigg and Sigel indicate that the need for love is the most important part of the native's being. Sympathy for others is a marked characteristic.

Those with Tyr in Sigel will direct energy well toward practical goals, but they may be rebuffed by setbacks, reacting in devious ways to overcome them. The Sigel/Thor combination brings confidence grounded in the personal *megin,* which Thor and Sigel represent. Loki's involvement with the sele of the sun-rune can be manifested as the capability to concentrate deeply on problems. This may be expressed as serious singlemindedness but tempered by humility. Urd's combination with this runic sele enters the frontiers of knowledge, both the "lost knowledge" of the ancient past, and the potential knowledge of the future. The Sigel/Aegir interface can bring the subject into contact with stupendous powers beyond his or her comprehension.

Tyr

Like As, Tyr is a "good rune," signifying an energetic nature. With Sól it can bring patience and the tactful qualities concomitant with the power of self-possession. It expresses understanding and a willingness to learn. There is also the tendency to judgment of events inherent in Tyr-Sól, which may led to self-sacrifice or even martyrdom. With Máni, Tyr allows the entry of psychic influences, though at the last resort they will be expelled at great personal cost. While this is happening, the subject can feel vulnerable, and may suffer from this feeling. With Odin, Tyr also admits external influences, but in this case, the subject learns from and incorporates the information for her or his own use. It is then used well and with the utmost energy. Thus, the subject can become very quick on the uptake and intuitively correct in many matters that cause others to stumble. With Frigg, Tyr can bring a subtle understanding of others' feelings. Tyr in his namesake doubly reinforces the power of the rune. However, there may be some indecision before important things need to be done, but the outcome will be one of positive action in the end. This combination also emphasizes energetic male sexuality. With Thor, Tyr may make the subject help others, but he or she may lose something in consequence of this, perhaps being used. With Loki, Tyr brings an unreal perception of present reality. The subject may take to "living in the past," and regretting times gone by. But, of course, this can be used positively in the "nostalgia industry." This combination may also bring feelings of persecution or having suffered injustice. With Urd, the tendency is to use the past in a creative way. Aegir and Tyr represent the renewal of primal knowledge, unlocking ancient energies in many ways.

Beorc

Beorc, the Goddess rune, with Sól brings out the nurturing qualities of the native. The waxing vigor of the Sun in springtime is manifested in the character, most probably as driving ambition to accomplish some "life's work." Our Lady Moon, in Beorc, is in her prime runic sele. In this sele, the phases of the Moon are paramount. The character transmitted depends entirely upon which phase is current when the Moon is in Beorc. This makes the combination appear eminently changeable and even seemingly capricious. Seasonal and lunar-phase-linked fluctuations of the emotions are predicted by this conjunction. Odin in Beorc brings a lively intellectual temperament, open to new influences. The imagination, even fantasy, may play a large part in the lives of individuals under this influence. Paradox may play some part, too. When in the sele of the Goddess, the planetary Frigg emphasizes female sexuality. This may be expressed in the bearing and rearing of children, or in the experience of many lovers. The purifying nature of Beorc may also be expressed here in professions such as nursing. Beorc with Tyr is equivocal, bringing uncertainty that may manifest paradoxically as bravado. This can be channeled into beliefs that one has a mission to "purify" some area of human life from perceived "contamination." The Thor/Beorc combination indicates emotional maturity and the qualities required for leadership. But this can be expressed in a "crusading spirit" that attempts to dominate others. One result of these tendencies may be overconfidence leading to setbacks. The sele of Beorc containing Loki can produce delays, making the subject accept things passively, and wait for "better days to come," or regret "times past." Like Loki, the present seems to be under a binding spell in this rune. Urd in Beorc attempts to break out, like the birch leaves of this springtime rune. This indicates that the native will always be trying something new, but that she or he will not succeed unless the time is right. Aegir and Beorc represents the reassertion of the Elder Faith in modern times—the return of the Goddess.

234 Interpretation of Runic Cycles

Ehwaz

As a rune, Ehwaz symbolizes the horse, the sacred animal of the sun in the Northern Tradition, expressing conjoining qualities. With Sól, it indicates a rightful pride in one's possessions and one's personal relationships. It brings creativity, with the production of useful new ideas, with a purposeful traveling toward a goal. It enhances the likelihood of accomplishing's one's perceived life's purpose. With Ehwaz, Máni brings out the unstable emotional qualities that are present in us all. Impulsive outbursts of emotion are tempered by independence and initiative. Odin and his steed, Ehwaz, create a bright, lively temperament in the native, who may well be a quick-thinking intellectual. Certain in their own correctness, natives will be forceful in their beliefs, and may insist on their way being the right one. With Ehwaz, Frigg's more negative aspects may become apparent, with self-centeredness being the worst of these qualities. Natives with this combination may well be aggressive in their lovemaking.

With Tyr, Ehwaz can produce an enormous capacity for self-aggrandizement, based upon self-reliance and aggression. This can produce a leader, but often it produces someone who has no notion of when he or she has actually achieved the ambition, which leads to attempts at ever-greater things and must inevitably result in failure. With Thor, Ehwaz tends to direct the considerable energy indicated by the planet into creative and successful joint endeavors. Loki riding upon Ehwaz signifies the inevitable return that all cycles must make, mitigating the impulsive nature of Man, bringing patience and endurance. With Ehwaz, Urd can indicate a rejection of past things, perhaps iconoclasm or revolutionary destruction. Aegir and Ehwaz are likely to engender novel forms of spirituality.

Man

With Sól, Man brings a full expression of human nature, both those beneficial to society, and those less desirable. The possibility of conceit or self-pride is very likely to be expressed in this sele, also opposition to necessary change. There is the possibility that through this, enemies may be made. But whichever qualities are manifested, whatever is done will be accomplished through the individual's personal internal strength. But there is likely to be a marked lack of long-term planning. When Máni stands in the sele of Man, although a humane rune, one of duality and combination, the changeable nature of the Moon is strongly present. Depending on the phase, this conjunction can bring either violent impulse or placid calm. The Odin/Man combination signifies the constructive power, that of taking natural materials and creating new artefacts from them. Man/Odin represents the clearly defined application of the intellect to creating the "man-made." Man with Frigg denotes the need for love and affection. A sensual and humane nature is indicated. Tyr and Man bring considerable energy, but this is accompanied by the tendency to "burn out" after a short time. This combination needs tempering with realism. The Man/Thor interface brings a well-balanced personality, able to consider both the good and bad points of anything before making a decision. This combination may bring material well-being and social respectability. Loki and Man combine to indicate an uncertain influence, almost completely at the mercy of time cycles. The business cycle may be important here. Urd's combination with the Man sele may bring resourcefulness and the unique human ability to persevere when there seems to be no hope. Aegir's combination with Man addresses the human need for spiritual things, bringing new revelations to challenge accepted theories and beliefs.

Lagu

Lagu is the rune of flow and growth, so Sól with Lagu reinforces the life-enhancing quality of this runic sele. In the native, it indicates single-minded strength of character, a person who carries through the idea to fruition, the project to completion. However, it can also indicate instability. With the Moon, Lagu brings a placid and lucid mind, and those qualities one needs for growing plants. With Odin, the flow of number and language is strong; natives with this sele can be expected to excel in these fields. However, deep insight sometimes leads to a tenacious hold on ideas, which may degenerate into bigotry. Frigg and Lagu indicate sensuality and attractiveness, leading to lasting love and emotional stability. With Tyr, Lagu can diminish the strong, go-ahead qualities of the planet, controling them and transmuting them into skills. With this combination, ability to work in harmony with the inherent qualities of materials, most notably in the crafts, is indicated. With Thor, Lagu can lead to dangerous losses of money in business or personal affairs. Money literally flows away. Loki's combination with the watery sele is also associated with business, more precisely with the business cycle. It indicates that the subject should invest or go into business at a favorable part of the cycle, and quit before the next depression arrives. If this advice is ignored, this combination can lead to overcompensation in the form of miserliness or unnecessary frugality. With Urd, Lagu represents a limiting principle in business terms, but can also bring determination to overcome limitations. Aegir and Lagu indicates a tide of new ideas and the physical manifestations of the creative principle.

Ing

The expansive sele of Ing with Sól present in it indicates the elevation or preferment of the individual in recognition of his or her personal qualities. It signifies almost unlimited potential, and a strong will combined with versatility, but tending toward opportunism. The Moon enters the sele to bring resourcefulness in changeability. But, according to the phase, there may well be disruptive changes indicated at some time in one's life. Odin and Ing combined bring an excellent combination for originality and inventiveness. There is the ability to see both sides of a question or argument. This conjunction is expressed in eloquence and literary abilities, as well as in the expansive side of the scientific endeavor. The planetary Frigg, when in the Ing sele, denotes a passive, rather capricious, sensuality. In Ing, Tyr brings equivocal qualities, which may be considered as "underachievement." People called "wasted talents" may well have the Tyr/Ing combination. In this sele, Thor's outgoing nature might indicate errors of judgment and possible financial losses. Spreading one's resources too thinly over too wide an area is possible. Loki's presence in Ing denotes unfavorable circumstances, usually from cyclical phenomena beyond the control of the subject. This combination may force the individual to new heights of ingenuity to overcome circumstances. With Urd in Ing, a restless nature is indicated, and with Aegir, Ing brings a sudden break from past methods, replacing them with new technologies that expand the boundaries of human experience.

Odal

The Sun in Odal, the sele of possession and enclosure, enhances the innate qualities of the subject. It brings personal control and integrity within the framework of natural law. There are tendencies, however, for the native to be exclusive and egotistical, perhaps unscrupulous. Máni in Odal seems to be unsettled, bringing uncertainty, dependent upon the state of the lunar phases. With Odin, the mercurial odylic force is in flow, bringing originality and considerable inventiveness. By the analytical use of the intellect, property and material security can be obtained. With Frigg, Odal may generate uncertainties over loyalty. Permanent relationships may be difficult to establish, but this combination may bring abilities in the literary field by way of compensation. With Tyr in Odal, established, grounded, critical abilities are indicated. Contentiousness, argument, and even defensive litigation may be the lot of the native. But the outcome should enhance one's property. Thor in Odal brings groundedness, a desire for knowledge and the stability that can stem from it. Loki's combination with Odal can bring intellectual prowess, but this may be tempered by introversion and unbridled skepticism. However, this combination is good for geometers, mathematicians, and engineers. With Urd, Odal's enclosure is breached, opening it to new, external, influences, while with Aegir it may be seen as manifesting in the worldwide nationalist movements of the twentieth century.

Dag

Dag is another solar rune, signifying the triumphant power of the height of the Sun at its midday/midsummer zenith. But it also encapsulates the other side of that triumphal apex in the moment of the commencement of the Sun's decline toward sunset and winter. It indicates an enhanced possibility for the native's creative powers, but also with the possibility of sudden change in direction. Love of spectacle is also indicated here. The lunar presence in Dag is another one whose character depends almost entirely upon the relevant phase of the Moon. Dag could bring restlessness to the point of neurosis, otherwise a balanced contentment. The "catastrophe" nature of Dag is demonstrated well by the Moon here. The planetary Odin in Dag is expressed by a sharp intellect whose judgment may be clouded by an inability to make decisions between alternative theories or conflicting observations. But the continuing questioning that accompanies these judgments will not be diminished. Dag and Frigg may be expressed as changeability, unpredictable moodiness, and an inability to form personal relationships that last. Tyr in Dag is expressed as a powerful nature, with the ability to tackle anything and succeed most of the time. But when frustrated, the subject may be exceptionally moody or angry. Thor in the daylight sele brings outgoing generosity and a hospitable nature. A parent with this combination will be protecting and nurturing. Dag with Loki denotes the kind of powerful, repressive discipline that nevertheless is always on the verge of collapse into anarchic disorder. With Urd, Dag indicates dispersion, opening doors, and carrying away of wealth from the home. It also brings the free interchange of ideas, without barriers. Finally, Dag with Aegir present carries with it the possibility of psychic powers manifested in a totally novel, modern way, radically breaking with tradition.

POSTSCRIPT

I have given here, for the first time in print, the basic principles of runic astrology, but judgment on the more complex elements must be deferred. At present, runic astrology does not have the long record of study that classical astrology possesses, so I will leave these other questions until a future occasion, or for others to pursue.

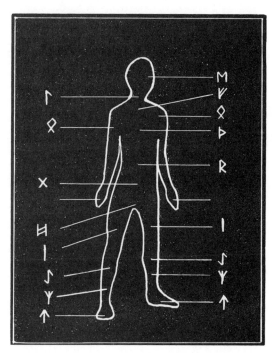

Fig. P.1. The ruling runes of the bodily parts, according to runic astrological correspondences.

The recognition of all sorts of cycles, not just astrological, is bound to grow as more and more data are assembled. The more subtle nature of each of the elements of the runic time cycles are bound to become more apparent as time passes.

> *Now must I ride the reddened ways,*
> *And my bay steed set to tread the sky;*
> *Westward I go to wind-helm's bridges,*
> *Ere Salgofnir wakes the warrior throng.*
> THE SECOND LAY OF HELGI HUNDINGSBANI
> (TRANS. BELLOWS)

THE RUNES AND THEIR CORRESPONDENCES

THE ELDER FUTHARK CORRESPONDENCES OF TREES, HERBS, COLORS, POLARITIES, AND ELEMENTS

RUNE NAME	TREE(S)	HERB	COLOR	POLARITY	ELEMENT	DEITY	SYMBOLIC MEANING
Feoh	elder	nettle	light red	female	fire/ earth	Frey/ Freyja	the primal cow, Audhumla
Ur	birch	Iceland moss	dark green	male	earth	Thor/ Urd	horns of the ox
Thorn	oak/ thorn	houseleek	bright red	male	fire	Thor	the thorn, hammer of Thor
As	ash	fly agaric	dark blue	male	air	Odin/ Eostre	the ash, Yggdrassil
Rad	oak	mugwort	bright red	male	air	Ing/ Nerthus	wheel under cart, fire of the torch
Ken	pine	cowslip	light red	female	fire	Heimdall Freyja/ Frey	primal fire of Muspellheim

RUNE NAME	TREE(S)	HERB	COLOR	POLARITY	ELEMENT	DEITY	SYMBOLIC MEANING
Gyfu	ash/elm	heartsease	deep blue	m/f	air	Gefn	sacred mark
Wyn	ash	flax	yellow	male	earth	Odin/ Frigg	wind vane, flag
Hagal	ash/yew	bryony	light blue	female	ice	Urd/ Heimdall	structural beams, the world, hailstone, serpent
Nyd	beech/ rowan	snakeroot	black	female	fire	Skuld	fire-bow and block
Is	alder	henbane	black	female	ice	Verdandi	icicle, primal ice of Niflheim
Jera	oak	rosemary	light blue	m/f	earth	Frey/ Freyja	sacred marriage, heaven/ earth
Eoh	yew/ poplar	bryony	dark blue	male	all	Ullr	vertical column of the Yew tree
Peorth	beech/ aspen	aconite	black	female	water	Frigg	the womb, a dice cup, a musical instrument (lyre)
Elhaz	yew/ service	sedge	white	m/f	air	Heimdall	the elk, the flying swan, open hand
Sigel	juniper/ bay	mistletoe	gold	male	air	Balder	the holy solar wheel
Tyr	oak	sage/ aconite	bright red	male	air	Tyr	the vault of the heavens over the cosmic pillar
Beorc	birch	lady's mantle	dark green	female	earth	Nerthus/ Holda	breasts of the Earth

RUNE NAME	TREE(S)	HERB	COLOR	POLARITY	ELEMENT	DEITY	SYMBOLIC MEANING
Ehwaz	oak/ash	ragwort	white	m/f	earth	Frey/ Freyja	Mother Goddess, two poles bound
Man	holly	madder	deep red	m/f	air	Heimdall/ Odin/Frigg	marriage of earth/ heaven
Lagu	osier	leek	deep green	female	water	Njord/ Nerthus	sea wave, waterfall
Ing	apple	selfheal	yellow	m/f	water/ earth	Ing (Frey)	the genitals
Odal	hawthorn	clover	deep yellow	male	earth	Odin	enclosed estate, land, property
Dag	spruce	clary	light blue	male	fire/air	Heimdall	balance (night, day)

THE RUNES OF THE ANGLO-SAXON ADDITIONS
TO THE ELDER FUTHARK

RUNE NAME	TREE(S)	HERB	COLOR	POLARITY	ELEMENT	DEITY	SYMBOLIC MEANING
Ac	oak	hemp	light green	male	fire	Thor	mark tree, boundary oak
Os	ash	"magic mushroom"	dark blue	male	air	Odin	mouth, speech, eloquence
Yr	yew	bryony/ mandrake	gold	m/f	all	Odin/ Frigg	yew tree, bow, midpoint
Ior	linden/ ivy	kelp	black	female	water	Njord	Jormungand, the world serpent
Ear	yew	hemlock	brown	female	earth	Hela	earth-grave
Cweorth	bay/ beech	rue	tawny	female	fire	Loge (Loki)	funeral pyre

RUNE NAME	TREE(S)	HERB	COLOR	POLARITY	ELEMENT	DEITY	SYMBOLIC MEANING
Cale	maple/ rowan	yarrow	white	female	earth	Norns	grail-cup
Stan	witch hazel/ blackthorn	Iceland moss	gray	male	earth	Nerthus	sacred stone
Gar	ash/ spindle	garlic	dark blue	male	all	Odin	spear of Odin

APPENDIX 2

RUNIC HALF-MONTHS

The beginning dates of the runic time cycle of the year is as follows, corrected for the Gregorian Calendar, times being local apparent time, averaged to the nearest hour:

Feoh	29 June	3:00
Ur	14 July	8:00
Thorn	29 July	14:00
As	13 August	19:00
Rad	29 August	0:00
Ken	13 September	6:00
Gyfu	28 September	11:00
Wyn	13 October	16:00
Hagal	28 October	22:00
Nyd	13 November	3:00
Is	28 November	8:00
Jera	13 December	14:00
Eoh	28 December	19:00
Peorth	13 January	1:00
Elhaz	28 January	5:00

Sigel	12 February	10:00
Tyr	27 February	16:00
Beare	14 March	21:00
Ehwaz	30 March	2:00
Man	14 April	7:00
Lagu	29 April	12:00
Ing	14 May	18:00
Odal	29 May	23:00
Dag	14 June	4:00

THE NORTHERN TRADITION PLANETARY HOURS

The traditional astrological planets control certain hours of the day. But unlike the Runic Hours, which are divided from the half to the half, they are divided from the hour to the hour. Their correspondences with the planetary deities of the Northern Tradition are as below. These hours are considered the best for performing actions that correspond to the attributes of the deities. When appropriate runic hours coincide with their planetary equivalents, these are especially powerful.

HOUR	SUNDAY	MONDAY	TUESDAY	WEDNESDAY	THURSDAY	FRIDAY	SATURDAY
00:00–01:00	Thor	Frigg	Loki	Sól	Máni	Tyr	Odin
01:00–02:00	Tyr	Odin	Thor	Frigg	Loki	Sól	Máni
02:00–03:00	Sól	Máni	Tyr	Odin	Thor	Frigg	Loki
03:00–04:00	Frigg	Loki	Sól	Máni	Tyr	Odin	Thor
04:00–05:00	Odin	Thor	Frigg	Loki	Sól	Máni	Tyr
05:00–06:00	Máni	Tyr	Odin	Thor	Frigg	Loki	Sól
06:00–07:00	Loki	Sól	Máni	Tyr	Odin	Thor	Frigg
07:00–08:00	Thor	Frigg	Loki	Sól	Máni	Tyr	Odin

HOUR	SUNDAY	MONDAY	TUESDAY	WEDNESDAY	THURSDAY	FRIDAY	SATURDAY
08:00–09:00	Tyr	Odin	Thor	Frigg	Loki	Sól	Máni
09:00–10:00	Sól	Máni	Tyr	Odin	Thor	Frigg	Loki
10:00–11:00	Frigg	Loki	Sól	Máni	Tyr	Odin	Thor
11:00–12:00	Odin	Thor	Frigg	Loki	Sól	Máni	Tyr
12:00–13:00	Sól	Máni	Tyr	Odin	Thor	Frigg	Loki
13:00–14:00	Frigg	Loki	Sól	Máni	Tyr	Odin	Thor
14:00–15:00	Odin	Thor	Frigg	Loki	Sól	Máni	Tyr
15:00–16:00	Máni	Tyr	Odin	Thor	Frigg	Loki	Sól
16:00–17:00	Loki	Sól	Máni	Tyr	Odin	Thor	Frigg
17:00–18:00	Thor	Frigg	Loki	Sól	Máni	Tyr	Odin
18:00–19:00	Tyr	Odin	Thor	Frigg	Loki	Sól	Máni
19:00–20:00	Sól	Máni	Tyr	Odin	Thor	Prigg	Loki
20:00–21:00	Frigg	Loki	Sól	Máni	Tyr	Odin	Thor
21:00–22:00	Odin	Thor	Frigg	Loki	Sól	Máni	Tyr
22:00–23:00	Máni	Tyr	Odin	Thor	Frigg	Loki	Sól
23:00–24:00	Loki	Sól	Máni	Tyr	Odin	Thor	Frigg

APPENDIX 4

CORRESPONDENCES OF THE DAYS OF THE WEEK

soterically, the days of the week have correspondences with runes, sacred trees, herbs, elements, an esoteric number, and a magic square, as below:

DAY	DEITY	"PLANET"	RUNE	TREE	HERB	ELEMENT	NUMBER	MAGIC SQUARE
Sunday	Sól	Sun	Sigel	Birch	Polygonium	Fire	1	36
Monday	Mani	Moon	Lagu	Willow	Chickweed	Water	5	81
Tuesday	Tyr	Mars	Tyr	Holly	Plantain	Fire	2	25
Wednesday	Odin	Mercury	Odal	Ash	Cinquefoil	Air	6	64
Thursday	Thor	Jupiter	Thorn	Oak	Henbane	Fire	3	16
Friday	Frigg	Venus	Peorth	Apple	Vervain	Earth	7	49
Saturday	Loki	Saturn	Dag	Alder	Daffodil	Earth	4	9

APPENDIX 5

ZODIACAL CORRESPONDENCES

ZODIAC SIGN	RULING PLANET	DEITY	DAY	STONE	ANIMAL	RUNE
Aries	Mars	Tyr	Tuesday	Diamond	Sheep	Eh
Taurus	Venus	Frigg	Friday	Sapphire	Bull	Ing
Gemini	Mercury	Odin	Wednesday	Emerald	Twin Ravens	Dag
Cancer	Moon	Máni	Monday	Agate	Crab	Ur
Leo	Sun	Sól	Sunday	Ruby	Lion	As
Virgo	Mercury	Odin	Wednesday	Sardonyx	Cat	Ken
Libra	Venus	Frigg	Friday	Chrysolite	Serpent	Wyn
Scorpio	Mars	Tyr	Tuesday	Opal	Scorpion	Nyd
Sagittarius	Jupiter	Thor	Thursday	Topaz	Aurochs	Jera
Capricorn	Jupiter	Thor	Thursday	Turquoise	Goat	Peorth
Aquarius	Saturn	Loki	Saturday	Amethyst	Eagle	Sigel
Pisces	Jupiter	Thor	Thursday	Bloodstone	Fish	Beorc

The final three signs have also been ascribed alternative correspondences with other planets:

Capricorn	Saturn	Loki	Saturday	Turquoise	Goat	Peorth
Aquarius	Uranus	Urd	Saturday	Amethyst	Eagle	Sigel
Pisces	Neptune	Aegir	Thursday	Bloodstone	Fish	Beorc

APPENDIX 6

THE EIGHT TIDES OF THE DAY

TIDES (TIMES)	ENGLISH	ANGLO-SAXON	NORSE
4:30–7:30	Morntide	morgen	morginn
7:30–10:30	Daytide or Undernoon	dægmæl, dægtid	dagtími
10:30–13:30	Midday or Noontide	Middæg, nontid	nóntíð, miðdagr
13:30–16:30	Afternoon or Undorne	ofernon	ofanverðr dagr
16:30–19:30	Eventide	æfentid	aftan
19:30–22:30	Nighttide	niht	nótt
22:30–1:30	Midnight	midniht	miðnætti
1:30–4:30	Uht	uhta, uhtantid	ótta

DAY MARKERS			
4:30	Rising	dægred	rismál
7:30	Day mark	dægmæl	dagmálastaðr
12:00	Noon	non	nón
16:30	Eykt		eyktarstaðr
19:30	Nachtmahlstatt (German), lit. "evening meal stead"		

THE TWELVE PALACES

According to Freya Aswynn (1990, 157–60), the twelve palaces listed by Odin in *Grímnismál* have the following correspondences:

PALACE	MEANING OF NAME	DEITY	ZODIAC SIGN
Bilskírnir	Lightning	Thor	Aries
Thrymheim	Thunder-Home	Skadi	Taurus
Fólkvangr	Field of Warriors	Freya	Gemini
Himinbjörg	Heaven Hall	Heimdall	Cancer
Breiðablik	Broad View	Balder	Leo
Sökkvabekkr	Stream of Time and Events	Saga	Virgo
Glitnir	Hall of Splendor	Forseti	Libra
Glaðsheimr	Shining Home (and Valhalla)	Odin	Scorpio
Ýdalir	Valley of Yews	Ullr	Sagittarius
Landviði	White Land (= Welsh *Gwynvyd*)	Vidar	Capricorn
Valaskjálf	Halls of Silver	Vali	Aquarius
Noatún	Shipyard	Njord	Pisces

THE SOLAR SYSTEM: ASTRONOMICAL DATA

The diameters of the major bodies of the Solar System (the 39 largest).

BODY	DIAMETER (KM)	DIAMETER (MILES)	REMARKS
Sun	1,392,530 km	(870,331 miles)	Stellar core of Solar System
Jupiter	142,984 km	(88,650 miles)	Planet
Saturn	120,000 km	(74,565 miles)	Planet
Uranus	51,800 km	(32,116 miles)	Planet
Neptune	49,500 km	(30,758 miles)	Planet
Earth	12,756 km	(7,926 miles)	Planet
Venus	12,104 km	(7,521 miles)	Planet
Mars	6,794 km	(4,212 miles)	Planet
Triton	6,000 km	(3,730 miles)	Satellite of Neptune
Ganymede	5,276 km	(3,278 miles)	Satellite of Jupiter
Titan	5,150 km	(3,200 miles)	Satellite of Saturn
Mercury	4,878 km	(3,031 miles)	Planet
Callisto	4,820 km	(2,995 miles)	Satellite of Saturn
Luna	3,476 km	(2,160 miles)	Satellite of Earth (the Moon)

BODY	DIAMETER (KM)	DIAMETER (MILES)	REMARKS
Io	3,632 km	(2,257 miles)	Satellite of Jupiter
Europa	3,126 km	(1,942 miles)	Satellite of Jupiter
Pluto	2,200 km	(1,375 miles)	Planet
Titania	1,610 km	(998 miles)	Satellite of Uranus
Oberon	1,550 km	(961 miles)	Satellite of Uranus
Iapetus	1,460 km	(905 miles)	Satellite of Saturn
Rhea	1,530 km	(951 miles)	Satellite of Saturn
Charon	1,200 km	(750 miles)*	Satellite of Pluto (or co-planet)
Umbriel	1,190 km	(739 miles)	Satellite of Uranus
Ariel	1,160 km	(721 miles)	Satellite of Uranus
Dione	1,120 km	(696 miles)	Satellite of Saturn
Tethys	1,050 km	(652 miles)	Satellite of Saturn
Ceres	1,003 km	(622 miles)	Asteroid
Pallas	608 km	(377 miles)	Asteroid
Vesta	538 km	(334 miles)	Asteroid
Nereid	500 km	(311 miles)	Satellite of Neptune
Encelad us	500 km	(311 miles)	Satellite of Saturn
Hygeia	450 km	(279 miles)	Asteroid
Hyperion	400 km	(248 miles)†	Satellite of Saturn
Mimas	390 km	(242 miles)	Satellite of Saturn
Euphrosyne	370 km	(230 miles)	Asteroid
Interamnia	350 km	(217 miles)	Asteroid
Davida	323 km	(200 miles)	Asteroid
Cybele	309 km	(192 miles)	Asteroid
Europa	289 km	(179 miles)	Asteroid

*Estimate.
†Longest dimension of an irregular body (240 km shortest).

GLOSSARY

The terms used in Northern Tradition runic work as dealt with in this book are derived, like the English language itself, from a multiplicity of sources. Many are from the old Norse, Celtic, and Scots languages, and some are specialist terms from the magical tradition of East Anglia. The following abbreviations are used to indicate these sources:

A-S	Anglo-Saxon	L	Latin
C	Celtic	M	Manx
E	English	N	Norse
E-A	East Anglian	R	Roman
F	French	Sa	Continental Saxon
G	Greek	Sc	Scots
H	Hebrew	W	Welsh

Æsir: the main divinities of the Northern pantheon (N).

Ætt: a group of eight, as in directions or runes (N) = *airt* (Sc); also: *ætt*, "quarter of the sky, direction, family, extraction"; *ætterni*, "belonging by birth or family to a place," and *ættmaðr*, "a relative, or kinsperson."

Ættcunning: knowledge of the qualities of the directions (N, E).

Airt: see *ætt*.

Arbor: a spindle for the transmission of rotational motion, as used in ancient astronomical mechanisms.

Archaeoastronomy: the archaeological study of astronomical remains, i.e., stone circles, or solar alignments.

Ásatrú: name given to the religion worshiping the *Æsir*.

Asgard: the abode of the *Æsir* (q.v.) (N *ásgarðr*).

Astrolabe: astronomical instrument used for taking the altitudes of fixed stars and planets.

Beltane: the May Day festival (30 April eve/1 May).

Bifröst: the Rainbow Bridge to Asgard (N).

Biorhythm: bodily cycle of a specific periodicity, affecting the physical, emotional, or intellectual capabilities of the subject (E).

Brigantia: Pagan festival of 31 January eve/1 February = Imbolc, Oimelc (C), Candlemas.

Bull's Noon: midnight, local time (E-A).

Caduceus: the winged staff of Hermes (G) = Mercury (R) = Odin (N).

Calas: Solidity, one of the three states of being in Bardic cosmology (W).

Candlemas: Christian version of Brigantia (q.v.)

Chime Hours: nodal center-points of the tides of the day, traditionally lucky times to be born.

Clog almanac: a traditional wooden calendar/calculator or rimstock (E).

Dægmæl: 7:30 a.m. by the sun (A-S).

Dægmælsceawere: professional time-teller in old England (A-S).

Dægmælspilu: local horizon solar marker (A-S).

Daemonium: the reverse quality of anything, its polar opposite (R).

Deal: the sacred pine tree (E-A).

Dies Ægyptiaci: "Egyptian Days," unlucky days in the traditional calendar (L).

Druid: literally "man of the Oak," a member of the Celtic Pagan priesthood (C).

Egyptian Days: *Dies Ægyptiaci* (q.v.).

Elder Futhark: the early, 24-character runic row (see Futhark and Futhork, below).

Election: likely, "In election to happen" (E-A).

Eneidvaddeu: execution, literally "reparation" (W).

Etruscan Discipline: the Etruscan system of laying out the landscape to reflect cosmological and magical principles.

Eykt: 4:30 p.m. real time (N, E).

Fate: see *Ørlög* and Wyrd (q.v.).

Fidchell: ancient Irish board game, parallel to Welsh *tawlbort* (q.v.) (C).

Fiducial: an agreed reference-point for comparative measurement, usually a fixed star.

Fifteen Stars: 15 "stars" especially important in medieval astronomy. They are Aldebaran, Algol, Algorab, Alphecca, Antares, Arcturus, Capella, Deneb Algedi, the Pleiades, Polaris, Procyon, Regulus, Sirius, Spica, and Vega.

Futhark: the runic alphabet, its name based on the first 6 characters, F, U, Th (Þ), A, R, K.

Futhork: the later expanded Anglo-Saxon and Anglo-Frisian runic row.

GHA: Greenwich Hour Angle, standard angular measurement for planetary position as used in nautical almanacs.

GMT: Greenwich Mean Time, standard time based on the British meridian at Greenwich, London.

Georgium Sidus: the planet Uranus (L, E).

Gnomon: artificial upright used to make a shadow with the sun for the purpose of time measurement.

Golden Number: key number in the calendar denoting a position in the 19-year Metonic Cycle (q.v.).

Great Year: the full period when in the precession of the equinoxes, the vernal point (q.v.) makes a complete circle through the constellations = 25,920 years.

Gregorian Calendar: the modern calendar, instituted by Pope Gregory XIII in 1582 (New Style). Adopted between 1582 and 1928.

Gwynn ap Nudd: literally, "light, son of darkness," Celtic lord of the Faerie kingdom and the underworld.

Half-month: a runic period lasting one-twenty-fourth of a year.

Hallowe'en: Christian festival of the dead (E) = Samhain (C) (q.v.).

Hamfar: traveling in an assumed shape or form different from one's usual natural form (N).

Harvests, Three: Lammas, Autumnal Equinox, and Samhain.

Heimdall: the watcher-god, guardian of the Rainbow Bridge, Bifröst (N).

High Noon: midday by the sun.

Hogmanay: the Scottish solar festival of the new year (Sc).

Howe: a burial mound, barrow (E).

Imbolc: see Brigantia.

Irminsul: the sacred world-pillar of the pagan Saxons, set up at what is now the town of Ober-Marsberg, Germany (Sa).

Jormungand: the world serpent = Midgard Serpent (N).

Jubilee: a festival of celebration and thanksgiving, held at 25-year periods (H).

Julian Calendar: calendar set up by Julius Caesar in 46 BCE (Old Style). Abandoned between 1582 and 1928.

Kenning: an oblique poetic reference or allusion, e.g., "The fishes' bath" = the sea (N, Sc).

Lammas: festival of the first loaf, from Anglo-Saxon *hlafmæsse* = Pagan festival of Lughnassadh, sacred to Lugh (C) = Odin (N).

LAT: Local Apparent Time, time measured from the actual visible position of the sun at any place.

Llwbr: a path (W).

Low Noon: midnight, local time.

Megalithic: literally, "big stones" (G): any human-made structure composed of large, roughly worked or unworked stones.

Megin: personal force, distinct from physical strength, the possession of which assures good fortune and success (N).

Messedagstav: "*Messedag* (mass day)-stave," clog almanac (q.v.) (Norwegian).

Metonic Cycle: the 19-year period, named after the ancient Greek astronomer, Meton, which marks the completion of a solar cycle.

New Style: dates expressed in the Gregorian (modern) calendar (q.v.).

Northumbrian Futhark: 33-rune row used in Northumbria (NE England).

Nowl: navel or conceptual center of the world (E-A) = Omphalos.

Nwyvre: the universal life force (W) = *önd* (q.v.).

Ogham: ancient Druidic stave-writing of Ireland and Britain (C).

Old Style: dates expressed in the Julian Calendar (q.v.)

Önd: the universal life-force (N) = Welsh *nwyvre* (q.v.)

Orlog: from *ørlög*, literally "primal layer" or "primal law"; that which makes "now" (N).

Otherworld: the area of consciousness beyond the everyday "this-world," ranging from states of expanded consciousness to other dimensions or universes.

Perron: geomantic marker, consisting of stone steps upon which is set a shaft surmounted by a globe, or, occasionally a cross (F).

Phoebe: the sun (E-A).

Pontifex Maximus: title given to the high priest of Roman religion, literally, "chief bridge-maker." It was taken over by the Roman Catholic Church, and the pope is still known as the *pontiff* (L).

Primstav: "primestave," see clog almanac.

Rimstav: "rimstock," Scandinavian clog almanac, sometimes transferred to a printed calendar (N, E).

Rismál: rising time, 4:30 a.m. real time (G, N, E).

Rune-hoard: abstract term for the greater collection of prehistoric and pre-runic signs, sigils, and symbols that became part of the Northern Tradition and appeared in later runic contexts, such as runestones or runestocks.

Runestock: see clog almanac.

Runic Hour: hour in the day corresponding to a specific rune.

Samhain: Pagan festival of death/rebirth, Eve of 31 October/1 November (C) = Hallowe'en (E).

Sele: a time of day, year, or a "mansion" of the Moon (E-A).

Shoat: the area along which runestones or slivers are thrown in rune-casting (A-S, E).

Sigrblót: the Norse-Icelandic festival of springtime (N).

Staple: geomantic mark-post at a crossroads or ford (E).

Svínfylking: Norse martial arts soldiers who fought in a squad in the shape of a wedge (N).

Tawlbort: traditional northern European board game of the Tafl variety, where a king and his men at the center are attacked by opponents from the four directions: a geomantic allegory (E).

Thing: a council assembly (N).

Thorrablót: the Norse-Icelandic midwinter festival of "Thorri's Offering" (N).

Tide: one of the eight time-divisions of the 24-hour cycle (A-S, E).

Trilithon: a megalithic (q.v.) structure composed of two upright stones on top of which a third horizontal stone is placed, as at Stonehenge.

Tynwald: the Manx parliamentary assembly (M).

Vé: a sacred enclosure, usually triangular in form (N).

Vébönd: consecrated fence around a sacred enclosure (N).

Vernal Point: marker of the spring equinox.

Völva: a wise woman (N).

Walpurgisnacht: Walpurgis' Night, May Eve (30 April) (Sa).

Wyrd: personal "fate" or "destiny," but also generally, "the way things go" (A-S).

Yule: the festival of midwinter, now amalgamated with Christmas (E, N, Sc).

BIBLIOGRAPHY

Agrell, Sigurd. 1931. *Senantik Mysteriereligion och nordisk Runmagi*. Stockholm: Bonnier.

———. 1934. *Lapptrummor och Runmagi*. Lund: Gleerup.

Alver, Brynjulf. 1970. *Dag og Merke: Folkeleg tidsrekning og merkedagstradisjon*. Oslo: Universitetsforlaget.

Amos, G. S. n.d. [ca. 1980]. *The Scratch Dials of Norfolk*. South Walsham, UK.

Andrews, Edson J. 1960. "Moon Talk: The Cyclic Periodicity of Post-operative Haemorrhage." *Journal of the Florida Medical Association* 46:1,362–66.

Anwyl, Edward. 1906. *Celtic Religion in Pre-Christian Times*. London: Constable.

Aswynn, Freya. 1990. *Leaves of Yggdrasil: Runes—Gods—Magic—Feminine Mysteries—Folklore*. St. Paul, Minn.: Llewellyn.

Baker, Margaret. 1974. *Folklore and Customs in Rural England*. Newton Abbot, UK: Rowman and Littlefield.

Bellows, Henry Adams, trans. 1923. *The Poetic Edda*. London: Oxford University Press.

Bertalanffy, Ludwig von. 1968. *General Systems Theory*. New York: Braziller.

Berthelot, Rene. 1949. *La pensee de l'Asie et l'astrobiologie*. Paris: Payot.

Bilfinger, Gustav. 1901. *Untersuchungen über die Zeitrechnung der alten Germanen*. Stuttgart: Liebich.

Bischoff, Michael. 1986. *Himmelszeichen: Eine bildreiche Kunde von Aberglauben und Ängsten*. Nordlingen: Greno.

Björnsson, Stefán. 1780. *Rymbegla sive Rudimentum computi ecclesiastici et annalis veterum Islandorum : in qvo etiam continentur chronologica geographica astronomica geometrica theologica nonnulla ex historia universali & naturali rariora.* Copenhagen: Stein.

Blacker, Carmen, and Michael Loewe, eds. 1975. *Ancient Cosmologies.* London: Allen and Unwin.

Brandon, Jim. 1983. *The Rebirth of Pan: Hidden Faces of the American Earth Spirit.* Dunlap, Ill.: Firebird.

Branston, Brian. 1955. *Gods of the North.* London: Thames and Hudson.

———. 1957. *The Lost Gods of England.* London: Thames and Hudson.

Brix, Hans. 1928. *Studier i nordisk Runmagi.* Copenhagen: Nordisk.

Brown, P. D. 2022. *Thirteen Moons: Reflections on the Heathen Lunar Year.* North Augusta, S.C.: Gilded Books.

Brown, P. D., and Michael Moynihan, eds. 2022. *The Rune Poems: A Reawakened Tradition.* North Augusta, S.C.: Gilded Books.

Browne, Thomas. 1716. *Christian Morals.* Cambridge: Cambridge University Press.

Buckland, Raymond. 1892. *Buckland's Complete Book of Witchcraft.* St. Paul, Minn.: Llewellyn, 1986.

Burnet, John. 1892. *Early Greek Philosophy.* London: Black.

Callander, J. Graham. 1910. "Notices of (1) a Seventeenth-Century Sun-Dial from Wigtownshire; and (2) a Stele, Discovered in Galatia, Asia Minor, Decorated with a Design Resembling the Mirror and Comb Symbols Found in Scotland." *Proceedings of the Society of Antiquaries of Scotland* 8, no. 4: 169–85.

Chadwick, H. M. 1899. *The Cult of Othin: An Essay in the Ancient Religion of the North.* London: Clay.

Chetwynd, Tom. 1986. *A Dictionary of Sacred Myth.* London: Unwin.

Christian, Roy. 1972. *Old English Customs.* Newton Abbot, UK: David and Charles.

Clark, Samuel. 1758. *The Laws of Chance.* London: Payne.

Clube, Victor, and Bill Napier. 1982. *The Cosmic Serpent: A Catastrophist View of Earth History.* London: Faber and Faber.

Cockayne, Oswald. 1864–1866. *Leechdoms, Wortcunning and Starcraft.* 3 vols. London: Longman, Green, Longman, Roberts, and Green.

Collin, Rodney. 1954. *The Theory of Celestial Influences.* London: Stuart.

Colum, Padraic. 1922. *The Children of Odin.* London: Harrap.

Cox, J. Charles, and R. M. Serjeantson. 1897. *A History of the Church of the Holy Sepulchre, Northampton.* Northampton, UK: Mark.

Cross, Launcelot (Francis Carr). 1914. *The Book of Old Sundials & Their Mottoes.* London: Foulis.

Cumont, Franz. 1956. *The Mysteries of Mithras.* New York: Dover.

Dewey, Edward R., and Og Mandino. 1973. *Cycles: The Mysterious Forces That Trigger Events.* New York: Manor.

Dickens, Bruce. 1915. *Runic and Heroic Poems.* Cambridge: Cambridge University Press.

Dornsieff, Franz. 1922. *Das Alphabet in Mystik und Magie.* Berlin: Teubner.

Drake-Camell, F. J. 1938. *Old English Customs and Ceremonies.* London: Batsford.

Du Chaillu, Paul B. 1889. *The Viking Age.* 2 vols. London: Murray.

Dürer, Albrecht. 1525. *Underweysung der Messung mit dem Zirckel un richt Scheyt.* Nuremberg: [Hieronymus Andreas Formschneider].

Düwel, Klaus. 2008. *Runenkunde.* Fourth revised and expanded edition. Stuttgart: Metzler.

Ebers, Edith, and Franz Wollenik. 1982. *Felsbilder der Alpen.* Hallein: Burgfried.

Eddy, J. A. 1976. "The Maunder Minima." *Science* 192:1189–1202.

Eisler, Robert. 1921. *Orpheus—the Fisher: Comparative Studies in Orphic and Early Christian Cult Symbolism.* London: Watkins.

Eliade, Mircea. 1949. *Le Mythe de l'éternel retour: Archetypes et repetition.* Paris: Gallimard.

Elliott, Ralph W. V. 1959. *Runes: An Introduction.* Manchester: Manchester University Press.

Ellis, Hilda, R. 1943. *The Road to Hel.* Cambridge: Cambridge University Press.

Ellis Davidson, H. R. 1964. *Gods and Myths of Northern Europe.* London: Penguin.

———. 1969. *Scandinavian Mythology.* London: Hamlyn.

Evans, George Ewart. 1971. *The Pattern under the Plough: Aspects of the Folk-life of East Anglia.* London: Faber & Faber.

Evans, James, and J. Lennart Berggren. 2006. *Geminos's* Introduction to the Phenomena: *A Translation and Study of a Hellenistic Survey of Astronomy.* Princeton: Princeton University Press.

Evans Wentz, W. Y. 1911. *The Fairy Faith in Celtic Countries.* London: Frowde.

Eysenck, H. J., and D. H. B. Nias. 1982. *Astrology: Science or Superstition?* London: Temple Smith.

Franz, Marie-Louise von. 1974. *Number and Time: Reflections Leading Towards a Unification of Psychology and Physics.* Evanston, Ill.: Northwestern University Press.

Garcia-Mata, C. and F. I. Schaffner. 1934. "Solar and Economic Relationships." *Quarterly Journal of Economics* 49:1–51.

Gardiner, Alan. 1961. *Egypt of the Pharoahs: An Introduction.* Oxford: Oxford University Press.

Gelling, Peter, and Hilda Ellis Davidson. 1969. *The Chariot of the Sun and Other Rites and Symbols of the Northern Bronze Age.* London: Dent.

Genzmer, Felix, trans. 1933. *Die Edda.* Jena: Diederich.

Gettings, Fred. 1985. *Dictionary of Astrology.* London: Routledge & Kegan Paul.

Gildas. 1978. *The Ruin of Britain and Other Works.* Edited and translated by Michael Winterbottom. London: Phillimore.

Gittleson, Bernard. 1976. *Biorhythm.* New York: Arco.

Gleadow, Rupert. 1968. *The Origin of the Zodiac.* London: Cape.

Gomme, G. L. 1883. *Folk-lore Relics in Early Village Life.* London: Stock.

Gorsleben, Rudolf John. 1930. *Die Hoch-Zeit der Menschheit.* Leipzig: Koehler and Amelang.

Grattan, J. H. G., and Charles Singer. 1952. *Anglo-Saxon Magic and Medicine.* London: Wellcome Medical Museum.

Graves, Robert. 1961. *The White Goddess.* London: Faber and Faber.

Green, Arthur Robert. 1926. *Sundials: Incised Dials or Mass-Clocks.* London: Society for Promoting Christian Knowledge.

Green, Patricia D. 1963. *Cult of the Cat.* London: Heinemann.

Grimm, Jacob. 1966 [1888]. *Teutonic Mythology.* Translated by James S. Stallybrass. 4 vols. New York: Dover.

Grønbech, Vilhelm. 1932. *The Culture of the Teutons.* Translated by W. Worster. 3 vols. London: Oxford.

Guénon, René. 1945. *Le Règne de la Quantité et les Signes des Temps.* Paris: Gallimard.

Guerber, H. A. 1985. *The Norsemen.* London: Guild.

Hamkens, F. Haye. 1971. *Der Externstein: Geschichte und Bedeutung.* Tübingen: Grabert.

Harding, Mary E. 1935. *Women's Mysteries, Ancient and Modern.* London: Longmans, Green and Company.

Harland, John. 1864–1865. "On Clog Almanacs, or Rune Stocks." In *The Reliquary* 5:121–30.

Hartman, Franz. 1889. *The Principles of Astrological Geomancy.* Boston: Occult Publishing Co.

Heggie, D. C. 1981. *Megalithic Science and Astronomy in North-West Europe.* London: Thames and Hudson.

Henderson, George. 1911. *Survivals in Belief among the Celts.* Glasgow: MacLehose and Sons.

Herrmann, Paul. 1929. *Das altgermanische Priesterwesen.* Jena: Diederich.

Higgins, Frank, C. 1923. *An Introduction to the Study of Masonic Archaeology.* New York: Pyramid.

Holmberg, Axel. 1848. *Skandinaviens Hällristningar.* Stockholm: Berg.

Howard, Michael. 1978. *The Runes and Other Magical Alphabets.* Wellingborough, UK: Thorsons.

———. 1985. *The Wisdom of the Runes.* London: Rider.

Jansson, Sven B. F. 1962. *Runes of Sweden.* Stockholm: Nostedt & Söner.

Jenny, Hans. 1974. *Cymatics.* 2 vols. Basel: Basilius.

Jones, P. K., and S. L. Jones. 1977. "Lunar Association with Suicide." *Suicide and Life-Threatening Behavior* 7, no. 1:31–39.

Jones, Prudence. 1982. *Eight and Nine: Sacred Numbers of Sun and Moon in the Pagan North.* Bar Hill, UK: Fenris-Wolf.

———. 1982. *Sundial and Compass Rose: Eight-fold Time Division in Northern Europe.* Bar Hill, UK: Fenris-Wolf.

Kaplan, Justin D. 1958. *The Pocket Aristotle.* Translated under the editorship of W. D. Ross. New York: Washington Square.

Keary, Charles. 1882. *Outlines of Primitive Belief among the Indo-European Races.* London: Longmans, Green.

Koestler, Arthur. 1972. *The Roots of Coincidence.* London: Hutchinson.

Kolisko, L. N. 1936. *The Moon and the Growth of Plants.* Translated by Marna Pease. London: Anthroposophical Agricultural Foundation.

Kosbab, Werner. 1982. *Das Runen-Orakel: Einweihung in die Praxis der Runen-Weissagung.* Freiburg-im-Breisgau: Bauer.

Lamb, H. H. 1977. *Climate, Present, Past and Future.* London: Methuen.

Langdon, Arthur G. 1896. *Old Cornish Crosses.* Truro: Pollard.

Larsen, Astrid Pilegaard, and K. Frank Jensen. 1979. *Spil og Spådom.* Copenhagen: Danmarks Paedagogiske Bibliothek.

Leonard, William Ellery. 1907. "The Fragments of Empedocles." *The Monist* 17, no. 3 (July): 451–74.

Lethaby, William. 1891. *Architecture, Mysticism and Myth.* London: Percival.

Leybourn, William. 1660. *The Art of Dialling Performed Geometrically by Scale and Compasses Arithmetically by the Canons of Sines and Tangents Instrumentally by a Trigonal Instrument Accommodated with Lines for That Purpose.* London: Tooke and Sawbridge.

List, Guido von. 1912. *Das Geheimnis der Runen.* Vienna: Guido-von-List Gesellschaft.

Lockyer, J. N. 1909. *Stonehenge, Astronomically Considered.* London: Macmillan.

Luce, Gay Gaer. 1971. *Body Time.* London: Temple Smith.

MacCulloch, J. A. 1948. *The Celtic and Scandinavian Religions.* London: Hutchinson.

Malory, Thomas. 1910. *Le Morte d'Arthur.* 2 vols. London: Dent.

Mann, Ludovic MacLellan. 1915. *Archaic Sculpturings: Notes on Art, Philosophy, and Religion in Britain 2000 B.C. to 900 A.D.* London: Hodge.

Marby, Friedrich Bernhard. 1955. *Der Weg zu den Müttern.* Stuttgart: Roland-Repro.

Mavrogordato, Alex. 1940. *The Structure of Civilisation.* London: Cranton.

Menaker, W. and A. Menaker. 1959. "Lunar Periodicity in Human Reproduction: A Likely Unit of Biological Time." *American Journal of Obstetrics and Gynaecology* 77:905–914.

Menon, C. P. S. 1932. *Early Astronomy and Cosmology: A Reconstruction of the Earliest Cosmic System.* London: Allen and Unwin.

Merne, John G. 1974. *A Handbook of Celtic Ornament.* Cork and Dublin: Mercier.

Montelius, Oscar. 1906. *Kulturgeschichte Schwedens.* Leipzig: Seemann.

Morgannwg, Iolo. 1862–1874. *Barddas.* Edited and translated by J. Williams ab Ithel. 2 vols. Llandovery: Welsh Mss. Society.

Müller, Werner. 1961. *Die Heilige Stadt, Roma Quadrata, himmlisches Jerusalem und die Mythen vom Weltnabel.* Stuttgart: Kohlhammer.

Naddair, Kaledon. 1987. *Keltic Folk and Faerie Tales: Their Hidden Meaning Explored.* London: Century.

Nietzsche, Friedrich. *Thus Spake Zarathustra.* 1909. Translated by Thomas Common. Edinburgh: T. N. Foulis.

Ó hUiginn, Tadhg Dall. 1922–1926. *The Bardic Poems.* Translated by Eleanor Knott. 2 vols. London: Simpkin, Marshall, Hamilton, Kent, and Co.

Olrik, Axel. 1922. *Ragnarök: Die Sagen vom Weltuntergang.* Translated by Wilhelm Ranisch. Berlin: De Gruyter.

———. 1930. *Viking Civilisation*. London: George Allen & Unwin.

Olsen, Magnus. 1928. *Farms and Fanes of Ancient Norway: The Place-Names of a Country Discussed in Their Bearings on Social and Religious History*. Translated by Th. Gleditsch. Oslo: Aschehoug.

Osborn, Marijane, and Stella Langland. 1982. *Rune Games*. London: Routledge and Kegan Paul.

Page, R. I. 1999. *An Introduction to English Runes*. Second edition. Woodbridge, UK: Boydell.

Pennick, Nigel. 1978. *Ogham and Runic: Magical Writing of Old Britain and Northern Europe*. Bar Hill, UK: Fenris-Wolf.

———. 1979. *The Ancient Science of Geomancy: Man in Harmony with the Earth*. London: Thames and Hudson.

———. 1980. *Sacred Geometry: Symbolism and Purpose in Religious Structures*. Wellingborough, UK: Turnstone.

———. 1981. *The Subterranean Kingdom: A Survey of Man-made Structures beneath the Earth*. Wellingborough, UK: Turnstone.

———. 1985. *The Cosmic Axis*. Bar Hill, UK: Fenris-Wolf.

———. 1987. *Earth Harmony: Siting and Protecting Your Home—a Practical and Spiritual Guide*. London: Century.

———. 1987. *Einst war uns die Erde heilig*. Waldeck-Dehringhausen: Heubner.

———. 1987. *Lost Lands and Sunken Cities*. London: Fortean Tomes.

———. 1988. *Games of the Gods: The Origin of Board Games in Magic and Divination*. London: Rider.

———. 1989. *Practical Magic in the Northern Tradition*. Wellingborough, UK: Thorsons.

———. 2015. *Pagan Magic of the Northern Tradition: Customs, Rites, and Ceremonies*. Rochester, Vt.: Destiny.

Pennick, Nigel, and Paul Devereux. 1989. *Lines on the Landscape: Leys and Other Linear Enigmas*. London: Hale.

Philostratus. 1911. *The Life of Apollonius of Tyana*, vol. 1. Translated by F. C. Conybeare. Cambridge, Mass.: Harvard University Press.

Piccardi, Giorgio. 1962. *The Chemical Basis of Medical Climatology*. Springfield: Thomas.

Rees, Alwyn, and Brinley Rees. 1961. *Celtic Heritage*. London: Thames and Hudson.

Reuter, Otto Sigfrid. 1934. *Germanische Himmelskunde*. Munich: Lehmann.

———. 1985. *Sky Lore of the North*. Translated by Michael Behrend. Bar Hill, UK: Runestaff.

Rhyne, W. P. 1966. "Spontaneous Haemorrhage." *Journal of the Medical Association of Georgia* 55: 505–6.

Rigby, Emma, Melissa Symonds, and Derek Ward-Thompson. 2004. "A Comet Impact in AD 536?" *Astronomy & Geophysics* 45, no. 1: 1.23–1.26.

Rimmer, Alfred. 1875. *Ancient Stone Crosses of England*. London: Virtue, Spalding, and Co.

Santillana, George de, and Hertha von Dechend. 1969. *Hamlet's Mill: An Essay on Myth and the Frame of Time*. Boston: Gambit.

Schneider, Karl. 1956. *Die Germanischen Runennamen: Versuch einer Gesamtdeutung*. Meisenheim: Hain.

Shippey, T. A. 1976. *Poems of Wisdom and Learning in Old English*. Cambridge: Brewer.

Small, J. W. 1900. *Scottish Market Crosses*. Stirling: Mackay.

Smith-Dampier, E. M., trans. 1920. *Danish Ballads*. Cambridge: Cambridge University Press.

Spence, Lewis. 1928. *The Mysteries of Britain*. London: Rider.

Spiesberger, Karl. 1955. *Runenmagie*. Berlin: Schikowski.

Stephens, George. 1866–84. *The Old-Northern Runic Monuments of Scandinavia and England*. 3 vols. London: Smith.

Storms, G. 1948. *Anglo-Saxon Magic*. The Hague: Nijhoff.

Syversen, Earl. 1979. *Norse Runic Inscriptions*. Sebastopol, Calif.: Vine Hill.

Tacitus. 2010. *Agricola and Germania*. Translated by Harold Mattingly. London: Penguin.

Taylor, Isaac. 1879. *Greeks and Goths: A Study on the Runes*. London: Macmillan.

Temple, Robert, K. G. 1984. *Conversations with Eternity*. London: Rider.

Thom, Alexander. 1971. *Megalithic Sites in Britain*. Oxford: Oxford University Press.

———. 1971. *Megalithic Lunar Observatories*. Oxford: Oxford University Press.

Thomas, David Morgan. N.d. *The Day-Book of Wonders*. London: Unwin.

Thorsson, Edred. 1984. *Futhark: A Handbook of Rune Magic*. York Beach, Me.: Weiser.

Tille, Alexander. 1899. *Yule and Christmas*. London: Nutt.

Turville-Petre, E. O. G. 1951. *The Heroic Age of Scandinavia*. London: Hutchinson.

————. 1964. *Myth and Religion of the North.* New York: Holt, Rinehart and Winston.

Twain, Mark. 1972. *Fables of Man.* Edited by John S. Tuckey. Berkeley: University of California Press.

Urton, Gary. 1980. *At the Crossroads of the Earth and Sky: An Andean Cosmology.* Austin: University of Texas.

Varagnac, André, and René Derolez. 1965. *Les Celtes et les Germains.* Paris: Bloud *et* Gay.

Verstegan, Richard. 1628. *Restitution of Decayed Intelligence in Antiquities.* London: Bill.

Virgil. 1916. *Eclogues, Georgics, Aeneid.* Translated by H. R. Fairclough. 2 vols. Cambridge, Mass.: Harvard University Press.

Wardle, Thorolf. 1983. *Runelore.* Braunschweig: [Wardle].

————. 1984. *The Runenames.* Braunschweig: [Wardle].

Watkins, Alfred. 1932. *Archaic Tracks Round Cambridge.* London: Simpkin Marshall, Ltd.

Webster, Graham. 1986. *The British Celts and their Gods under Rome.* London: Batsford.

Wheatley, Paul. 1971. *The Pivot of the Four Quarters: A Preliminary Enquiry into the Origins and Character of the Ancient Chinese City.* Edinburgh: Edinburgh University Press.

Whitlock, Ralph. 1979. *In Search of Lost Gods: A Guide to British Folklore.* Oxford: Phaidon.

Wittgenstein, Ludwig. 1922. *Tractatus Logico-Philosophicus.* London: Kegan Paul, Trench, Trubner & Co.

Wright, Dudley. 1924. *Druidism: The Ancient Faith of Britain.* London: Burrow.

Zaehner, R. C. 1957. *Mysticism Sacred and Profane: An Inquiry into Some Varieties of Praeternatural Experience.* Oxford: Oxford University Press.

Zeller, Otto. 1977. *Der Ursprung der Buchstabenschrift und das Runenalphabet.* Osnabrück: Biblio-Verlag.

INDEX